Praise for *The Mackay MBA of Selling in the Real World*

"Harvey Mackay's new book is his best yet—and that's saying a lot. It is relevant, easy to apply, and an absolute must-read. Miss it at your own peril. A genius work in practical terms."

—Larry King

"I advise people to never eat alone, but this book makes a perfect dining companion. Feast on this extraordinary advice."

—Keith Ferrazzi, author of *Never Eat Alone*

"Harvey Mackay is THE Dean of Sales, and his *Mackay MBA of Selling in the Real World* is the ultimate post-graduate course primer in the area of sales."

—James G. Ellis, dean of the Marshall School of Business at the University of Southern California

"If anyone can 'write the book' on sales success, it's Harvey Mackay. He is a proven leader in sales. My advice: Follow the leader to a stellar sales career."

—John C. Maxwell, author of the *New York Times* bestseller *The 21 Irrefutable Laws of Leadership*

PORTFOLIO / PENGUIN

THE MACKAY MBA OF SELLING IN THE REAL WORLD

Harvey Mackay is the author of six *New York Times* bestsellers (three of which went to number one), including *Swim with the Sharks Without Being Eaten Alive*. His books have sold more than ten million copies worldwide. They have been translated into forty-six languages and distributed in eighty countries.

Mackay is a nationally syndicated columnist for United Feature Syndicate (twenty years) and one of America's most popular and entertaining business speakers. He's been named one of the top five speakers in the world by Toastmasters International.

Mackay is chairman of MackayMitchell Envelope Company, a $100 million company he founded at age twenty-six. He and his wife, Carol Ann, have three children and eleven grandchildren.

ALSO BY HARVEY MACKAY

Swim with the Sharks Without Being Eaten Alive

Beware the Naked Man Who Offers You His Shirt

Dig Your Well Before You're Thirsty

Pushing the Envelope: All the Way to the Top

We Got Fired! . . . And It's the Best Thing That Ever Happened to Us

Use Your Head to Get Your Foot in the Door

THE MACKAY MBA OF SELLING IN THE REAL WORLD

HARVEY MACKAY

Portfolio / Penguin

PORTFOLIO/PENGUIN
Published by the Penguin Group
Penguin Group (USA) Inc., 375 Hudson Street,
New York, New York 10014, USA

USA | Canada | UK | Ireland | Australia
New Zealand | India | South Africa | China

Penguin Books Ltd, Registered Offices: 80 Strand, London WC2R 0RL, England
For more information about the Penguin Group visit penguin.com

First published in the United States of America by Portfolio/Penguin, a member of Penguin Group (USA) Inc., 2011
This paperback edition with new material published 2013

Pages 65–66: Excerpt from article by Jim Rohn, *Success* magazine. By permission of *Success* magazine.
Pages 241–42: Selections by Bob Dilenschneider. By permission of the author.

THE LIBRARY OF CONGRESS HAS CATALOGED THE HARDCOVER EDITION AS FOLLOWS:
Mackay, Harvey.
The Mackay MBA of selling in the real world / Harvey Mackay.
p. cm.
Includes bibliographical references and index.
ISBN 978-1-59184-387-0 (hc.)
ISBN 978-1-59184-623-9 (pbk.)
1. Selling.   2. Selling—Psychological aspects.   I. Title.
HF5438.25.M312 2011
658.85—dc23 2011021789

PRINTED IN THE UNITED STATES OF AMERICA
1   3   5   7   9   10   8   6   4   2

Set in Adobe Garamond Pro
Designed by Joy O'Meara

Dedication

To the merchant in us all . . . each and every one.

From the five-year-old proprietor of a lemonade stand . . . to the GE sales maven pitching a 250-megawatt turbine dynamo.

From the English lit teacher bending a teenager's ear on the charm of the written word . . . to the community volunteer fighting her heart out for a wetlands wildlife sanctuary.

Forget the Death of a Salesman *and embrace the Life of the Salesperson!*

Negotiating and persuading is what we do 24/7. The aspiration: to execute it expertly . . . and with an irresistible touch of class.

Praise for Harvey's Six *New York Times* Bestselling Books:

Lou Holtz—"Harvey Mackay may be the most talented man I have met."

Billy Graham—"Harvey's business acumen shows through on every page . . . There's so much warmth, wisdom, and wittiness in this book that it would be well for everyone to read every page."

Ted Koppel—"Harvey Mackay takes you on an easy reader ride to success in the business world. He got his; now, in a burst of compassion, he's drafted the guidelines so that you can get yours."

Rabbi Harold Kushner—"Harvey Mackay has no equal when it comes to understanding what makes people tick."

Gloria Steinem—"He is fast, smart, funny—and frighteningly right."

Tom Peters—"Harvey Mackay joins Bob Townsend (*Up the Organization*) as master of brief, biting, and brilliant business wit and wisdom."

Donald Trump—"Harvey's uncanny ability to get people to talk and reveal their darkest and brightest hours is unsurpassed."

Stephen Covey—"A mother lode of timely, hard-earned, bite-size, street-smart golden nuggets . . . invaluable for job seekers, employed or unemployed."

Mark Victor Hansen and Jack Canfield—"Enjoy Harvey's cookbook for success—it gives the reader the best of his wisdom—truly, the best kind of chicken soup for anyone and everyone in business and in life."

Ken Blanchard—"I *love* this book! Mackay strips away the veneer and hits us between the eyes with the naked truth about succeeding in the real world. Impossibly, he delivers more in his second book that in his record-shattering first."

Larry King—"Harvey Mackay is the only person I'll listen to while standing in shark-infested waters . . . real stories from the real world with real solutions."

Norman Vincent Peale—"Harvey Mackay is one of the greatest writers of our time."

Contents

IMAGINE

STICK WITH IT

SETBACKS

REACH OUT

TICK TOCK

EXCEL

Acknowledgments

Any MBA worth its salt covers a lot of turf, and *The Mackay MBA of Selling in the Real World* is no exception.

Ron Beyma should add mind reader to his list of credits. Every author needs a trusted friend who is part cheerleader, part salesman, part word-smith, part taskmaster—and fully committed to success. Ron was my "academic adviser" on this MBA project, but he probably feels like he was the one taking the exams!

The G in Greg Bailey's name could just as well stand for Mr. Get It Done. Every day he plows through millions of details with impeccable skill and inexhaustible energy. This book is further proof. If ever there was an administrative powerhouse who could translate strategy into finely nuanced action, he's the one. Perhaps Greg's most amazing gift is his diplomacy and ease in mobilizing my varied team of supporting professionals.

My sister and editor Margie Resnick Blickman's flawless eye for detail remains as acute and valuable as ever. What dedication and authority! Her ability to shape stories and draw wisdom from them is indispensable, and her flair for packaging take-home value is unmatched.

Jan Miller is a literary agent with a definitive grasp of today's publishing world. A forceful negotiator and a creative partner, she sets the standard in her profession for navigating a book from drawing board to marketplace.

Mary Anne Bailey's skill is her faultless feel for the finishing touch in drawing together a book's every detail into one seamless package.

Penguin Group's Portfolio imprint is the A-team among publishing mavens. Under the formidable leadership of Adrian Zackheim, this comes as no surprise. Adrian is committed to nurturing fresh generations of editorial talent. Newcomer Jillian Gray is ample proof that Adrian knows how to place responsibility in able hands. Jacquelynn Burke, Natalie Horbachevsky, Michael Brown, and Julia Batavia are other talents in this all-star squad. Allison Sweet McLean's publicity skills for Portfolio are poised to help us make the desired dent in the publishing marketplace. And I can't forget Will Weisser, Adrian's second in command.

Every successful book venture today requires outside expert promotional resources. Mark Fortier of Fortier Public Relations has become the new beacon in book publicity, and the strategy he has mapped out is nothing short of catalytic. Cathy Paper's extraordinary market mastery is indispensable to me. Joe Soto and Taylor Hinkle are my social media gurus who are a step ahead of every trend.

For more than half a century Neil Naftalin has been my cornerman when it comes to crunching the definitive number and checking the elusive fact. It's hard to imagine where I would be without his precision . . . or his friendship.

Jan Beyma is a behind-the-scenes researcher with keen diligence, who knows both readers' expectations for clarity and the subtleties of the Web.

Most people do judge a book by its cover, and that's no bad path when you have a talent like Rachel Roddy etching out the design. The winning book covers she has crafted fill the Success Wing of publishing's hallowed halls.

No team member has been more influential in making me a recognizable icon in the media marketplace than photographer Judy Olausen. There's only one way Judy makes all of her subjects look . . . and that's better!

Punctuating text with the inimitable artwork of the *New Yorker* and *Peanuts* adds the talents of the world's perkiest illustrators. Hats off to Cartoon Bank administrator Merrideth Miller for arranging their presence.

Pivotal new business forces deserve special attention. For that reason, I am particularly indebted to Sam Richter and Alex Mandossian for their authoritative, cutting-edge Internet and digital age contributions.

Scott Mitchell, CEO of MackayMitchell Envelope Company, continues to evolve a business built on the principles in this book. I salute Scott and the entire MackayMitchell Envelope team for what they achieve.

And, while they're always mentioned last, know that they are first in my heart: That's the inspirational engine stoked by my remarkable wife, Carol Ann, and our three wonderful kids: David, Mimi and Jojo and their families.

Author's Note

Because I write anecdotally and use real-life situations in all my work, I feel that using gender-specific language lends authenticity to each chapter, and it's easier on the eyes. Obviously, the message in each of these pieces is not aimed solely at a male or female reader. Have fun with what I'm offering here—and learn from the experience of both genders along the way.

I've structured this book to be inviting to read cover to cover. Chapters are short. Lessons are sprinkled in with stories.

The Mackay MBA beats a path up the ladder of excellence. Some of the hardest lessons are saved for last.

My readers have a special fondness for morals and aphorisms—some term it "refrigerator door" wisdom. I call these nuggets Fortune Cookies, because some of them really *can* make you a fortune if you put them to work.

Quickies are sprinkled liberally throughout. Some of them are stories. Some are short-form studies. All are diversions, many on the lighter side.

My vision for this book: An MBA to give you an analytic map for success. *The Mackay MBA* will prime you on the street-smart psychology you need to succeed, especially in the world of sales.

Snack on this book and dip into its lessons regularly and at random. That may be the best way to learn about business . . . and about life.

Harvey Mackay

Foreword

As I've done in a couple of my other books, I start by thanking you for buying this book. Now I want you to do me a favor: Don't—**DO NOT**—*read* this book.

Rough it up!

Study it! Underline it!

Highlight it!

Plaster it with Post-its!

Don't wait to put these ideas, concepts, tools and philosophies to work. They don't pay off in wisdom. They pay off in results. These are the tested practices that have grounded my career for over a half century of selling and business leadership. This book won't revolutionize what you *know* about salesmanship. It will revolutionize and *actualize* the salesperson within you.

Welcome to a world of selling as you have never known it . . . and, even more, my best wishes for a happy and successful life!

Harvey Mackay

"It's the whole kindergarten thing, Mom. I'm alone
in there, swimming with the sharks."

Introduction

Once you meet Harvey Mackay, you never forget him. From the day I met him, it didn't take long before I respected Harvey and loved him like a sibling. A coach is fundamentally a salesperson. Before I became a coach, I was a salesperson in the business world, and one of the most important lessons I ever learned was: "You don't *sell* anyone. You help people get what they want."

I've never met anyone who understands sales better than Harvey, because he has spent his entire life helping people get what they want. In this masterpiece, Harvey gives readers what *they* want: an unrivaled command of sales.

Swim with the Sharks and Beyond

In 1988, Harvey Mackay decided to put all he had learned about salesmanship, management, motivation and negotiation into a book. He called it *Swim with the Sharks Without Being Eaten Alive*. It became a #1 *New York Times* bestseller and launched Harvey's public speaking career. Today Harvey is the author of six *New York Times* bestsellers, and two of his books—*Swim with the Sharks* and *Beware the Naked Man Who Offers You His Shirt*—have ranked among the *New York Times'* top 15 inspirational business books of all time. His motivational business books have sold more than 10 million copies, are distributed in 80 countries worldwide, and have been translated into 42 languages.

Swim with the Sharks launched a remarkable international speaking career for Harvey. For more than two decades, he has been speaking once a week somewhere in the world to a Fortune 1000 company or a leading business association. He is one of America's most popular and entertaining business speakers. In 1993, he was voted by Toastmasters International as one of the five top speakers in the world, and he is a member of the National Speakers Association's Hall of Fame. He has also addressed students at many of the top business schools—Harvard, Stanford, Wharton, University of Chicago, University of Southern California and Notre Dame.

Harvey has been a nationally syndicated columnist for United Feature Syndicate since 1993, author of a weekly business article which appears in 60 newspapers and magazines across the country with a combined circulation of more than 10 million. "It's called a business column," Harvey stresses, "but it's really about life lessons." The diverse backgrounds of the thousands who send him letters and e-mails each year vouch for this.

Harvey's books and columns are used in more than 200 universities and can be found in libraries all across the United States. In addition to his widespread writings and public speaking engagements, Harvey has counseled and mentored more than 500 students and young adults.

Playing-Field Psychologist Without Rival

When Harvey Mackay recruited me to revitalize the University of Minnesota football team in December 1983, he greeted me at the Twin Cities airport in a raccoon coat. I wasn't at all sure I wanted to take this plunge. The windchill must have been 30 below outside, but Harvey was all fire and gumption. Then and there I knew I was up against a psychological talent with major-league reach.

Harvey persuaded me to come to Minnesota, whatever my misgivings about the climate. The decision was the right one. To this day, I stand in awe at the wonderful detail and engineering that he used to anticipate and overcome any objection I could have had. He knew his prospect to the core. Every detail was concocted into the equation. Every appeal was introduced effortlessly at just the right moment to make it persuasive.

Those early negotiations sealed what has become a lifelong friendship. Ever since, I have spent a lot of time with Harvey on the golf course, and the excellence of his competitive thinking dazzles there as well. I've played at least a hundred rounds of golf with him. Not once has he ever lost the appetite to battle on. Vince Lombardi never lost a football game, the great coach maintained; he just ran out of time.

So it is with Harvey. Ever ready to play the next nine holes, he's sure he can spot that chink in your game or in your psyche that will turn his fortunes. Given the time and the chance, I'm sure he would. Harvey knows how to pay attention to every psychological signal and motivational cue. What's even better, he knows how to teach others to listen with that same finely tuned ear.

You know what takes my breath away about Harvey's competitive zeal? His infinite capacity to learn. I knew he had a marathon coach and a speech coach, and that was impressive enough. On Amen Corner at Augusta, Harvey had just sunk a beauty of a putt on the 13th hole one afternoon. When I asked him how, he muttered offhand, "Lou, having a putting coach helps." He then proceeded to tell me about the tips he'd picked up from Stan Utley at Grayhawk Learning Center in Scottsdale. A *putting* coach, you ask? When mere inches make the difference, Harvey will find the master who will put that precious edge to his advantage. And the teacher in Harvey gives him a special satisfaction in sharing his knowledge of inside resources with others.

Lessons . . . and the Long View

Harvey has described his philosophy of life as being built on these four cornerstones: Be a good husband. Be a good father. Be a good businessperson. Give back to your community—in both time and money—for the good fortune that you've had. His definition of success is just as straightforward: "Have a predetermined goal and successfully carry it out over a long period of time—and have a terrific time doing it," Harvey says.

For example: "If you're a street cleaner," he says, "be the best street cleaner you can be. If you're a hairstylist, be the best hairstylist you can be. If you're a CEO, be the best CEO you can be." This attitude, Harvey believes, is something you have to foster early in life. "I've never met a successful person who hasn't had to overcome either a little or a lot of adversity in his or her life," Harvey explains. "Move mountains to find a mentor. No one can do it all on their own . . . even the Lone Ranger had Tonto." Harvey believes in lifetime education, and that education must be America's #1 priority. Why? Harvey's answer: "The best way I've heard it stated is, 'If you think education is expensive, try ignorance.'"

When asked what it takes to be successful, Harvey says you must start with a mission statement. Harvey's is simple: "My goal is to be successful. To achieve that goal, I will never stop learning, growing, changing or giving of myself. End of mission statement. Hit the start button to a whale of a lifetime."

Harvey has made giving back to his community a priority in his life. For many years, he was the chairman of the task force that made a reality of the Hubert H. Humphrey Metrodome in Minneapolis, Minnesota, and he was proud to be asked to throw out the first baseball there. He played a key role in landing the 1992 Super Bowl for Minneapolis, and he was a catalyst in obtaining an NBA franchise, the Minnesota Timberwolves, for the city. Harvey also co-chaired the Save Gopher Sports campaign, which in 2002 raised nearly $3 million to save three varsity sports—men's and women's golf and men's gymnastics—from extinction at the University of Minnesota. The men's golf team miraculously went on to win the NCAA championship that year.

Harvey has been a board member of more than 20 nonprofit organizations committed to helping people and communities, and has served as president of many of these organizations. Harvey was a member of the Board of Trustees of Robert Redford's Sundance Institute for 12 years; he has also served on the boards of the Minnesota Orchestra and the Guthrie Theater, as well as Allina Health Systems and the Minnesota chapters of the American Cancer Society and the American Heart Association.

From 1979 to 1981, Harvey was elected by his peers to lead the Envelope Manufacturers Association. He has been inducted into the Sales and Marketing Executives International's Academy of Achievement Hall of Fame as well as the Minnesota Business Hall of Fame. He has served as president of the University of Minnesota National Alumni Association and as president of the Minneapolis Chamber of Commerce.

In 2004 Harvey received the coveted Horatio Alger Award, which is given to distinguished Americans "who demonstrate individual initiative and a commitment to excellence, as exemplified by remarkable achievements accomplished through honesty, hard work, self-reliance and perseverance." The ceremony marking his membership took place in the chambers of the U.S. Supreme Court. And in 2007 he received the prestigious Ellis Island Medal of Honor. Previous recipients of these two awards include U.S. presidents, senators, kings, queens, business legends, entertainers and superstar athletes . . . not to mention one former college football coach.

From the podium he kids that in high school he was so skinny he could tread water in a test tube, yet Harvey has run 10 marathons in the last 15 years, including those in Boston and New York, and he is a former #1-ranked senior tennis player in the state of Minnesota. Harvey is a prostate cancer survivor and has never given a speech without mentioning how vitally important it is for every man to get a PSA test after the age of 45.

And here's what Harvey has to say about the family he and his wife have raised: "Friends and family have told me for years that I married over my head. And guess what? It's true. My incredible wife, Carol Ann, has a list of achievements that dwarfs mine. Our best accomplishment together is our three children, David, Mimi and Jojo, and our 11 wonderful grandchildren, who are the very heart of my life."

Harvey was once asked to capture in a nutshell his advice on living. He said: "Do what you love. Love what you do. And deliver more than you promise."

Lou Holtz

Lou Holtz—a living legend—is one of the greatest coaches in college football history. His unforgettable leadership of the football program at the University of Notre Dame made him a national icon. He is the only coach in NCAA history to lead six different universities to bowl games, one of the reasons why he was inducted into the College Football Hall of Fame in his first year of eligibility. Today viewers of all ages applaud the insights and wisdom of his contributions as the dean of college football analysts on ESPN.

THE MACKAY
MBA OF SELLING
IN THE
REAL WORLD

Prologue:
Sales Superstardom

The Ingredients

What Makes a Good Salesperson?

I've been a salesman all my life, and I've been hiring sales reps for nearly as long. So I think I know a thing or two about sales. I am often asked to identify the traits of a sales superstar. Here's my recipe:

- **Hungry fighter.** If I had to name only three traits that make a great sales representative, they would be:

hungry fighter,

hungry fighter and

hungry fighter.

That's how much I think of this trait. Every good salesperson I've ever encountered is driven. They have a strong work ethic and a high energy level. They work harder and longer than their peers. When the economy is poor, they are still out there pounding the pavement, making calls.

- **High integrity.** I've always believed that telling the truth is the best policy. In business, especially today, it's a must. A few years back, the Forum

Corporation in Boston studied 341 salespeople from 11 different companies in 5 different industries. Their purpose was to determine what separated the top producers from the average producers. When the study was finished, the results were startling. It was not skill, knowledge or charisma that divided the pack. The difference came down to one trait: honesty. When customers trust salespeople, they buy from them!

• **Positive attitude.** Your attitude, not your aptitude, will determine your altitude. Success is 90 percent mental. You can alter your life by altering your mind. In tough economies, it may not be your fault for being down, but it is certainly your fault for not getting up. You have to be a believer to be an achiever.

• **Authoritative.** Strong sales reps know their products backward and forward. They also know their competitors' products and are prepared to point out the differences.

• **Prepared.** I still remember the old Boy Scout motto, "Be prepared." Well, it's true. It takes a lot of unspectacular preparation to produce spectacular results.

• **Reputation.** You can't buy a good reputation—you must earn it. If you don't have a positive reputation, it will be difficult to be successful in whatever you do.

• **Likability.** I have never known anyone to buy from someone they don't like. Are you genuine? Pleasant? Easy to talk with?

• **Good first impression.** You never get a second chance to make a good first impression. Are you neat and well groomed? Underdressed or overdressed?

• **Goalsetter: measurable, identifiable, obtainable, specific and in writing.** Winners set goals; losers make excuses. Goals give you more than a reason to get up in the morning; they are an incentive to keep you going all day.

• **Service mentality.** I've often said the sale begins when the customer says yes. Good salespeople make sure the job gets done on time—and done right. There's one thing no business has enough of: customers. Take care of the customers you've got, and they'll take care of you. You must have a fanatical attention to detail!

- **Great listener.** You can't learn anything with your mouth open. For too many people, good listening means, "I talk, *you* listen." Listening is a two-way process. Yes, you need to be heard, but you also need to hear others' ideas, questions and objections. If you talk at people instead of *with* them, they're not buying in—they're caving in. Believe it or not, being a good listener is more important in sales than being a good talker.

- **Sense of humor.** It is impossible to overrate the importance of a sense of humor. When there are inevitable setbacks along the way, learn to laugh about them.

- **Thirst for self-improvement.** You don't go to school once for a lifetime. You are in school all your life. Good salespeople are constantly working to become better. They take courses, read books, listen to audiotapes and inhale everything they can to improve. We live in the information age, so it's easy to take every opportunity to learn and grow at any hour of the day.

Study this list. Commit to developing or improving these traits, and prepare for a spectacular career!

Mackay's Moral: A salesperson tells, a good salesperson explains . . . and a great salesperson demonstrates.

YOU

Chapter 1

The Early Bird

The *San Francisco Chronicle* used to call me monthly to participate in a discussion on a particular subject for their Sunday edition. One month the subject was "What job taught you the most lessons?"

I had to think about that for a while since I've had only a couple of jobs in my adult life. My first job out of college was for an envelope company, where I toiled for nearly five years. I learned plenty in that job, of course, but most significantly that I wanted to own my own company. In 1959, I bought a struggling envelope company, and the rest is history. I learn something new in this job every day.

After giving it some thought, I realized that the job that really taught me a lot was the paper route that my father, who headed the Associated Press bureau in St. Paul, Minnesota, encouraged me to sign up for when I was 10.

Here are some of the lessons I remember learning at that young age:

- **Hard work**. Seven days a week, I had to get up at 4 a.m., when it was pitch dark and often snowing or raining, and deliver my papers by 6 a.m. There were no days off. And nine months of the year I had school to look forward to after my route.
- **Promptness**. Be on time. Customers expected to crack open the morning paper at the same time as they did their three-minute eggs.
- **Focus**. When you know you have to get up early every morning, you know you have to get your homework done and get to bed

early. It helps to think about the rewards of hard work. I was constantly saving for something, and if I focused on that, the work seemed easier. I've always felt that if you put your mind to it, you can do anything.

- **Persistence.** You deal with all kinds of people, including many who don't like to pay their bills. But you have to keep after them. You learn that there are good days and bad days at work, but you work on all of them regardless. Pretty soon the bad days get better.

- **Customer service.** You learn how to deal with people face-to-face on a paper route. Sometimes you have to apologize for things that are out of your control, which is a tough thing to teach to anyone, especially a 10-year-old. But this is what I had to do when newspapers were late getting to me, or when other elements like the weather caused havoc, and I was in turn late getting papers delivered.

- **Quality control.** Who likes a wet newspaper? We didn't have little plastic bags to put papers in back in those days. And it was important to remember who wanted the paper between the doors, in the milk box or under the mat.

- **Accountability.** I was accountable for my route to make sure my customers received their newspapers in a timely fashion and that they paid their bills. It's pretty cut and dried, especially when you are a one-man show.

- **Handling money.** Collections and keeping financial records were also important, as well as learning how to handle money. A 10-cent boo-boo was as important to me then as a thousand-dollar mistake is now. The adding-and-subtracting end of the business also helped with math class.

- **Salesmanship.** Most important, I learned my #1 skill: the art of selling. If people paid in advance, I earned more from the newspaper office. If I could get my customers to pay for the newspaper one or two months in advance, I was in candy heaven. Likewise, if I could get new subscribers, I made more money—a good incentive for anyone. I learned that I loved to sell, and knew it would be my life's work.

Now, after 50-plus years of working with another kind of paper, I can honestly say that the job that launched my career was pivotal. Everyone has to start somewhere. You never forget your first job.

Today the business of delivering papers is usually handled by people old enough to have a driver's license. More and more, the news itself is delivered to us on the Internet. But the same classic lessons I learned about business as a paperboy are being learned by young people in their first jobs everywhere, whether behind the register of a convenience store or tending to tots, lawns or gardens.

No matter where you go to work, you are not an employee—you are a business with one employee: you. Nobody owes you a career. You own it, as a sole proprietor. You must compete with millions of individuals every day of your career. You must enhance your value every day, hone your competitive advantage, learn, adapt, move between jobs and industries—retrench so you can advance and learn new skills.

Mackay's Moral: It's never too early to learn this lesson: A student of life always does the homework.

Quickie #1
Integrity Deflates Easily

Ethics and integrity must be the cornerstone of every sales professional's existence. Let me tell you a true story about Professor Bonk, who taught chemistry at Duke University. The lessons: First, integrity is always right. Second, dishonesty can be very risky business.

One year, three guys were taking chemistry and all getting solid A's going into the final exam. They were so confident that the weekend before finals they decided to go up to the University of Virginia to party with some friends. Due to bad hangovers, they slept all day Sunday and didn't make it back to Duke until early Monday morning.

Rather than taking the final exam then, they explained to Professor Bonk that they'd gotten a flat tire on their trip to Virginia and didn't have a spare, so they didn't get back to campus until late Sunday night. They wanted to delay the exam until Tuesday.

Professor Bonk thought this over and then agreed they could make up the final on the following day. The three guys were elated and relieved. They studied that night and went in for the test the next day. Professor Bonk placed them in three separate rooms, handed each of them a test booklet, looked at his watch and told them to begin.

They opened up the test booklet and saw that the first question, about OXYGEN, was worth 5 points.

They all thought this was going to be easy. Then they turned the page and saw the second question, worth 95 points:

Which tire?

Chapter 2

Believe in Yourself

Another professor I want to mention stood before his class of 30 senior molecular biology students, about to pass out the final exam. "I have been privileged to be your instructor this semester, and I know how hard you have all worked to prepare for this test. I also know most of you are off to medical school or grad school next fall," he said to them. "I am well aware of how much pressure you are under to keep your GPAs up, and because I know you are all capable of understanding this material, I am prepared to offer an automatic B to anyone who would prefer not to take the final."

The relief was audible as a number of students jumped up to thank the professor and departed from class. The professor looked at the handful of students who remained, and offered again, "Any other takers? This is your last opportunity." One more student decided to go.

Seven students remained. The professor closed the door and took attendance. Then he handed out the final exam.

There were two sentences typed on the paper: "Congratulations, you have just received an A in this class. Keep believing in yourself."

I never had a professor who gave a test like that. It may seem like the easy way out of grading a bunch of exams, but it's a test that any teacher in any discipline could and should give. Students who don't have confidence in what they've learned are B students at best.

The same is true for students of real life. The A students are those who believe in what they're doing because they've learned from both successes and failures. They've absorbed life's lessons, whether from formal education or the school of hard knocks, and they've become better people. These are the people you look for when you're hiring or promoting, and they're the ones you keep if you're downsizing. Your organization needs that brand of thinking.

Psychologists say that, by the age of two, 50 percent of what we believe about ourselves has already been formed; by age six, it's 60 percent, and at eight years, 80 percent.

Wouldn't you love to have the energy and optimism of a little kid? There is nothing you couldn't do or learn or be.

But you're a big kid now, and you realize you have some limits. Don't let the biggest limit be yourself. Take your cue from Sir Edmund Hillary, the first person to reach the summit of Mount Everest: "It's not the mountain we conquer, but ourselves."

Remember the four-minute mile? People had been trying to achieve it since the early days of civilization. In fact, folklore has it that the Greeks had lions chase the runners, thinking that would make them run faster. They also tried drinking tiger's milk—not the stuff you get down at the health food store, but the real thing. Nothing worked. So they decided it was impossible. And for thousands of years everyone believed it.

It was physiologically impossible for a human being to run a mile in four minutes. Our bone structure was all wrong. Wind resistance too great. Inadequate lung power. There were a million reasons.

Then one man—one single human being—proved that the doctors, the trainers, the athletes and all those before him who'd tried and failed were all wrong. And miracle of miracles, in the three years *after* Roger Bannister did it, approximately a dozen other runners broke the four-minute mile.

A few years ago in New York, I stood at the finish line of the Fifth Avenue Mile race and watched 13 out of 13 runners break the four-minute mile in a single race. In other words, the runner who finished dead last, that 13th runner, would have been regarded as having accomplished the impossible just decades earlier.

What happened? There were no great breakthroughs in training. Human bone structure didn't suddenly improve. But human attitudes did.

On May 6, 1954, Bannister ran the first sub-four-minute mile in recorded history at 3 minutes, 59.4 seconds. Let's turn the clock back from now. In the last six decades, the four-minute barrier has been reduced by nearly 17 seconds. But that's hardly the whole story. New Zealander John Walker was the first person to run 100 sub-four-minute miles during his career, and American Steve Scott has run the most sub-four-minute miles, with 136.

Believe in yourself, even when no one else does.

Currently the mile record is held by Hicham El Guerrouj, who set a time of 3 minutes, 43.13 seconds in Rome in 1999. Another advance in this incredible progression: In 1994, 40 years after Bannister's breaking of the barrier, the Irish runner Eamonn Coghlan became the first man over the age of 40 to run a sub-four-minute mile.

You *can* accomplish your goals . . . if you set them. Who says you're not tougher, smarter, better, harder-working or more able than your competition? It doesn't matter if *they* say you can't do it. What matters—the only thing that matters—is if *you* say it. Until Bannister came along, we all believed the experts. Bannister believed in himself—and changed the world. If you believe in yourself, well, then there's nothing you can't accomplish. So don't quit. Don't ever quit.

Mackay's Moral: If you believe, you will achieve.

Quickie #2
Bet on You!

Whatever you do, don't be like Melvin. He went to church every day for three months and kept praying to God to please let him win the lottery.

A bolt of lightning.

Melvin asks, "God, is that You? I am a simple man. All I want is one thing. Please let me win the lottery."

And God tells him: "Do me a favor . . . Meet me halfway . . . Buy a ticket."

Believe in yourself . . . even when no one else does. Don't just sit around and wait for things to happen!

Chapter 3

One Person:
All the Difference

All my life my father pounded into me: One person can make all the difference in the world. I can't think of a better example than my good friend Jon Wefald, president emeritus of Kansas State University. In 1986, Jon Wefald was made the 12th president of the school. In a brilliant career, the following is what he accomplished:

- Enrollments increased from 16,500 in 1986 to more than 23,500 in 2009. In 1984, the administration prior to Wefald's had predicted that enrollments would fall to about 11,000 or 12,000.
- The campus added a total of 2.5 million square feet of new space, including 26 new structures.
- All in all, Kansas State University has been developed into one of the most beautiful university campuses anywhere in America.
- Today K-State is at the forefront of animal health research.
- The university is vitally involved with the United States Army and the Pentagon to become a national leader in the effort to solve the crisis that might be caused by agro-terrorists.
- The academic prestige of the university has grown enormously over the past 20 years, and Kansas State is now regarded from coast to coast as an excellent land-grant university. A total of 125 K-State students have won Rhodes, Marshall, Truman, Goldwater

and Udall scholarships since 1986, which puts K-State ahead of other public universities winning those awards during that period.

- Jon Wefald was part of a handful of university presidents instrumental in developing the Big 12 Conference, which has become one of the top athletics conferences in the nation.

- K-State became a top 10 football team during the past decade, having gone to 11 straight bowl games from 1993 to 2003. By beating the University of Oklahoma for the Big 12 Championship in Kansas City in December 2003, K-State won its most important football game yet.

- The women's basketball team won the Big 12 Championship in 2004. The women's volleyball team has been to eight straight NCAA tournaments.

All in all, the progress Jon Wefald made at Kansas State University during his tenure as president was extraordinary. Better said, it was breathtaking!

How did he do it? Jon is one of the greatest salespeople I have ever met.

In the two decades we have known each other, I'll bet Jon has sent me more than 50 letters about his dreams, goals and vision for the university, and how he was going to accomplish them. When he invited me to address the Kansas State University MBA program (and stay overnight at the president's mansion), I saw firsthand a leader admired by staff, faculty, administration and students.

Jon Wefald took stock of his considerable assets. He tirelessly put them to work to advance his organization. Inevitably the glow he created reflected on him personally.

Mackay's Moral: What sets you apart gets you ahead. Make it work for you. Then make it sell for you too.

Chapter 4

Loyalty in Little Things Is Huge

When the going gets tough . . . the tough sometimes just dig in their heels.

Take Amador Barbosa, a Latino American war hero and member of what Tom Brokaw called "The Greatest Generation"—the men and women whose courage won us World War II. Amador, in his 80s, told Manny Lopez of the *Kansas City Business Journal* of an incident that happened while he was clearing German land mines by a roadway.

An American truck carrying explosives was ordered to stop because of the mine threat. Barbosa and his buddies were ordered to empty the truck of its high-risk cargo. Suddenly enemy bullets rained down on the truck. The Germans were trying to blow up the truck and the roadway so they could flee more easily. The truck caught fire, but Barbosa—true to his mission and to his team—continued to unload the burning crates of grenades and bazooka shells. For this he earned the Soldier's Medal—which is, by the way, two notches above a Purple Heart—for risking his life to save someone else's.

That's extraordinary loyalty. In a world where careers have become as portable as smartphones, even *ordinary* loyalty is fast disappearing from the business landscape. It shows. Loyalty is the foremost ingredient in long-term sales relationships. The lack of it is why more and more deals are struck on price alone.

One of the first qualities I look for in both employees and friends is loyalty. Someone can be a great worker, but if he isn't loyal, his employment puts the company in jeopardy. Without loyalty, a "friend" is really only an acquaintance. When someone is my friend, I make a 100 percent commitment, 100 percent of the time. And I expect the same from others.

A testament to that is the Wall of Service at MackayMitchell Envelope Company, where every employee's picture is displayed. You would be in awe of the tenure of our employees. We have employees with up to 45 years of service. Among our retirees are many whose entire careers were spent with us.

My philosophy is this: Employee loyalty begins with employer loyalty. Your employees should know that if they do the job they were hired to do with a reasonable amount of competence and efficiency, you will support them. You will take an interest in their career advancement and give them the tools they need to perform effectively. In return, you as the employer can expect that your workforce is prepared to give its best effort every day.

It goes beyond the "I'll scratch your back and you scratch mine" notion. There is a common goal that can be reached only if everyone pulls together for the good of all.

Loyalty is as compelling a sales priority as it is a personal trait.

Fostering employee loyalty is the first step to creating customer loyalty. Most businesses depend on loyal customers for their bread and butter, and occasionally for their gravy as well. We all have customers who will buy from us even when they can get a lower price somewhere else, or quicker turnaround, or better service.

But change all those "ors" into "ands" and your customers will start to question your loyalty to them. The same holds true for employees. You can't keep them guessing how they will be treated and expect them to give their best to you.

I couldn't agree more with Frederick Reichheld, author of *Loyalty Rules!*, who believes that loyalty is the fuel that drives financial success. Based on extensive research into companies from online start-ups to established institutions such as Harley-Davidson, Enterprise Rent-A-Car, Cisco, Dell, Intuit and more, Reichheld reveals six bedrock principles of loyalty upon which leaders build enduring enterprises.

1. **Play to win/win.** Never profit at the expense of partners.
2. **Be picky.** Membership must be a privilege.
3. **Keep it simple.** Reduce complexity for speed and flexibility.
4. **Reward the right results.** Worthy partners deserve worthy goals.
5. **Listen hard and talk straight.** Insist on honest, two-way communication and learning.
6. **Preach what you practice.** Explain your principles, then live by them.

Could it be simpler?

John Akers, former chairman of IBM, puts loyalty in this context: "We've all heard shortsighted businessmen attribute a quote of Vince Lombardi: 'Winning is not the most important thing; it's the only thing.' Well, that's a good quote for firing up a team, but as an overarching philosophy it's just baloney. I much prefer another Lombardi quote. He expected his players, he once said, to have three kinds of loyalty: to God, to their families and to the Green Bay Packers, in that order."

Mackay's Moral: Employees should be encouraged to ask questions, but they should never have to question your loyalty.

Chapter 5

Find Mentors

Well, the truth is, we're not all Roger Bannisters or Jon Wefalds or Albert Einsteins . . . and we don't have to be first to succeed. As a famous politico once said, "It's the pioneers who get all the arrows."

In the restaurant business, for example, you never want to be the first operator in a location. Usually the place has to pass through three or four sets of hands before there's a fit between a restaurant, its location and the market that's being served.

The trick is to benefit from the Bannisters without having to take the arrows. The people who ran the four-minute mile *after* Bannister had succeeded in large part because they had Bannister as a role model to prove it could be done. When Bannister accomplished it, the others were able to psych themselves up and do the same thing.

Jim Pollard, the "Kangaroo Kid" of the Minneapolis Lakers (before they moved to Los Angeles), was my role model from how he laced his shoes to how he cradled a rebound one-handed, even to his running style. I still run that way today . . . albeit a tad slower.

As an undergraduate at the University of Minnesota, having Professor Harold Deutsch as my academic adviser was a personal milestone. I took Professor Deutsch's class on the history of World War II. He had been one of the interpreters at the Nuremberg Trials. To say he made history come alive would be an understatement. He did not teach history; he was part of history. His class met every Tuesday and Thursday. You came early because it was SRO—standing room only. And it was no snap course. Professor

Deutsch was a wonderful mentor to me and made me realize how important it is for everyone to have a mentor in life.

Professor Deutsch and my college golf coach at Minnesota, Les Bolstad, both taught me how to stay focused and to set realistic goals. They also taught me the arts of persuasion, leadership and visualization.

Who (or what) is psyching *you* up? If you think about why you are the way you are, chances are it has a lot to do with trying to be like someone you've admired. You've observed and imitated that person's mannerisms. Sometimes, to win his or her approval, you've patterned your whole lifestyle after that person. And you didn't become permanently cynical just because you discovered at age fourteen that Mom and Dad weren't perfect and that Simon and Garfunkel were right: Joe DiMaggio *has* gone and he ain't ever coming back. (In case you don't remember who Simon and Garfunkel were, don't worry. One day, they won't be coming back either.)

You never stop needing role models.

The superstars in any field keep right on holding role models in front of their eyes long after they've become role models themselves. They study them, copy them, compete with them—even try to surpass them. It doesn't end with childhood. They constantly goad themselves to meet new challenges. They top old role models, then find new ones. They top themselves, and they set new goals. What better way to measure yourself, to feel good about yourself and achieve, than trying to be like the people you admire?

Mackay's Moral: Look at yourself in the mirror. If you like what you see, capture the same positive energy every morning of your life.

Chapter 6

Practice Right
So You Can't Get It Wrong

Practice makes perfect . . . not true. You have to add one word: Perfect practice makes perfect.

I wish I had coined that phrase, but I didn't. Vince Lombardi did. Practice something time and time again and—if you don't know what you are doing—all you are really doing is perfecting an error. You have put a ceiling on how good you can become.

A golfer can go out and play eight days a week. He can practice eight days a week. And if he doesn't know what he is doing, all he is really doing is perfecting his errors—eight days a week.

I have studied the Russian, Chinese, Japanese and Arabic languages and, quite frankly, people think I am a heck of a linguist. Actually, I am a lot slower learner than most of the people with whom I started my language classes. But there is one marked difference: I finished. They didn't.

The difference that matters is *what* you learn, not how fast you learn it.

For Japanese, it might take 200 hours. Russian, 300 hours. Mandarin, 400 hours. But eventually that breakthrough occurs.

It's kind of like a stonecutter hammering away at his rock perhaps 100 times without making a dent in it. And yet on the 101st blow, the rock splits in two. It was not that blow that did it, but what followed all that had come before. If you're not willing to practice—and practice until you get it right—you will never make the 100 blows that cause the breakthrough on the 101st.

A perfect example of this was when my son, David, and I were taking Japanese lessons from the Berlitz language school in preparation for a four-week stay in Japan. At the time, he was an undergraduate student at Stanford University and right at the peak of his learning curve. I was somewhat over the hill and would not be considered a fast learner. However, it made no difference whatsoever because of my perseverance. After two weeks into the class, David was on page 75 of the text and I was on page 30. By the end of the course, he had learned approximately 35 percent more than I had because of his speed and young brain. To overcome this, I had to spend an extra three weeks of studying to catch up with him. In the end, we both left with the same Japanese vocabulary. I just had to pay a higher price.

Look at the great athletes and musicians. There are no walk-ons at the Super Bowl or Carnegie Hall . . . or in corporate boardrooms, for that matter. The level of performance in those exalted places is only partially a reflection of talent. There are two other qualities that are indispensable in making it to the top: determination and expert coaching.

Over a lifetime I've had numerous coaches to help me bring out whatever God-given talent and potential I have. I've had coaches for:

- public speaking
- writing
- ideas/creativity
- computers/social media
- foreign languages
- marathon running
- golf (including putting)
- downhill and waterskiing
- swimming
- dancing (thanks to my wife, Carol Ann)
- table tennis
- bowling

- stretching
- boxing
- scuba diving
- ice skating
- basketball
- volleyball . . . and many, many others.

Whatever it is you do, you can be better at it if you just keep on learning. I certainly have not mastered the art of making envelopes, selling envelopes or developing new envelopes.

The minute I persuade myself that I have learned all there is to learn about a subject and can relax, that's the moment my competition will hand me my head and slam me into the pavement. The annals of business are filled with stories of companies which thought they had it made and could milk their enterprises as cash cows without having to bother about improving their products or services. It's amazing how fast they found their markets disappearing.

Apply this lesson to your own business. Hire people who are still learning, people who feel that learning is a lifelong process, either in the classroom, in the office or at home. Show them you want them to grow—and your business will grow too.

Right after communism fell in the early 1990s, I made a seven-day lecture tour to Moscow. I will never, ever forget a Help Wanted sign I spotted. It translated, "Inexperience Wanted!" In short, they didn't want anyone who had been practicing bad habits. They wanted a new and fresh employee that they could train properly.

Mackay's Moral: All the world's a stage, and most of us need more rehearsals.

PRACTICE—The Fortune Cookies

No matter how long a doctor has been treating patients, he is still practicing.

———————————

Theory may raise people's hopes, but practice raises their income.

———————————

A man prepared has won half the battle.

———————————

A pint of sweat will save a gallon of blood.—*George Patton*

———————————

A winner is someone who recognizes his God-given talents, works his tail off to develop them into skills and uses these skills to accomplish his goals.—*Larry Bird*

———————————

Before everything else, getting ready is the secret of success.
—*Henry Ford*

———————————

Amateurs practice until they get it right. Professionals practice until they can't get it wrong.

———————————

Everybody wants to be on a championship team, but nobody wants to come to practice.—*Bobby Knight*

———————————

Failure to prepare is preparing to fail.—*John Wooden*

———————————

Good, better, best; never rest till good be better, and better, best.

———————————

Chapter 7

Learn from Legends

At MackayMitchell Envelope Company, we just celebrated our first half century in business. One of the reasons we made it this long is our phenomenal sales force. They are all A+ students. But one was the genuine professor emeritus of sales.

Harry Goldfarb decided at the tender age of 25 to flog envelopes. Fifty-five years later, he was still at it. And were we ever lucky he was still on our team until the day he died. I'd hate to have had him working for the competition.

When I bought this near-bankrupt company way back when, Harry came with the furniture. I had long since gotten rid of the furniture; Harry was not disposable. He passed away at the age of 80, but he was 80 going on 21, and retirement was not in his vocabulary. If you don't use it, Harry would tell you, you'll lose it.

So what is it that separated him from the pack? He was the essence of the hungry fighter. A competitor. A guy who believed second is last. And yet, in his own quiet, inimitable style, he was a class act all the way—with his family, customers and company peers. In short, everybody loved Harry. If Harry met 100 people, all 100 people would not like him . . . they would *love* him! He had instant credibility.

The amazing thing is these exact words could have been written about Harry when he was 80, when he was 75, when he was 25.

Well . . . you get the picture.

Harry didn't change one-tenth of 1 percent during his 55-year selling career. Not in the eyes of his peers or his customers.

How did he do it?

Sincerity, dogged persistence, fanatical attention to detail, sense of humor and a lot of giggles . . . He knew *thine* enemy (our competitors) and was completely knowledgeable about the envelope business. He was truly the dean of the Minneapolis–St. Paul envelope community. You might take an order away from him, but you'd *never* pick off one of his accounts. Why? Because he would never, never, never give up.

Remember, when Harry started in this racket, it cost only two cents to mail a letter. Envelopes looked pretty much like they do now. He had no competition from fax machines or e-mail. And people actually wrote letters.

Sure, Harry remembered the good old days, but he didn't live in the past. He provided good old-fashioned service. And he found that as times and technology changed, service was still the glue that made the deal stick.

That was the indomitable Harry spirit I knew. And it's lacking in too many people today who choose sales as a career.

Shortly before Harry passed away, I phoned one of his accounts and asked the buyer, "Why have you stayed with Harry all these decades? I know it's at least 35-plus years."

She didn't miss a beat.

"That's easy. Harry's a prince. Over the years he's hauled envelopes in his car up to our office . . . actually bought envelopes from your competitor when you were out of stock to satisfy us . . . opened your factory on a Saturday to get out a dated mailing . . . and never has made a pit stop at our office without his million-dollar smile."

We were just wild about Harry, and still are.

I was honored to speak at Harry's funeral. "When God made Harry," I said, "He didn't do anything else that day. He was the most tenacious yet easygoing bulldog I ever knew."

Mackay's Moral: If you have a Harry in your shop, treasure him or her. They know what taking care of business is all about.

Chapter 8

Sell Yourself

The three toughest sells: Company. Product. Self.

A new salesperson takes over a sales territory from a salesperson who's just been fired. He calls on the CEO of the XYZ company. The CEO greets him thus: "Let's get something straight. I don't like your company. I don't like your products. And I don't like you. Don't let the door hit you on your way out."

The new salesman smiles at the CEO and says to her, "Gee, I wish I had 100 prospects like you!"

The CEO looks at him and says, "Perhaps you didn't hear me. I said I don't like your company, I don't like your products and I don't like you. Now I want you out of here."

The salesperson says, "Yes, I understand, and I still wish I had 100 prospects like you."

The CEO is having a hard time believing what's going on. "I must be missing something," she says. "Why on earth do you wish you had 100 prospects like me?"

"Because I have 500," the salesman replies.

Having 100 prospects who don't like you, your company or your products can make it difficult to get started each day, but that's precisely what makes winners out of people—overcoming obstacles, large and small, to come out on top.

But any salesperson with an ounce of sense must take a serious look at objections potential customers raise. Is the company the problem? Are deliveries late or incorrect? Is price an ongoing issue? Are guarantees offered and honored? Do you have support from your supervisors to do a little extra for your customers? Does this company have a reputation for making customers want to continue to do business with you?

> **In sales, you have good days and bad days. The trick is to convince yourself every morning that it's going to be a good day.**

If you're having a difficult time answering these basic questions to your satisfaction, your customer will show you the door—and you should run right through it and find another company to work for.

How about the products you're selling? Good? Great? The best? Reliable? In demand? Too cheap or too expensive? Weird colors/shapes/sizes? The old line about being able to sell ice to an Eskimo doesn't really apply to the folks out there who are trying to keep their customers happy day after day. Sooner or later the smooth talkers are exposed. Sooner or later the products they sell are no longer in demand. If you really want to make a good living in sales, you must have superior products that customers want. It's that simple. Your company and your products are easy enough to change . . . it's the "you" factor that determines whether you were born to sell.

The tough question—what is it your (potential) customers don't like about you? You might gather a few good friends and try your pitch, demonstrate your products and use all your best lines. These are people who like you, after all. Chances are, they'll tell you that you're doing everything just fine. I've always said, people buy from people they like.

The opposite is true too. Consider this story: Two salesmen are walking down the street together. One says to the other, "Do you see that SOB across the street?" The other sales rep says, "Yeah. I don't sell him either."

If you really have a deep-down burning desire to improve, you need to go back to the people who said no to you in their offices. Beg if you must, but ask for a few minutes of their very valuable time to find out where you messed up. Ask first about your company and your products, and make note of any objections to what you're selling.

Then move to *how* you're selling. Give them a few leads, if they are reluctant to be critical.

Was I too arrogant?

Too pushy?

Too condescending?

Too obnoxious?

Did I listen to your needs?

Did I waste your time?

Did I do my homework?

Is there someone else I should be talking to?

What are you looking for in a supplier?

May I call on you again in a few months?

Is there another reason you won't do business with my company or me?

Pay attention to the answers. And even if you never get a nickel's worth of business out of your tough calls, you will have information that is far more valuable. I call that constant, immediate, unfiltered feedback. Remember it . . . but more importantly, use it.

Mackay's Moral: You can't direct the wind . . . but you can sure shift the sails.

Chapter 9

The Well-Pressed Impression

Gail Madison is an etiquette consultant who knows the inside-out of impression psychology. Graduates of the prestigious Wharton School have benefited from her wisdom. The following is a dialogue we had on front-running sales etiquette in today's sales world.

Gail, you're all for turning up the psychological awareness monitor a couple of notches, aren't you? Share a tip or two about the first moments of a sales encounter.

When you're in a prospect's office, don't touch anything. Don't array your materials on their desk or move the items already on it. Be respectful and don't invade that person's space.

In sales meetings, the sales mentality focuses on closing the deal. You also stress the importance of "conversational closures" along the way. What do you mean by that?

It's okay to comment on a photo, but that begins a conversation, and you have to finish it once you've started it. If you ask, "Is that a picture of your family?" then you have to finish off the inquiry with some positive comment.

Imagine a friend is visiting your home and asks, "Did you recently decorate your house?" You say yes, and they say nothing. What do you conclude? Their choice not to follow up implies a pretty clear opinion as to what they think of your design or renovation work.

A good question to a prospect can trigger an avalanche of a response. So many salespeople don't know what to do when this happens. Naïveté or just plain inexperience makes them regard their own question in a self-defeating way. They just keep bulldozing down their list.

It's so key to listen during a presentation. After you ask a question or make a statement, if the other person wants to talk . . . let 'em go, go, go!

Outside of the occasional word or two of acknowledgment—"I understand" or "I see"—to show that you're tracking, don't interrupt. Be present . . . nod your head . . . make eye contact. Jot down important points you might want to make later.

The longer you let them talk, the more you'll learn about who they are and what they want. Human beings work on emotion and vanity. So many young salespeople feel they need to overcome client objections the instant they are tabled.

Let the client run with the ball. By investing attention and energy in trying to control, you miss a lot.

You're saying: Don't misinterpret the purpose of your own questions. Don't focus on how well the prospect answers exactly the question you asked. Questions are tools to gather positioning information in a broader sense.

That's right. People do indeed show their true colors if you let them go long enough. You'll truly learn where you need to go next.

And demonstrating the capacity to listen is essential in itself. It may be the single most convincing reason you'll get or not get the business. Any other tips about conducting a well-oiled conversation?

Salespeople often assume they have said something when they actually haven't. A lot of people think they have mentioned a consideration, but all they've done was to think it. Be sure to monitor your own remarks as well as the other person's.

Another definite don't: Never ask a question that could be easily answered by a company's website.

You not only demonstrate your ignorance, but your laziness as well. Doing this sort of advance research remains a competitive edge. It's not yet a norm, though it will be soon. Scouting the Web about a company also demonstrates a mind-set. This is the kind of preparedness that people equate with attentive service.

Let's move from conversation to clothing. Some young people assume that the dress standards for the sales side of IT and high-tech firms are as loose and free-spirited as the in-house program-development skunkworks. This is hardly the case. Even in the most creative and laid-back companies, sales-people have to play by different rules, don't they?

At Wharton, lots of students interview with high-tech giants. The IT people may dress in T-shirts and jeans, but it's suits for sales. Even when interviewing for jobs in the same company, successful candidates will wear different outfits for different departments. The process can get funny . . . and even entail a couple of changes of clothing in a locker!

If you're in sales, you have to be attentive to appearance issues. The suit remains the symbol of authority. The statistical evidence is overpowering. Students do better for teachers who dress up. Employees work longer and harder for people in suits.

Every day, you interact with promising young people just starting out in sales and management. What challenges are you seeing out there these days?

Recently I worked with a high-tech genius kid. We didn't go so far as a suit, but he's now wearing a sport coat, tie and dress shirt. And he's turned into a different person, far more comfortable with his new self. The strange thing is that he always really has liked clothes. Add to that a little military bearing in the walk, and you're talking shades of Bond. James Bond. Impressive.

Given the unclear standards of our time, young women have it particularly tough, don't they?

I recently saw a young woman make a presentation. She was trying very hard to get her point across, but she looked like an unmade bed. Her hairstyle was a ringer for Morticia in the *Addams Family*, and she wore awful pants that kept creeping up her legs.

That's just one kind of problem. When dress codes aren't clear, it's much harder for women than for men, and women can end up wearing really inappropriate things. We are just more inclined to associate women's clothing with their personalities. Too-tight clothing or too-high heels often get young women (and their careers) into trouble.

Are flamboyant dressing and an overbearing personal style still to be found on the contemporary sales landscape?

Polyester and striped shirts and loud ties died in the '70s. Ralph Waldo Emerson's wise words are worth remembering: "Who you are speaks so loudly I can't hear what you're saying."

If you go to an art gallery, the walls are white for a reason. You want to showcase the art. The props of prosperity and an attentive lifestyle matter too: shined shoes, the quality pen in your pocket or purse, the obvious taste and attainment signaled by a fine briefcase. Apparel awareness shows you're both a game player and a team player.

The age-old correlation survives: The connection between appearance and respect from others and personal confidence in yourself. If salespeople studied this more in others, they would more easily recognize the potential for improvement in themselves.

You and I are both bothered by how people squander time and powers of observation while waiting in the lobby of a company.

That goes for salespeople who are waiting to meet a prospect as well as those who are up to bat for a job interview. Observe the dress protocols, especially of leadership figures. The reception areas are a laboratory for this. What do the executives dress like?

How about meals themselves? There's a dining psychology for sales that's every bit as important as the menu and the ambience. What's your take on the top priorities?

Set up the environment ahead of time. You remain in control and make the choice of dining spot, but learn and respect client preferences in advance. Make sure you have a great table. Tip the maitre d' or whomever, in advance if you don't know them, for something special such as having the table moved.

The prospect or customer should have the best seat in the house, looking out into the restaurant. Lingering, misguided tradition argues for having the customer face the salesperson or the wall to better control the customer's attention. That's just rude.

An attentive waitstaff says a lot about your personal authority and charm. Make the guest feel honored and well cared for. Achieving that feeling may take some time and research, but it's a worthwhile investment. Allow the guest to walk ahead of you. In general, be deferential.

On an imaginary time chart of the restaurant dining event, when should business be brought up?

A rule of thumb is 30 minutes after the encounter begins. However, the real-world agenda can change this dramatically. If you both know what you're there for and you have an established relationship, you can cut to the chase: "Since we have limited time, would it be all right if we moved to the business matters?"

There you go. Announce the time-management decision and move ahead.

Some people bring their iPad or brochures or a sheaf of papers to the dining table. If paper is absolutely necessary, one summarized sheet is the maximum.

I agree. Not bringing anything is best. Follow up with e-mail or mail after the meeting. Focus on the discussion. Props like this make a mess.

Amen! No brochure flopping into the butter, no matter how proud you are of the document.

How about follow-ups after a lunch or dinner? A brief note remains a standard gambit among my business colleagues.

A letter or an e-mail will work. Keep true to that length. A special note on e-mail protocol: Do not send a lengthy message in an e-mail, because it won't be read. Put it in an attachment. And you better know what you're talking about. The attention span is not only shorter these days, it's also more demanding. Lastly, don't be afraid to pick up the phone. That can be your best reassurance of clear communication.

Are there social signals salespeople give off about being too hungry for the business?

Nothing is more obnoxious than being hounded by the salesperson who throws cards and documents at you.

The most self-destructive sales behavior is the badly managed conversation. Overly aggressive salespeople interrupt and persist in trying to control the conversation. If the customer or prospect attempts to redirect the dialogue, the clumsy salesperson will mount a verbal wrestling match. Pushy salespeople constantly try to manipulate the topic back to what they want to talk about. They are so sure they have what you want. At the same time, they don't have a clue as to who you are.

How about receiving prospects or customers in the office?

Treat them as though they are guests in your home. Be the gracious host. Offer coffee or tea, or water. Offer food. It says, "I'm happy to have you here." And it matters. Even if they decline your offer, there's a dividend for showing you put thought into their coming, and their comfort.

The vanity and biases of the older salesperson can sometimes be hard to rein in. Let's say such a person is calling on a young client or prospect who is a nonstop techie. Throughout the conversation, the targeted customer is constantly diverting himself with his laptop or smartphone. What does a salesperson do when persistently relegated to secondary attention?

Don't take it personally. Today's kids—some of them extraordinarily successful and powerful—are so used to doing multiple technical things at once, and they're good at it. They don't mean the slight personally. They're probably hearing you. It's just that older people have a hard time believing that's possible. Keep going as though it weren't happening.

I learned this message the hard way. During a presentation, I got fed up with the constant clicking from someone in the audience using her smartphone. I asked her to stop messaging while I was talking. She explained she was taking notes. The group had understood this all along, but I didn't. I was humbled and said, "Hey, I'm such a dinosaur, I didn't even know you could do that." I was the person shamed, and rightly so.

Another antiquated trapping of the salesman of yore: the backslapping, gut-busting joke. From a diplomacy and social awareness standpoint, where does humor fit into the social tool kit these days?

A sense of humor is really important, but you have to temper it with the right language. Unless you're a highly paid stand-up comic, I'm not sure that joke telling is the way to get across your appreciation for humor.

People don't know their audience today, and it is much less homogeneous than it once was. You might have strong views on a particular politician, for example, and automatically assume the rest of the world shares your outlook. But don't bet the farm on it.

It's like threading a needle. The person across from you might be sizing you up and making a mental note: "This person takes unnecessary risks for a small payoff."

That's right. Your listener might be fuming and thinking, "How dare you? You have no idea what my political or religious views might be."

We've all witnessed people making toasts at weddings that they thought were hilarious while the rest of the guests were wincing or rolling their eyeballs. You have to be experienced, wise and very confident to pull humor off successfully.

Self-deprecating humor deserves a special comment. This can work for a guy. But when a woman says something negative about herself to a guy, men tend to believe it. Guys think, "She's probably right." Men can go back and forth with self-deprecating humor, and they don't really believe it.

If jokes have become more dangerous, are well-told stories and anecdotes more Important?

Absolutely. Holidays are a great time for younger people to collect stories. Older generations seem more gifted at telling them. Telling and applying a story well is a gift. People pay good money just to be around individuals who can spin memorable stories.

For salespeople, stories are often great tools to show how well a company works as a team, to support customer goals or overcome challenging situations.

Mackay's Moral: You'll achieve success if you learn to impress.

"You don't get an office. You get cargo pants."

Chapter 10

LinkedIn and Facebook: The New Handshake

Do you think of yourself as a research subject?

If you sell, I guarantee you: You are other people's homework.

It's likely if they are prospects . . . and almost certain if they are customers.

People buy from people they trust and like. People buy from people with shared values and interests. People buy from people with mutual personal and professional connections. They don't buy from shadowy characters with blotchy, checkered Web profiles. It's never been easier to nail the answer to the question "What is this person really like?" And believe me, anyone can and will find out.

> **Google, LinkedIn and Facebook are the universal first stops in Web searches.**

Typically LinkedIn (linkedin.com) is used by business professionals to create a virtual business network. Many regard Facebook (facebook.com) as a personal social network, but its use as a business tool is rapidly increasing. Why? Precisely because it reveals the personal side some naïve folks think they can hide.

Many people believe that what they post on LinkedIn and Facebook is private. "Isn't my personal information only searchable and viewable by those who have been invited into my network?" Dream on. And you say you've polished up your Facebook pitch? That's less than half the story. What's the buzz that others have to say about you?

Sam Richter, president of SBR Worldwide and senior vice president/chief marketing officer at ActiFi, regularly briefs me on the hottest Internet trends. He's a national authority on using the Web for sales preparation and sales intelligence. Sam's "Know More!" training program teaches executives around the globe how to find information and put it to use to gain an edge in sales, business development and account management. He has created some free online tools that will help you find online information in ways that you probably never thought possible. Check them out at knowmorecenter .com.

How do I know the Sam Richter approach works? Because we have given presentations together around the country, and our company uses his system. So what I'm about to describe for you is the Web world according to Sam.

LinkedIn is one of the most powerful business research tools for salespeople, to some degree even surpassing Google in its ability to help you find information on executives and other businesspeople. LinkedIn has hundreds of millions of members, and its membership is growing every day! Understanding the power of LinkedIn is critical to your business and personal success.

LinkedIn helps you build a virtual network of business executives:

- who know you (your first-level connections),
- plus a network of executives who know the people who know you (your second-level connections),
- and a network of people who know the people who know the people who know you (your third-level connections).

The network multiplication can be a nonstop snowball. Once you're registered, you invite people into your network. As people accept your invitations and as you accept theirs, everyone's network is shared.

In his highly praised books and educational programs (www.samrichter .com), Sam describes in detail how to use LinkedIn:

- as an intelligence-gathering tool for building highly qualified lead lists,
- for researching prospects and clients and mining their business relationships,
- and for researching companies prior to sales calls.

There are even tricks on how to use LinkedIn and Google in combination to get information on executives, even when you are not connected with the individual at any level!

Prior to any sales call, the smart salesperson uses LinkedIn to research company contacts as well as the company itself. With LinkedIn's mobile application—available for free—you can conduct research on the fly, within minutes of meeting with someone. There's no excuse not to do it.

Sam also offers some awesome tips for using LinkedIn as an intelligence-gathering tool. They include:

- Use LinkedIn's people search engine to locate an individual's profile and study it prior to any meeting. Look at the person's work background and educational history, and focus on whom you share as a connection.
- See if anyone has recommended the person you looked up and what they say about this individual. Does the recommendation seem genuine? Is it detailed? Rule of thumb: The more specific a recommendation is, the more believable.
- Use LinkedIn's advanced search features to find people at certain companies, with certain job titles, within certain industries, living in specific regions or any combination of these options. You can even search profile keywords to see if an individual has expertise in a specific area.
- Use LinkedIn's company search feature to find LinkedIn company profiles. Why is this important? In a flash, you're armed with a snapshot of the kind of people this company hires. Sam points out this can be a real edge in selling insurance or financial services.

- Integrate your blog, Twitter feed, presentations, videos and other digital assets you're proud of into your LinkedIn profile. Make it easy for prospects to see your good work.
- Join LinkedIn groups and participate in the discussion. Don't promote yourself or your company. Instead, offer informative answers that highlight your expertise.
- Search for questions posted by LinkedIn users and answer them in LinkedIn's question-and-answer area. Again, make your answers informative, not self-promotional. People will eventually seek you out.

Even more popular than LinkedIn is Facebook. Facebook is now the most popular site on the Internet, and more searches are done on Facebook each month than on Google!

Before you post anything on the Internet, ask yourself: "How would I feel if this appeared on the front page of tomorrow's newspaper?"

While LinkedIn has always been a business networking site, Facebook has been primarily a social network site that people use to connect with their friends. However, many companies now have Facebook fan pages and are increasing their presence on the site. More and more, companies are researching their vendors, salespeople and business partners on Facebook. Does an individual's professional persona compute, given their personal activities chronicled on Facebook?

Sam recommends keeping your personal Facebook network "tight": Invite and accept invitations only from your true friends. Make sure to carefully review your Facebook privacy settings and "lock them down" so only your Facebook friends can see your information, posts and photos.

Even then, it's still important to think before you post something on Facebook. Always remember: It's possible for others outside your network to find your information. Do you really want prospective business partners to read about your political beliefs, learn what you had for breakfast this morning or see that July 4th party photo of you in the red bathing suit?

For your business network, connect with prospects and clients via Facebook's fan pages. A fan page is typically created and managed by your company's marketing department. Or, if you run a small business, you can easily create a fan page yourself. Your company can be "liked" by an unlimited number of fans!

The impersonal Web has made the art and science of selling much more personal. To cite Sam, "The good news is, you control the message."

Mackay's Moral: What makes the Web possible is all about technology. What makes the Web powerful is all about psychology.

Quickie #3
Your Ultimate Makeover

Google yourself on the Web. Put your name in quote marks. If you have a common name, you may have to add a few other cues, such as company name, city of residence or alma mater.

If the only hit that pops up is a Facebook photo of you in a toga guzzling a yard of beer or toking off a bong, you're in trouble. If the only hits are a listing in the church choir's roster for an Easter service three years ago and a mention in the news that you witnessed an auto wreck last spring . . . well, you're like most of America.

But you can change all that. People want to do business with others who are Web-certified entities:

- **Create a clear, positive posting for LinkedIn.** You can be invited to join LinkedIn or create your own account. To participate in Groups, find one you're interested in and click the moderator to ask if you can join the dialogue.
- **Contribute an article to a publication.** It doesn't have to be a business piece. Maybe it's a community project, or a remembrance of an unforgettable coach on a memorial site. Write something meaningful that demonstrates you have good taste and judgment.
- **Give a talk and publicize it.** Many community organizations need speakers, and you may have the opportunity to post your talk on their website. The early-20s youngster of one parent I know joined a disaster relief group in Haiti after the 2010 earthquake. Despite initial misgivings about the young person's safety, the experience proved positive for all involved. The parent went online to describe her hesitations and the evidence. Not an easy choice, but the comments showed a mother who was forthright and thoughtful.
- **Tweet intelligent tips.** The best way to create Twitter traction, I think, is to recommend sites and gems on the Web that you find useful yourself. Don't pretend you're a star. Tweet others a fresh edge on camping in Nova Scotia or organizing their garage.

"I can't explain it—it's just a funny feeling that I'm being Googled."

Chapter 11

Sharpen
Your Best Selling Points

My last book, *Use Your Head to Get Your Foot in the Door*, was dedicated cover-to-cover to helping people find a job. It works no matter what your profession. If you're shopping for a spot in sales, some of its principles are worth noting:

1.   **Showcase your network.** The buff on your footwear still counts, but the depth and dazzle of your personal network may be the ultra-shoeshine of the 21st century.

- Is your network current and relevant to your career position today?
- When asked, can you access key people in it quickly?
- Are you a broad-based player or does your network expose you as narrowly fraternizing just with sales cronies? Remember, a network with depth earmarks people who are comfortable crossing departmental lines to solve problems.
- Are you regularly in touch with high-quality endorsers and references to inform them about your job status and goals?

2.   **Manage marketplace buzz.** Salespeople must always factor in a phantom reference which—positive or negative—may be the most influential factor in getting a job: *marketplace buzz.* Have honest, credible explanations, for example, as to why your company lost a key account and why you're out of a job.

3.   **Show resilience.** The New Economy demands the ability to claw back from sometimes head-spinning setbacks. That's true for everyone, but for no segment is it truer than for salespeople. Because, as you know, salespeople need to show resilience. If you think in terms of the Gold Rush, then you'd be pretty depressed right now, because the last nugget of gold would be gone. But the good thing is, with innovation, there isn't a last nugget. Every new thing creates two new questions and two new opportunities.

4.   **You can't exaggerate the risk of exaggerating.** P. T. Barnum was famous for his brassy statement "If I shoot at the sun, I might hit a star." Flush this instinct out of your system. People are no longer so forgiving about exaggeration, especially about claims in your résumé. Today you can find out anything about anyone in a flash.

5.   **Demonstrate social network command.** Networks like LinkedIn are the sales frontiers of the future. If you're absent or fleetingly represented in such key social networks personally, how can you hope to persuade a potential employer that you would know how to exploit social networks when selling their products or services?

6.   **Think teamwork, not territory.** In *Use Your Head*, I quote psychologist authorities who stress how crucial teamwork is in the new world of work. It's not just a taste for style. Teamwork-intensive organizations are leaner and more efficient.

For Carol Ann's and my anniversary, our entire family was thrilled as we hosted the gang on a photo safari to Kruger National Park in South Africa. During the months of preparation beforehand, we stitched together careful plans to stake out what are known as the "Big Five" in the African wilds:

- lions
- leopards
- rhinos
- elephants
- Cape buffaloes.

But what about all those other keen animals like giraffes and hippos? We rearranged our priorities and scored some stunning photographic shots of hyenas, impalas and even a couple of the park's 200 elusive chee-tahs.

Our bunch came away with a lot of take-home about territorial behavior. Is it any surprise the "Big Five" are exceedingly territorial? Is it any surprise that many "Big Five" subspecies are nearly extinct?

So it is with salespeople. Many salespeople try to show off how territorial they are, thinking that exceptional salespeople flash their fangs to defend their turf.

Mackay's Moral: Either you learn the psychological tracks of the modern seller or you make yourself a candidate for extinction.

Quickie #4
So You Aren't Johnny Depp . . .

Do you lack the dazzle of Angelina Jolie's lagoon-blue eyes or the regal command of Meryl Streep's screen poise? Come up short on George Clooney's suave or Daniel Craig's rippling abs?

Well, you don't have to rate first billing to be billing first.

Call attention to your strengths, recognize where you fit in the team, and you're guaranteed to shine.

When actor Karl Malden, born Mladen Sekulovich, died in 2009, the *New York Times* hailed him as "the uncommon everyman." Malden frequently shared credits with the likes of Marlon Brando and George C. Scott. With an epic schnoz, Malden knew he could never command center stage, but he swore he would run the last mile "to be #1 in the #2 parts I was destined to get."

So it was in *On the Waterfront* and *Patton* . . . and he was second to no one in a string of high-credibility endorsement ads for American Express.

Decide where your psyche fits in the cast and shine. That may mean:

- Be known for your reliability and steadiness of vision.
- Remain the unflappable source of judgment in crisis and turmoil.
- Execute the impossible when logistics degenerate into spaghetti.

James Mason, another stellar silver-screen #2, once said, "How do I wish to be remembered, if at all? I think perhaps just as a fairly desirable sort of character actor." Hollywood and the critics remembered him *their* way when his colleagues nominated him for three Oscars and three Golden Globes.

Chapter 12

Better Humble Than Stumble

In the history of the world, there has never been a city that juices itself more on ego than Tinseltown. That said, I remain a huge movie buff and religiously watch the Academy Awards telecast. I'm even more interested because my son, David, is a film director and producer in Hollywood.

The curious thing? For the very cream of the entertainment profession, genuine humility flows in their blood. Stars with staying power understand exactly how reliant they are on the support of others.

Two of the most memorable lines during the 2008 Oscar ceremonies came from the year's Best Actor and Best Actress, Sean Penn and Kate Winslet.

"I want to be very clear," Sean Penn admitted, "I do know how hard I make it to appreciate me." While few would refer to Penn as humble, that had to be the understatement of the year! Kate Winslet was disarmingly honest: "I'd be lying if I said I hadn't made a version of this speech before. I was probably eight years old staring into the bathroom mirror, and this would have been a shampoo bottle," she said as she held up her Oscar.

Danny Boyle, who won Best Director for *Slumdog Millionaire*, went onstage and started jumping up and down. The movie was originally slated to be released only on DVD, and he said he promised his kids that if he ever won an Oscar, he would accept it in the joyous spirit of Tigger from *Winnie the Pooh*. Never forget that winning moments are also made of keeping promises to the people who've helped get you there.

I've been speaking to business groups for decades now, but I remember the first time my wife, Carol Ann, heard me give a speech. I knew she would be my harshest critic, so I practiced a great deal. I delivered what I thought was a great speech. Many people came up to me afterward and complimented me. In the car on the way home, I turned to Carol Ann and asked, "Sweetheart, how many great speakers do you think there are in the world today?"

She smiled and replied, "One fewer than you think, dear."

Mackay's Moral: The sound carries farther when others blow your horn.

Chapter 13

Be Yourself

At a Woodrow Wilson Foundation dinner in 2006, I was invited to be the emcee. Here's what I said to kick off the occasion:

> "I asked my wife, Carol Ann, what kind of words might suit the occasion. 'Whatever you do,' she said,
> - 'Don't try to sound intellectual,
> - Don't try to be sophisticated . . . or charming.
> - Just be yourself!' "

The roar of the crowd confirmed how worldly wise Carol Ann's advice was.

Being yourself is hardly as easy as it sounds. For salespeople, sounding phony is a career kiss of death. Learn who your real self is and let it shine in the best possible light.

There are two myths about being yourself that deserve to be vaporized:

1. **I can like everyone, if I set my mind to it.** No, you can't. And not everyone you meet will like you either. For every person you meet who says, "There are no strangers here, only friends we haven't met," there's another who says, "Good fences make good neighbors." There will be people who just never warm up to you, and there will be people you won't want to get to know no matter how pleasant or charming they seem. The wise salesperson

knows the difference between being friendly and polite to everyone versus sensing when there is real chemistry.

2. **People who like each other are more likely to agree.** If only that were true. You can pick up many business magazines and find stories about how two friends went into business together and wound up mortal enemies. Good friends will either learn to discuss only those things they agree about or else just agree to disagree when they have differences. U.S. Senators Orrin Hatch and the late Ted Kennedy were good friends, but you never heard either one praising the other's political beliefs during Senate debates.

As Raymond Hull, Laurence J. Peter's collaborator in *The Peter Principle*, put it: "He who trims himself to suit everyone will soon whittle himself away."

The doorway to being yourself is liking yourself. It is hard to have confidence in a salesperson who doesn't like herself or himself.

Mackay's Moral: Oscar Wilde had it right: "Be yourself.
Everyone else is already taken."

Chapter 14

Trust Is a Must

People in business don't have to like each other, but they *do* have to trust each other. At MackayMitchell Envelope Company, we don't tolerate anything less than honest negotiations and delivery guarantees.

An envelope is a very standard commodity. Sure, the paper, the glue, and the size can vary. The end product can probably be duplicated by a hundred companies. But nobody can match us day in and day out, job after job, envelope after envelope, smile after smile. Our customers know we'll do what we promise. They've even occasionally forgiven us for an honest mistake because they know we'll make good on our word.

We also don't do business with vendors who are less than up-front. It could eventually affect how we deliver to our customers, and we don't like to lose customers. Our sales force wouldn't stick around for long if we made their job harder. Can you blame them?

Ethics are not remote, pie-in-the-sky considerations. Every time you're tempted to short quality standards or fudge a delivery date, it can have ethical consequences.

Imagine a third grader running to his father and saying, "Daddy, what does 'ethics' mean?"

His father tells him to go look it up in the dictionary.

A few minutes later, the little boy comes back and says, "I looked it up, but I still don't know what it means."

His father says, "Look, son. Let's say one of my customers leaves a $100 bill in his suit pocket at our dry cleaning business. Here's the ethics: Do I tell my partner?"

How many people associate politicians with telling the truth? At a congressional hearing, when was the last time you heard the truth, the whole truth and nothing but the truth?

We all have our own opinions of what has happened, but how would you like to be remembered as the president that 80 percent of the population didn't trust? With those numbers you may be able to keep your job in politics, but I can't think of another profession where you could get the same result.

Mackay's Moral: Mark Twain put it well when he said, "I am different from George Washington. I have a higher, grander standard of principle. Washington could not lie. I can lie, but I won't."

"*Wait, those weren't lies. That was spin!*"

Chapter 15

Discover Your Potential

Flea trainers have observed a strange but predictable habit of fleas. Fleas are trained by putting them in a cardboard box with a top on it. The fleas will jump up and hit the top of the cardboard box over and over and over again. As you watch them jump and hit the lid, something very interesting becomes obvious. The fleas continue to jump, but they are no longer jumping high enough to hit the top.

When you take off the lid, the fleas continue to jump, but they will not jump out of the box. They won't jump out because they can't jump out. Why? They have conditioned themselves to jump just so high.

People very often do the same thing. They restrict themselves and never reach their potential. Just like the fleas, they fail to jump higher, thinking they are doing all they can do.

Your past is not your potential.

In the words of Charlie Brown, "The greatest burden in life is to have a great potential."

Far too many people exist in a world of "what is" rather than applying their energies to "what can be."

To reach your potential, the primary ingredient is desire. Many people fail to succeed because they don't know what they want or they don't want it in the worst way. In other words, they aren't willing to work for it . . . they don't want to pay the price.

It's like the woman who said to a world-class musician, "I'd give anything to be able to play like you." And the musician said, "I don't think you would, because not many people are willing to make the commitment."

Desire isn't enough. You must have the will to prepare. Preparation means yearning, learning, reading, listening, organizing and expanding your thinking. It involves rigorous training of your mind and body to achieve success.

The playwright George Bernard Shaw understood this. A reporter interviewed him shortly before his death and asked, "Mr. Shaw, you have visited with some of the most famous people in the world. You've known royalty, world-renowned authors, artists, teachers and dignitaries from every part of the world. If you could live your life over and be anyone you've known, or any person from history, whom would you choose to be?"

Shaw replied, "I would choose to be the man George Bernard Shaw could have been, but never was."

> There are a lot of excuses for not being the person you have
> the potential to become. One of them is negativity. . . . It's
> the naysayers who say it can't be done.

In the 1940s, not all aeronautical engineers or physicists were convinced that a human could break the sound barrier. But famed pilot Chuck Yeager believed it could be done . . . and he flew right through it.

Another reason that many people don't realize their potential: They don't seize the opportunity to display their talents.

Look at Paul Hornung, the Hall of Fame running back for the Green Bay Packers. Hornung had won the Heisman Trophy as a quarterback at Notre Dame, but Green Bay already had a star at that position in Bart Starr. Hornung didn't get much playing time for a couple of years, until the Packers' new coach, the legendary Vince Lombardi, realized that Hornung had some additional abilities, some hidden assets. Lombardi already knew Hornung was big, but he also found out he could run with the ball and was especially good inside the 20-yard line.

The results were dramatic. In 1961, the Packers began their famous string of championship wins, including Hornung being named the NFL's Most Valuable Player.

Most companies have hidden assets, a vast potential of value-creating people just waiting to be discovered and unleashed. The Japanese watchmaker Seiko makes sure that its top people get an opportunity to thrive. The company has adopted a formal performance appraisal system to help determine whether a person is promotable. If an employee gets an outstanding appraisal on three successive occasions, then the company pays special attention to that person.

Top managers have the responsibility for reviewing those who are promotable and for selecting and appointing managers. This performance appraisal system is helping Seiko to build up a pool of potential management talent. How do you suppose Seiko would rate you?

Mackay's Moral: The undeveloped piece of property with the greatest potential can still be found between the ears.

Quickie #5
Be Yourself, Then Improve Yourself

I've always been fascinated by the Japanese carp otherwise known as the koi. It's a fish with seemingly unlimited growth potential. If you put the koi in a small fishbowl, it will grow to be only two or three inches long. In a larger tank or a small pond, it will reach six to ten inches. Put it in a bigger pond, and it gets to be a foot and a half. But if the koi is placed in a large lake, where it can really stretch out, it can grow up to three feet long. The size of the fish is proportional to the size of its home.

Well, it works that way with people too. We grow according to the size of our world. Not physically, of course, but mentally. You too can be a mental giant!

Is it up to your supervisor to prepare you for a promotion? Maybe a little, but the real responsibility belongs much closer to home. You have to let your boss know that you're always ready for a new challenge and will do whatever it takes to prepare. You want to be qualified before the next job opens up, not disappointed after. You want to be interesting at the office and after hours. Your coworkers and friends can hear the same stories only so many times.

Grow. Stretch. Transform yourself.

A simple bar of iron is worth about $5. Made into horseshoes, the value rises to about $50. Transform it into needles, and now you're talking $500. But if you take that bar of iron and make it into springs for a Swiss watch, it could be worth a half-million bucks. You started with the same raw material; the value grew as the material was formed and developed.

It's the same with people.

Chapter 16

Super Sellers
Are Customer-Centric

For years, companies have contended how customer-centered they have become. Major corporations are now flexing muscle behind their boasts. The newest addition to the executive C-Suite is the CCO—Chief Customer Officer.

The CCO's portfolio consolidates under one roof the lifeblood customer-centric activities, such as sales, marketing, customer service, even billing. This new twist is called "customer experience management." Studies are starting to show the results you would expect: increased satisfaction, improved loyalty and more frequent referrals.

Tierney Remick is Global Market Managing Director for the high-power search firm Korn/Ferry International. She continues to be a valued interview guest in my books. Tierney has a surefire grasp of what stratosphere-level companies are after when they're on the prowl for talent at the top. Here's what she shared with me about the new way sales is connecting with the C-Suite.

What characterizes the new breed of executive sales leadership?

Clearly there's a business strategy dimension today in top-level selling that didn't exist earlier. A strategic business mind is required, one that understands better the viewpoint of the audience. The goal is to create a more constructive commercial dialogue and relationship, not just one based on personality.

Has top-level sales moved beyond closing the individual deal?

Absolutely. Everything is so integrated today. Customers, clients, even competitors. Look only at the end of the deal, and you miss the real opportunities.

How has the personal outlook of a successful top salesperson changed?

Besides having the key strategic instincts, there's a focus on what broader business issues need to be addressed. Not only on how they'll affect my organization, but how will they impact the business relationship that we're nurturing with the customer? For example, how do we ensure the relationship is transparent when it needs to be?

What about technical edges like reading people, managing a negotiation, or leaving a distinctive impression?

Historically, successful outcomes tended to be "I win. You lose." Today it's win/win. That requires both sides to understand where there has to be give-and-take and how this influences the personality on the other side of the table. You need an intuitive understanding of where your counterpart is coming from and must have empathy for their point of view.

Top-level salespeople couple high empathy with high IQ. This can create a sense of partnership that will extend deals further. Many CEOs are incredibly effective salespeople, and the most successful ones radiate the feeling that they genuinely care about the customer.

As the importance of empathy grows, doesn't this create natural advantages for women in top-level selling?

You would think so. Many characteristics, such as high empathy, high intuition and strong win/win negotiation are typically considered feminine characteristics. There's also a multicultural, multigender sensitivity that makes a difference in today's world. This probably wasn't the same 10–15 years ago. We're working in a global community. In many societies, there are as many women as men in business, and they are of all ages.

How important is it for the top salesperson to be a seamless part of the company's overall identity . . . as if this person jumped out of the company website?

The individual has to be a very strategic ambassador of the company—

however the company wants itself to be presented—in all that he or she does or says. But that's true for all senior executives today. With the increasing technical complexity of business, top CIOs (Chief Information Officers), as another category, have the same responsibility.

Are major sales at the top more likely to involve a team?

In the best organizations, the CCO sits at the strategic leadership table with the other functions. All activities are thought through from an integrated perspective: "Whatever I sell will have an impact on the customer relationship, including technology and operations." That entails constant awareness of business in the broader sense.

Let's say a fast-moving consumer goods company is making a sales presentation to a huge retailer. The seller's CCO may well be accompanied by the CEO and the CIO. Functional integration is critical.

It seems that more and more execs, including those at the very top, handle the logistics of their business life through BlackBerrys and smartphones. With so many transactions managed today via mobile devices, does this require a different sort of preparation and presence of mind?

Technology is frequently one-sided interaction. It's too easy to assume everything can be done using technology. Executives shine if they retain that personal accountability and communication effectiveness required face-to-face and voice-to-voice. If the senior sales officer loses the reality of touch-contact skills with partners, it won't work.

You have to be in command of the technical arsenal, but you can't let it intrude on your personal style. You certainly can't lean on gadgetry as a substitute for human warmth.

Sole reliance on technology diminishes a person and becomes a distraction.

Two decades ago, the classic sales executive, even at the very top, was prized for his or her skills as an interpersonal motivator. Is today's top seller a more analytical breed than in the past?

Certainly the analytical reach is expected to be deeper. Sales executives are being held accountable for the return-on-investment (ROI) impact of their decisions. All sales are not equal. Top sellers need to have the financial acumen to differentiate the good deal from the bad one. Will the transaction's ROI be truly profitable? If it's not, and you choose to do the deal anyway, you need to know the bottom-line impact and exactly why you're doing it.

How about career pathing for a CEO? Is a substantial career assignment in marketing/sales regarded as important preliminary experience for a future CEO/COO?

Yes, because of the interaction with customers and prospective partners. Those are routine activities for a CEO. No company sits by itself anymore.

Mackay's Moral: If you're aiming for a top job in sales, customer-centric spells career-centric.

"No, Thursday's out. How about never—is never good for you?"

Chapter 17

Celebrate the Child in You

Kids get excited about life. They see everything with fresh eyes, knowing they will find something new and different every time they look. Adults, on the other hand, look for what they know and expect. Imagine what we're missing!

We've forgotten the enthusiasm, the sense of surprise at experiencing new things, the fascination with solving puzzles. All are traits radiated by a great salesperson.

My friend the late Jim Rohn was a master speaker and motivator. He encouraged folks to "practice being like a child." Jim said there are four ways to be more like a child, no matter how old you are.

- **Become curious.** "Learn to be curious like a child. Kids can ask a million questions. You think they're through. They've got another million. . . . Kids use their curiosity to learn. Have you ever noticed that while adults are stepping on ants, children are studying them? A child's curiosity is what helps them to reach, learn and grow," he said. Children let their imaginations run wild and aren't afraid to try unconventional ideas. Children don't have to be taught to "think outside the box." Most kids I know hate being confined. They are experts at pushing the envelope!

- **Get so excited you hate to go to bed at night.** Reawaken that can't-wait-to-get-up-in-the-morning feeling—the feeling that you're so excited that you're about to explode. At your next family gathering, heed the request of a sweet Irish grandmother I know: "Put me at the kids' table," she would say, so that she could eat fast and get back to the fun and games. "Kids are so much more interesting than adults" is her wholehearted attitude.

• **Believe.** Faith is childish, Jim maintained. "Adults too often have a tendency to be overly skeptical. Some adults even have a tendency to be cynical." Adults need proof that something is good before they will believe it. Kids track the world differently, according to Jim. As he put it, "Kids think you can get anything. Notice the difference?"

• **Trust.** "Have you heard the term 'sleep like a baby'? That's it," Jim said. "Childish trust. After you have gotten an A+ for the day, leave it in somebody else's hands."

> **The "trust" inventory may be the shortest supply chain in today's business world.**

Can you trust that your customers will pay for their orders? Can you trust your vendors to come through on time? Can you trust your staff to show up ready to work every day? In a child's world, trust and a nonthreatening environment go hand-in-hand.

Yet this isn't about being gullible or naïve. Study successful salespeople, as I have for decades, and you will be constantly amazed at the youthful energy that keeps them hopping. Energy, imagination and a credible sense of innocence—all boost a salesperson's likability and trustworthiness.

"Curiosity, excitement, faith and trust," Jim Rohn said. "What a powerful combination to bring back into our lives."

Mackay's Moral: Grow up and think like a kid again.

SUCCESS—The Fortune Cookies

Everyone wants to win on Saturday afternoon when the game is played. It's what you do the other six days that decides the outcome.
—*Lou Holtz*

If you want a place in the sun, expect a few blisters.

Every accomplishment begins with the decision to try.

Effort is what makes the impossible possible, the possible likely and the likely definite.

You don't say "Whoa!" when you're in a horse race.

Life is like a game of tennis: The player who serves well seldom loses.

Anyone can win . . . once.

While on the ladder of success, don't step back to admire your work.

A successful person is usually an average person who took a chance.

Not doing more than average is what keeps the average down.

The only place where *success* comes before *work* is in the dictionary.

Success is doing what we like to do and making a living at it.

The two hardest things to handle in life are failure and success.

_____

Success is a journey, not a destination.

_____

The real opportunity for success lies within the person
and not in the job.

_____

It's harder to be a success when your parents already are.

_____

There aren't any rules for success that work unless you do.

_____

For the real winners, there are no finish lines.

_____

Winning is a habit. Unfortunately, so is losing.

_____

IMAGINE

Chapter 18

Visualize Success

One of the best ways to use your imagination is to visualize or fantasize success. Long ago I came to realize that projecting myself into a successful situation was the most powerful means of attaining my personal goals.

That's what a placekicker does when he comes on the field to kick a winning field goal. Three seconds left in the game . . . 80,000 screaming fans . . . 30 million people watching on TV . . . and the game is still in the balance. As the kicker begins his moves, he makes the hundred tiny adjustments necessary to achieve the mental picture he's formed in his mind so many times—a picture of himself kicking the winning field goal.

The ability to project is a common trait among all great athletes. They have vision. They see things happening a split second before they actually do.

Jack Nicklaus, one of the greatest golfers of all time and a PGA Tour Hall of Famer, was asked about his tremendous success, especially in making crucial tournament-winning putts. He thought about it for a bit and said, "I never missed a putt in my mind."

Nicklaus is not considered to be the best at hitting his woods, long or short irons, or even at chipping and putting. But almost everyone considers him the greatest thinking golfer of all time. There has simply been no equal at the mental part of golf, which for me is half the game.

Thomas Watson Sr. was 40 when he took over as general manager of a little firm that manufactured meat slicers, time clocks and simple tabulators. He had a vision for a machine that could process and store information long before the computer was a commercial reality. To match his lofty vision, Watson renamed his company International Business Machines Corporation. Toward the end of his life, Watson was asked at what point he envisioned IBM becoming so successful. His reply was simple: "At the beginning."

Fred Smith's vision for a nationwide overnight express air-delivery service was first unveiled in the early '70s in a term paper for an economics class at Yale University. Unfortunately, his professor didn't share Smith's excitement, and gave him a C. Smith, however, took the idea and created an exceptional company known as Federal Express.

> **Success is no surprise to visionary people. They know what they want, determine a plan to achieve it and expect positive results.**

The renowned religious leader Billy Graham prayed, "God, let me do something, anything, for You." That attitude allowed Billy Graham to find a vision that drove his life.

The ability to visualize something better in the world is the cornerstone of countless other success stories. For example:

- Henry Royce was unwilling to accept anything but automobile perfection, and the Rolls-Royce remains an emblem of the exceptional today.
- Orville and Wilbur Wright were inspired at a children's birthday party when they saw a toy with a wound-up rubber band take to the air. They turned that inspiration into a reality.
- Marie Curie held high her commitment to scientific excellence in spite of doubters, and she made important discoveries until the day she died.

Such successful people were able to visualize—above and beyond the majority of folks—a condition that was just right. They taught us that a vision begins with imagination coupled with a belief that dreams can one day be realized.

And a man by the name of Viktor Frankl owed his 92-year-long life to his ability to project himself. He was a renowned Viennese psychiatrist before the Nazis threw him into a concentration camp. I heard him speak some years ago, and he held the audience spellbound.

Viktor Frankl's words: "There's one reason why I'm here today. What kept me alive in a situation where others had given up hope and died was the dream that someday I'd be here telling you how I survived the concentration camps. I've never been here before. I've never seen any of you before. I've never given this speech before. But in my dreams I've stood before you in this room and said these words a thousand times."

Mackay's Moral: People begin to become successful the minute they decide to be.

Chapter 19

Putt for Survival

Like a million other people, Major James Nesmeth dreamed of improving his golf game from his usual score in the 90s. Circumstances forced him to quit the game completely for seven years—never teed it up, never swung a club. And yet, the next time he played he shot an incredible 74!

Nesmeth did think about the game during those seven years . . . In fact, that's probably what saved his life. You see, Nesmeth spent those years as a prisoner of war in North Vietnam, confined in a cage that measured approximately four and a half feet high by five feet long.

For most of his imprisonment, he saw no one, spoke to no one and could barely move. At first, he spent most of his time praying for his release. But as the weeks dragged on, he realized he would lose his sanity or even his life if he didn't keep his mind active. He learned to visualize.

Want to change reality big-time? Learn to fantasize!

Nesmeth decided to play golf. He pictured his favorite golf course and played 18 holes every day. He dreamed every detail, from his clothes to his golf clubs to all the sights and smells of the course. He imagined different weather conditions, different cup placements, different seasons. He held the club and experimented with different grips. He saw his swing improve. He watched the ball sail down the fairway, and he rejoiced as he sank every putt.

Nesmeth took his time, every day, to "play" a full round. Four hours a day, seven days a week, for seven years. All this time, his physical condition was deteriorating, as you could see in the horrifying pictures taken of the POWs as they were freed. But this guy kept his mind in tip-top shape. And the first time he played after his release, he shaved 20 strokes off his game—all because of the power of visualization.

Tom Fatjo knew what he wanted to do, and through "creative dreaming" he turned a $500 investment and a used garbage truck into the country's largest solid-waste disposal company. Says Fatjo, currently chairman and CEO of WCA Waste Corporation: "In the beginning stages of developing our first garbage company in Houston, I used to imagine trucks, a whole fleet of blue trucks, running out of our lot onto the streets of Houston in the early morning mist. In my imagination I could 'see' the trucks and the men as they wound their way around the streets of our town." He visualized his dream as already being a reality.

Half a century ago, who could have imagined putting a man on the moon? President John F. Kennedy, of course, gave America that vision in 1960, with the goal of achieving it in 10 years. While some folks scoffed at the idea, millions of others shared the president's dream. The rest is history.

Visualization can help you to survive . . . and to succeed.

Visualization allows you to see your ideal tomorrow. It doesn't do the planning and it doesn't anticipate the obstacles. It gives you a real idea of what is possible, if only you want it badly enough. The journey may not be simple, but it's worth every mile if you remember where you started and have a clear destination in mind.

A farmer hired a neighbor's teenage son to help him do the spring plowing. The farmer believed in letting people do their work without unnecessary supervision, so he helped the boy get the tractor going and went off to work in another field. The inexperienced teenager was eager to impress his new boss, and kept looking over his shoulder to make sure he was plowing straight furrows. But though he checked his progress frequently, he was discouraged to see a very crooked row when he reached the edge of the field.

He tried and tried, but just couldn't keep the rows straight. When the farmer came to check his progress, he identified the problem immediately.

Helping the boy off the tractor, the farmer told him, "You can't plow a straight row if you continually look back. You must keep your eyes focused straight ahead. And always remember where you've been."

Mackay's Moral: Vision is not so much what you think as how you think. If you can visualize it, you can make it happen.

Quickie #6
Farsighted

Helen Keller was totally blind by the age of 19 months. Yet Keller graduated *cum laude* from Radcliffe College and went on to become a brilliant author, activist and lecturer. During a speech she once gave to college students, an audience member naïvely asked her, "Tell me, Ms. Keller, is losing your eyesight the worst thing in the world that can happen to anyone?"

"No," she said. "It's losing your vision."

Eyesight, you see, is what we perceive in front of us; vision is seeing all the way down the road.

Chapter 20

Rain Can *Make* Your Parade

Retired Indianapolis Colts coach Tony Dungy is a master of helping those around him visualize victory. He's been that way ever since his high school playing days, which is one reason I worked so hard to help recruit him for the Minnesota Gophers, where he was a college gridiron star. In fact, I was extremely proud when Tony wrote in his blockbuster 2007 book, *Quiet Strength,* "Harvey, I wouldn't be here if it weren't for you."

It's no surprise that his quarterback Peyton Manning is a big believer in practice and preparation. You might recall the constant, relentless, sidewinding rain at the 2007 Super Bowl in Miami between Indianapolis and the Chicago Bears. The terrible weather was ideal for the Bears' running game, but conditions looked bad for Indianapolis, which plays in a 60-degree indoor stadium.

However, just the opposite happened. The Bears turned the ball over five times and quarterback Rex Grossman bobbled two snaps, losing 10 yards on one to kill a scoring drive. Indianapolis recovered the other fumble. Manning encountered no such game-changing calamities. Why? Every season Manning practices the "wet-ball drill" with his starting center, currently Jeff Saturday. Manning fills a bucket full of water, grabs a football and heads out to the field. He dips the ball into the bucket and practices snap after snap.

Manning said his center hates the wet-ball drill, and he admitted getting a little bored with it himself. But they still do it every year. When asked about the infamous wet-ball drill in the raucous Colts locker room after their Super Bowl win, Saturday laughed and said, "Not my favorite drill. But it paid dividends tonight."

When you visualize, anticipate negatives and how you will overcome them. Then create a practice plan that makes your response instantaneous.

At every meeting I hold with my managers, we end with the same exercise. We go around the room, and I ask each one to anticipate what could go wrong. If it does, I ask, what are you going to do to fix the problem?

What matters *isn't* that a customer pounces on you with an overwhelming objection, for instance. What matters is that you'll deliver an unbeatable answer with utter confidence when that objection comes sailing at you.

Mackay's Moral: Anticipating catastrophe
is the surest way to avert it.

Chapter 21

You Gotta Have a Dream!

Martin Luther King Jr. had a dream. Robert Fulton had a dream. Henry Ford had a dream. America was built by dreamers. In the movies, the cop always wants to retire to a good fishing lake; the big-city newspaper reporter wants to pack it in and buy a small-town newspaper. Dreams like this are part of American folklore. The military used to sell the dream of retirement after 20 years. Join at 18, see the world and retire at 38.

There are many who have had dreams but have never gotten off our duffs and taken the action step to translate them into reality. How many people have claimed that they had thought of the Hula Hoop or the Pet Rock but just never quite got around to doing anything about it?

Dreams can be great motivators. They can be harmless, like betting a buck or two on the lottery, or they can be dangerously self-deluding. We all know salespeople who spend a lifetime chasing that million-dollar sale with the commission so large they could retire tomorrow—if they could just get over that last tiny hurdle.

Leo was that type of salesperson. He worked on one of those once-in-a-lifetime deals for months, and was so close to finalizing it he ordered a new Lexus LS and made a huge pledge to a charitable organization. All of you salespeople reading this know that the bigger the sale, the more that can go wrong with it. Something did go wrong, and Leo never closed the deal. Imagine his embarrassment when he had to back out of both his purchase and his pledge.

You should never, and I mean never, spend a commission until the check arrives.

Whatever the dream, whether it's early retirement, your own business, or a second home, it's a lot easier to achieve if you approach it as a long-term goal. Dreams are just dreams unless you have a plan. And since many dreams involve big bucks, you need a financial plan, not just a career plan.

> **Embrace risk, but do so wisely. It takes just as much intelligence and effort to hang on to your money as it does to make it work hard for you.**

Don't put all your thought and energy into climbing the greasy pole and then taking a casual approach to the money you're making. Too many people are smart about their careers and dumb about their money. And even career-smart people can find that their jobs aren't quite as secure as they thought they were.

Mackay's Moral: A dream is just a dream.
A goal is a dream with a deadline.

Chapter 22

Don't Miss Miss America

I was one of the judges for the Miss America pageant in 2001, when Miss Oregon, Katie Harman, won the contest. I learned two valuable lessons about the selection of candidates.

Almost everybody knows that the judges are entrusted with picking the Miss America that *America* would pick, not the one who catches their eye or lights their particular fire. Each contestant is judged within five different categories. It's the composite score that matters and each element is weighted. By the way, in the finals competition, the breakdown is 30 percent for talent and just 20 percent for swimsuit fitness.

> **In today's business world, the bigger the decision, the more likely it is to be made by a committee.**

In the same way, all big business decisions rest on multiple measures. If you're being judged, know the criteria that count. Learn the weightings and the balance game. If you knock your head out pushing one or two overwhelming traits, you can easily knock yourself out of the race.

When I met that bevy of talented, attractive women in Atlantic City, I also came away with one overwhelming impression: These were 51 individuals, not a batch of Stepford Wife clones. In sales, we often cripple ourselves with Dream Team–style thinking. We create superficially similar pairings:

- Our best salesperson is assigned the biggest account.
- The nerdiest client draws the geeky sales superstar.
- Meanwhile, the century-old business gets the rep in the pinstripe suit.

Chemistry doesn't work that way. Sometimes the biggest account will run so smoothly that it can do just fine when paired with a competent and attentive administrator. Sometimes tomorrow's money is best made if the top salesperson digs into a scruffy up-and-comer at the cusp of a new industry. Occasionally a carefully placed techno thoroughbred is just the right live wire. She can be the ideal ticket to overhaul the account of a business whose buying habits are helping to embalm that company into eternity.

Mackay's Moral: Mr. and Miss America may date each other. That doesn't mean they are meant for each other.

Quickie #7
Out of the Cubicle,
but Definitely Online

Promo magazine reported on a DoubleClick study done in the last few years on moms and Internet behavior. DoubleClick's findings: "Eighty-nine percent of household moms use the Internet at least twice a day, and 86 percent say they rely on search engines to find Web information." On their daily agenda: price comparison, product info and . . . where did you say that store was and how do I get there?

What does this tell us? Among other things:

- If you're in sales, chances are next to nil that your product will be bought by its ultimate customer without being influenced by the Internet. And it's likely to be researched or shopped on the Internet at several levels before the final sale.
- Internet presence is no add-on. A poor Internet presence will sink your ship.
- The Internet has become the bloodiest competitive arena since the Roman Colosseum. Regularly searching your rivals should be as routine as that morning workout.

The question used to be if the customer was computer literate. No longer. Customers automatically find their way to the Web today. The challenge has morphed into a whole new monster. When a potential buyer finds your Web message:

* Will it be informative and engaging?
* Is it easy to navigate?
* Does it capture the reality of your products and services in a convincing way?

Like it or not, your Internet identity is already part of your sales equation. How big a plus or minus is the only question.

Chapter 23

Inching Ahead Your Goal Line

All of us know that it's easy to get sidelined or distracted in trying to reach our goals. A study released in 2007 reported that 29 percent of American women and 19 percent of American men were on a diet. This may not be a bad idea, since one recent U.S. study said that more than 60 percent of Americans are overweight.

Did you ever notice how your diet goal always seems to run into a snag . . . or, should I say, snack?

Let me tell you a story about a portly fellow who used to wear the grapes in those ancient Fruit of the Loom underwear commercials. He became obsessed with losing weight and went on a crash diet, losing more than 100 pounds within three months. However, the dramatic weight loss left him hospitalized.

After recovering, he decided to learn how to lose weight safely through good nutrition and proper exercise. He was so thrilled with what he learned, he set a goal to share his knowledge with others who are troubled with obesity, and he determined to make it fun and entertaining. Today Richard Simmons is recognized all over America for his weight-loss crusade. He couldn't have done it without setting goals and sticking to them.

> **Great goals make you stretch, not snap.**

You must stay focused on your goals above all else. Truly dedicated individuals won't let anything interfere with attaining their goals. That's why so few people become champions. It's not easy.

The late Red Auerbach, famed Boston Celtics coach, was one of the most successful basketball coaches in history. He believed that the basic principles for success were the same in business as athletics. At the top of his list was setting goals.

Good teams always have common goals. When you find that goals of certain members differ from the team's, then the team will usually not do well. That's why teams with outstanding individual talents sometimes do poorly, while others are able to blend average abilities into championships.

I witnessed this firsthand at the 2000 Olympics in Sydney, Australia, when the huge underdog Lithuanian basketball team took the U.S. Dream Team to the final seconds before losing.

Goals give you more than a reason to get up in the morning; they are an incentive to keep you going all day. Goals tend to tap the deeper resources and draw the best out of life. Achieving goals is a significant accomplishment.

Most importantly, goals need to be realistic: beyond your immediate grasp but within your reach in the foreseeable future.

I remember a particular *Peanuts* cartoon in which Charlie Brown is having a bad day. He's just struck out swinging. In disgust, he shouts, "Rats!" Back in the dugout, he buries his face in his hands and laments to Lucy, "I'll never be a big-league ballplayer. All my life, I've dreamed of playing in the big leagues, but I just know I'll never make it."

Lucy responds, "You're thinking way too far ahead, Charlie Brown. What you need to do is set yourself more immediate goals."

"Immediate goals?" asks Charlie.

"Yes," says Lucy. "Start with this next inning when you go out to pitch. See if you can walk out to the mound without falling down." Baseball is a game rich in wisdom. Look at all the specialists: designated hitters, set-up relief pitchers, closers, and on and on.

The lesson is clear. Want to excel in life? Master what you do, and, for sure, master one thing at a time.

Mackay's Moral: You have to get to the plate before you can hit one out of the park.

PEANUTS featuring "Good ol' Charlie Brown" by SCHULZ

STRIKE TWO!

STRIKE THREE!

Tm. Reg. U.S. Pat. Off.—All rights reserved
© 1972 by United Feature Syndicate, Inc.

RATS!

I'LL NEVER BE A BIG-LEAGUE PLAYER! I JUST DON'T HAVE IT! ALL MY LIFE I'VE DREAMED OF PLAYING IN THE BIG LEAGUES, BUT I KNOW I'LL NEVER MAKE IT...

YOU'RE THINKING TOO FAR AHEAD, CHARLIE BROWN...WHAT YOU NEED TO DO IS TO SET YOURSELF MORE IMMEDIATE GOALS...

7-2

IMMEDIATE GOALS?

YES

START WITH THIS NEXT INNING WHEN YOU GO OUT TO PITCH...

SEE IF YOU CAN WALK OUT TO THE MOUND WITHOUT FALLING DOWN!

Chapter 24

The Bucket List

In Rob Reiner's 2007 film *The Bucket List*, Morgan Freeman plays a talented historian who earns his way as a mechanic. Jack Nicholson is a billionaire intent on persecuting his valet. Both are on the exit list with terminal lung cancer. They meet in treatment and resolve to do a series of things—some oddball, some serious—before they kick the bucket.

This concept was first introduced to me many years ago by Coach Lou Holtz. He originally had a list of 107 items that he methodically crossed off—like dining at the White House or appearing on the *Tonight* show when Johnny Carson was host. By 1998, Lou and his wife, Beth, had achieved 99 of the original goals! But that hasn't stopped the Coach from ramping up the list. When I checked with him in 2011, he had added three new goals: becoming a member of the College Football Hall of Fame, owning his own plane and celebrating his 50th wedding anniversary.

Since seeing *The Bucket List*, I've thought that every salesperson ought to have a list like this. It epitomizes the idea of s-t-r-e-t-c-h so central to our profession. In case you're not sure how to begin, here are eight candidates you might want to weigh:

1. Sell something to the person you think might be the toughest customer in the world (maybe Bill Gates, Steve Jobs, Warren Buffett . . .) and map out exactly how you might do it.
2. Use your selling skills to sell your town on a major community

project. Imagine what that project might be: It could be a hospital dedicated to treating a particular disease that's taken a loved one from you . . . or a major-league stadium. Hey, I've actually done that, and learned more in the process than a postgraduate fling at Harvard could ever have given me.

3.   Having become such a sales maven, imagine you're endowing a major foundation. What would its goals be? How would you channel the giving? Which one person would you support in their work to better the world?

4.   Imagine you're a celebrity CEO salesman on TV. Your chauffeured Bentley has just pulled up to the AFTRA office on Wilshire Boulevard to get your union card. You'll need it if you're going to act in a TV ad. You're about to embellish the tradition trail blazed by Chrysler's Lee Iacocca, Orville Redenbacher, Wendy's Dave Thomas or Frank Perdue. Imagine you're the next Ron Popeil announcing, "But wait! There's more!" What would you pitch and how would you manicure your delivery?

5.   Your sales skills are so coveted that you become a feature personality profile in *Inc.* and *Fortune.* Which of your unique skills and traits have the press beating down your door? What incredibly useful app did you invent for smartphones that has made the lives of millions of salespeople simpler and more effective . . . something that no one else could ever imagine?

6.   The White House is calling. You are asked to apply your salesmanship and negotiation skills to resolving a major global conflict. Where would it be and how would you tackle it? Which of your many protégés will you recruit to staff the mission with the best available talent?

7.   Ultimately you leave business altogether for a second career in politics. Harry Truman learned his diplomacy steps in a Kansas City haberdashery business. A string-tied Ronald Reagan peddled 20 Mule Team Borax laundry products on '60s TV. My friend John Y. Brown became governor of Kentucky after

building the foundation of today's KFC empire with unsurpassed salesmanship charm. What office would you seek and what would be your platform?

8. Make a list of the 10 people you want to meet in your lifetime. Use the Six Degrees of Separation theory, try LinkedIn or Facebook, write a fan letter and ask for a meeting. But don't assume everyone is out of reach.

Mackay's Moral: Flights of fantasy help you soar in reality.

Chapter 25

Fantasy Sparks Reality

A mother once asked Albert Einstein how to raise a child to become a genius. Einstein advised her to read fairy tales to the child.

"And after that?" the mother asked.

"Read the child more fairy tales," Einstein replied, adding that what a scientist needs most is a curious imagination.

Imagination is important not only for scientists, but also for anyone looking for new and better ways to do what they're already doing. And who isn't in favor of that?

Imagination is what keeps the engine of a good salesperson crackling with vitality.

L. Frank Baum, author of *The Wonderful Wizard of Oz*, surely had an active imagination. His Oz characters and story line are evidence of that. But did you know that in his more than 55 novels, 82 short stories and 200 poems, he also envisioned such later inventions as the laptop computer, the color television and the wireless phone? By the way, Baum died in 1919, long before any of these gadgets could have been practically produced.

"Imagination has brought mankind through the dark ages to its present state of civilization," Baum once wrote. "Imagination has given us the steam engine, the telephone, the talking-machine and the automobile, for these things had to be dreamed of before they became realities. So I believe that dreams—daydreams, you know, with your eyes wide open and your brain machinery whizzing—are likely to lead to the betterment of the world. The imaginative child will become the imaginative man or woman most apt to create, to invent, and therefore to foster civilization."

Your imagination can take you to plenty of places you've never been. But if you haven't used it for a while, try these ways to awaken your imagination:

- **Ask questions.** What if I shake up the order of my presentation or even make such simple adjustments as changing the graphics in my PowerPoint? When I go to my chief competitor's website, what one product or service feature do I admire most, and how much will it cost me to build in an option equally as good?

- **Take risks.** You might admire the way a whiz in the engineering department constantly comes up with new ideas. Invite that person to coffee and ask how he or she does it. Start a project—like beefing up product quality control for outsourced components—that will require you to learn new technical skills.

- **Be curious.** Read different business news sources on the Web in the morning. (There are dozens!) Try that exotic ethnic restaurant your #1 client has been raving about. Read that book recommended by the college prof you most admired. Talk to someone who has served in a combat zone or in the thick of a humanitarian relief mission, and imagine yourself in that situation.

- **Expect the unexpected.** Instead of lamenting that things didn't turn out exactly as you planned, figure out how the surprise results might be even better. Entrust a younger colleague with editing a sales pitch, and you might find a breezy new way to present your case to Gen-X customers with shorter attention spans.

- **Build a model without instructions.** Take a pile of Legos and see what you can create. Play with Play-Doh. Make a food sculpture. Choose a color and note how many objects are that shade. Get on your hands and knees and look around from a child's point of view.

Mackay's Moral: Imagination's one and only rule:
If you can imagine it, you can do it.

STICK WITH IT

Chapter 26

The ABCs of Determination—
Any Body Can

Determination is what keeps us hammering away. Determined people pos-sess the stamina and courage to pursue their ambitions despite criticism, ridicule or unfavorable circumstances. In fact, discouragement can often spur us on to greater things.

Consider Sylvester Stallone and his phenomenal success. As a child, Stallone was frequently beaten by his father and told he had no brains. He grew up lonely and confused. He was in and out of various schools. An adviser at Drexel University told him that, based on aptitude testing, he should pursue a career as an elevator repair person.

Stallone decided to pursue acting, but his abnormal life led to one failure after another. He remained determined to learn his chosen craft and decided to try his hand at writing. After watching Chuck Wepner, a relatively unknown fighter, go the distance against the champion Muhammad Ali, Stallone was inspired to write the script for *Rocky*—in less than four days. As Vince Lombardi said, "It's not whether you get knocked down. It's whether you get up again." Five *Rocky*s later, Stallone is a champion . . . of determi-nation.

Determination turns ordinary into extraordinary.

Thousands of businesses that statistically should have failed are success-ful today because of the determination of their owners. Consider:

- Coca-Cola sold only 400 Cokes in its first year.
- Apple Computer was rejected for aquisition by Hewlett-Packard and Atari.
- Inventor Chester Carlson pounded the streets for years before he could find backers for his Xerox photocopying process.

Like many military heroes before and after him, General Ulysses S. Grant had such a fierce sense of determination that President Lincoln saw him as indispensable, even after setbacks. Following Grant's defeat at Shiloh, newspapers throughout the Union demanded his removal, and Lincoln's friends pleaded with him to give the command to someone else. But Lincoln said, "I can't spare this man. He fights. He's got the grip of a bulldog, and when he gets his teeth in, nothing can shake him off."

Look at Mother Teresa. Through her quiet determination, the tiny nun brought world attention to the plight of the poor.

The roots of President Teddy Roosevelt's determination started with a childhood ailment. Severe asthma limited his ability to play like other kids, and as he lay in bed struggling to breathe, Roosevelt was afraid to go to sleep for fear he wouldn't wake up. Yet he was determined to become strong both mentally and physically. His desire to become self-sufficient fortified him through a daily exercise routine and hours of weight lifting. He became an avid reader and absorbed books on every conceivable subject. As a Harvard student, Roosevelt became known for his energy and enthusiasm.

Don't let a setback be a monkey on your back.

If your switch is off more than on, it's time to examine what's making you less than motivated. Is it the job itself? Find something to love about it, or find a different line of work. Is it the fear of failure? Then you haven't been paying attention: Failure is an opportunity to learn and improve—and boost your enthusiasm. Are you bored? Burned out? Ready for a different challenge? Jump at the chance to try something new. Life's too short to hate what you're doing! Find something you can be passionate about, and work at it until you can't imagine doing anything else.

Sometimes in life you have to go for it . . . to test yourself. I saw this exhibited firsthand in December 2006 when I was driving my good friend Muhammad Ali back from a surprise party we'd thrown for his wife, Lonnie. It was also the evening for the premiere of a television documentary called *Ali Wrap*. Unfortunately, we were 15 minutes late arriving home to view the show from the start. It was approximately a 25-yard walk from the car to the front door, which the champ negotiated with his walker. As we entered his house, you could see the giant TV screen some 15 yards away with bigger-than-life images of Muhammad.

The moment Muhammad's eyes hit that screen, he thrust his walker to the ground, made a mad dash for the sofa and plopped himself down to watch the show. I stood there dumbfounded—I couldn't believe my eyes. To the best of my knowledge, he hadn't taken a step without his walker in many months. No human being ever knows what's really inside until ultimately challenged to throw all caution to the wind and go for it.

I'd like to have a dollar for every salesperson who threw in the towel, bagged it and quit in their first year.

It's a good thing the following four Hall of Fame coaches didn't think that way. Look at their first-year NFL records:

- Tom Landry   Dallas Cowboys   0-11-1 in 1960
- Chuck Noll   Pittsburgh Steelers   1-13 in 1969
- Bill Walsh   San Francisco 49ers   2-14 in 1979
- Jimmy Johnson   Dallas Cowboys   1-15 in 1989

They all got massacred in their first *and* second years in the NFL. Incidentally, they also won a total of 11 Super Bowls among them.

Today we live in a culture of instant gratification, where the attributes of patience and determination are hard to find. We need to be more like the young college graduate determined to find a position with a reputable company. She faced continual rejection in the interview process, yet her determination helped keep her goals in mind. One busy personnel manager, flooded with applications, suggested the hopeful applicant check back in 10 years. "No problem," the young woman responded. "Would a morning or afternoon interview work best for you?"

Mackay's Moral: Be like a postage stamp. Stick to it until you get there.

DETERMINATION—The Fortune Cookies

You don't quit trying when you lose; you lose because you quit trying.

Success is putting your "knows" to the grindstone.

A can-do attitude is the mind's paintbrush—it can color any situation.

People never fail at anything—they just give up.

There's no future in saying it can't be done.

The will is as important as the skill.

He who doesn't hope to win has already lost.

There's no defeat except in no longer trying.

Race to the finish . . . or *walk* to the finish—just finish.

Quitters never win. Winners never quit.

Trying times are no time to quit trying.

A person without determination is like a knife without an edge.

In most cases, *IQ* is less important to a person's education than *I will.*

You can't get anywhere unless you start.

When something can't be done, watch someone do it.

Chapter 27

Quitters: Never Winners

There are three things you must do to be successful:

1. Don't quit.
2. Don't quit.
3. Don't quit.

When I graduated from the University of Minnesota in 1954, I was kind of cocky and thought I knew it all . . . I thought I'd be able to start at the top and work my way up.

I started as an envelope salesman. My first boss threw the Yellow Pages at me, saying, "Lotsa luck, kid." I just couldn't make a sale. One day I asked an old grizzly, "Sid, how many times do you call on a prospect before you just give up?"

And he answered, "It depends on which one of us dies first."

I'm constantly asked what I think is the secret of success. Well, it's a lot of things, but—as I've said—here's what is at the top of my list: 1) You need to be a hungry fighter, and 2) a hungry fighter never quits. I've learned over the years that success is largely hanging on after others have let go.

When you study the truly successful people, you'll see that they may have made plenty of mistakes, but when they were knocked down, they kept getting up . . . and up . . . and up. Like the Energizer Bunny, they keep going . . . and going . . . and going.

What's most amazing? Stars who rise up from a wallop to the breadbasket don't stay slouched over. Many go on to tower over their professions:

- Michael Jordan was cut from his high school basketball team.
- Henry Ford failed and went broke five times before he finally succeeded.
- Ernest Hemingway is said to have revised *The Old Man and the Sea* manuscript 80 times before submitting it for publication.

Sales success is getting up more than you fall down.

I love the story about the high school basketball coach who was attempting to motivate his players to persevere through a difficult season. Halfway through the season he stood before the team and said, "Did Michael Jordan ever quit?"

The team responded, "No!"

He yelled, "What about the Wright brothers? Did they ever give up?"

"No!" hollered back the team.

"Did Muhammad Ali ever quit?"

Again the team yelled, "No!"

"Did Elmer McAllister ever quit?"

There was a long silence. Finally one player was bold enough to ask, "Who's Elmer McAllister? We never heard of him."

The coach snapped back, "Of course you never heard of him—he quit!"

Even Babe Ruth, considered by sports historians to be the greatest baseball player of all time, failed on many occasions. He struck out 1,330 times.

Or how about Brett Favre? He threw more interceptions than any NFL quarterback in history, yet he also threw more touchdown passes than any quarterback in NFL history.

Sir Winston Churchill provides a very special example. I was fortunate to personally learn the details of this memorable—and often misquoted— oration from Churchill's grandson Winston S. Churchill III, who has written a book titled *Never Give In! The Best of Winston Churchill's Speeches.*

Sir Winston, himself a person who never quit during a lifetime of defeats and setbacks, delivered the shortest and most eloquent commencement address ever given. Despite a difficult time with the entrance exam at his preparatory school, Harrow, and undistinguished academic performance there, Churchill was asked to address the school's graduating students in 1941. He gave a speech of less than 50 words, thundering at its peak: "This is the lesson: Never give in, never give in, never, never, never, never—in nothing, great or small, large or petty—never give in!" He sat down to a thunderous ovation.

Mackay's Moral: Big shots are only little shots
who keep shooting.

Chapter 28

The 10,000-Hour Investment

Malcolm Gladwell's *Outliers: The Story of Success* continues his steady stream of thought-provoking bestsellers. This book will make a lot of people feel much better about not achieving instant success. Gladwell maintains it takes about 10 years, or 10,000 hours, of practice to attain true expertise.

"The people at the very top don't just work harder or even much harder than everyone else," Gladwell writes. "They work much, much harder." Achievement, he says, is talent plus preparation . . . and the preparation part of the formula looms far larger than we normally assume.

Gladwell cites The Beatles' rise to fame as unassailable evidence. They had been together seven years before their famous arrival in America. They'd spent a lot of time playing in strip clubs in Hamburg, Germany, sometimes for as long as eight hours a night. John Lennon said of those years, "We got better and got more confidence. We couldn't help it with all the experience playing all night long." Overnight sensation? Not exactly. Estimates are that the band performed live 1,200 times *before* their big breakout success in 1964. By comparison, most bands don't perform 1,200 times in their careers!

Gladwell quotes neurologist Daniel Levitin, who has extensively studied the formula for success:

The emerging picture from such studies is that 10,000 hours of practice is required to achieve the level of mastery associated with being a world-class expert—in anything. In study after study of composers, basketball players, fiction writers, ice skaters, concert pianists, chess players, master criminals, and what have you, the number comes up again and again. Of course, this doesn't address why some people get more out of their practice sessions than others do. But no one has yet found a case in which true world-class expertise was accomplished in less time. It seems it takes the brain this long to assimilate all that it needs to know to achieve true mastery.

Two computer giants, Bill Joy, who cofounded Sun Microsystems, and Bill Gates, cofounder of Microsoft, are also proof of the 10,000-hour theory. Who can argue that their hard work didn't pay off big-time?

As Malcolm Gladwell puts it, "Practice isn't the thing you do once you're good. It's the thing you do that makes you good."

My purely unscientific observations support this in spades. Our sales reps at MackayMitchell Envelope Company seem to hit their prime after several years of hard work. And I believe it's more than getting comfortable in the job, because I've also seen the opposite scenario: sales reps who initially seemed like naturals at selling who couldn't peddle water in the desert.

Why?

They thought they could get by on their good looks, their winning personalities or their pedigrees. The notion of investing 10,000 hours didn't apply to them—or so they thought. We'll never know, because they aren't working for us anymore.

Hanging loose to cash in on the jackpot, confident you're a born winner? Heed Honest Abe Lincoln's foolproof advice:

"Things may come to those who wait. But only the things left by those who hustle."

While you're working at it, do what the Liverpool moptops did so well. Don't just work hard—press yourself to work smarter every minute you're clocking time.

Mackay's Moral: Some people dream about success,
and others wake up and do something about it.

Quickie #8
Hubris the Humorless

In ancient Greece, Alcibiades was telling Pericles how Athens should be governed. Annoyed by the young man's tone, Pericles said, "Son, when I was your age, I talked just the way you are talking."

Alcibiades looked Pericles in the face and replied, "How I should like to have known you when you were at your best."

Ah, the arrogance of youth. To put the story in context, Pericles is often referred to as "the first citizen of Athens" for his many achievements: his promotion of art and literature, his championing of democracy, and his sponsorship of an ambitious building project that included most of the surviving structures on the Acropolis, including the Parthenon. Alcibiades, on the other hand, was also a statesman and orator.

The respective lengths of the Wikipedia entries for these two suggests history is still duking it out as to who was greater, but Pericles has the clear edge in the impact of his achievements. Alcibiades, defeated at the Battle of Notium, ultimately exiled himself. Contributing to his downfall were the great, unchecked expectations he allowed to be circulated about himself before being thrashed by the Spartans.

In the dictionary, Alcibiades could be the personification of "hubris." Hubris means extreme haughtiness, exaggerated pride or arrogance. Hubris has lost touch with reality. That's why powerful people so often overestimate their competence or capabilities.

Recent headlines illustrate hubris to the extreme: the disgraced governor of Illinois flailing to defend his actions in 2010 . . . the CEO of BP complaining days after the Gulf oil-rig explosion and resulting massive oil spill that he wanted his life back. Hubris lives on—an odd affliction that makes its observers sicker than the self-centered souls it afflicts.

Chapter 29

Compassion Uplifts You Too

A Native American grandfather was talking about how he felt to his grandson. "I feel as if I have two wolves fighting in my heart," he said. "One wolf is the vengeful, angry, violent one. The other wolf is the loving, compassionate one."

The grandson asked him, "Which wolf will win the fight in your heart?"

The grandfather answered, "The one I feed."

According to one definition, compassion is an emotion that is a sense of shared suffering, most often combined with a desire to alleviate the suffering of another and to show special kindness to them. Compassion essentially starts with empathy. Compassionate acts consider the suffering of others and attempt to alleviate it as if it were one's own. In this sense, compassion is the cornerstone of the Golden Rule.

Where does compassion fit in business? Will it hurt the bottom line? Will it make our company look soft, like a pushover?

The answers: at all levels, no and definitely not. Compassion and profitability are not mutually exclusive. On the contrary, companies that are perceived as people-oriented and good corporate citizens have a far better chance of succeeding than those that put profits ahead of people.

When I was interviewing New York City Mayor Michael Bloomberg for my book *We Got Fired! . . . And It's the Best Thing That Ever Happened to Us*, the mayor told me that one thing he never forgot was the people who called him after he was fired by Salomon Brothers.

"I remember the exact list," Bloomberg said. "If any of them end up in trouble, I'll call them. If you see them on the way up, you should see them on the way down. Whenever someone gets fired or has some real problems, I always call to tell them my thoughts are with them. And if I can be of any help whatsoever, please let me know."

Michael Bloomberg is right about being there at the dark moments. I have always tried to call people when they were down, or to do what I could to help them get back on their feet and succeed. I believe compassion should be a vital part of our character.

> **There is a big difference between compassion and sympathy. Sympathy sees and says, "I'm sorry." Compassion feels and declares, "I'll help." Compassionate people really care.**

There are scientific studies suggesting there are physical benefits to practicing compassion. People who practiced compassion produced 100 percent more DHEA, a hormone that is thought to counteract the aging process, and 23 percent less cortisol—the "stress" hormone.

When you're happy, you make others more happy. Why? Because compassionate people are more positive, plain and simple. Compassionate people radiate vibes that make the people around them happy to be where they are. And every skilled salesperson knows that a happier prospect is more receptive and more inclined to be a repeat customer.

Confucius said wisdom, compassion and courage are the three universally recognized moral qualities of a person. I'm not a big philosopher, but who could disagree with that?

Mackay's Moral: Helping someone up won't pull you down, and could very easily pull them to your side.

Chapter 30

Enthusiasm: Only You Can Ignite It

Charles Schwab was one of the first managers to win a salary of $1 million annually. That was in the 1920s, mind you, and his boss was a tough businessman named Andrew Carnegie, a man not known for wasting a dollar. Why did Carnegie give Schwab such a princely salary? Schwab headed Carnegie's United States Steel Company, and under his direction it was the absolute tops in all of industry for its day.

What was Schwab's secret? "I consider my ability to arouse enthusiasm among my people the greatest asset I possess," said Schwab, "and the way to develop the best in a person is by appreciation and encouragement. I believe in giving a person incentive to work. So I am anxious to praise but loath to find fault. I am hearty in my approbation and lavish in my praise."

Automaker Henry Ford was like-minded. Very early in his career, even after failure upon failure, Ford remained enthusiastic. "You can do anything if you have enthusiasm . . . Enthusiasm is the spark in your eye, the swing in the gait, the grip of your hand, the irresistible surge of your will, and your energy to execute your ideas. Enthusiasm is at the bottom of all progress! With it, there is accomplishment. Without it, there are only alibis."

"Enthusiasm is one of the most powerful engines of success," wrote the American essayist Ralph Waldo Emerson. "When you do a thing, do it with your might. Put your whole soul into it. Stamp it with your own personality.

Be active, be energetic, be enthusiastic and faithful, and you will accomplish your object. Nothing great was ever achieved without enthusiasm."

One of the paradoxical things about life is that everyone dies . . . but not everyone fully lives. Too many people have what we might call "near-life experiences." They go through life bunting, so afraid of failure that they never try to win the big prizes . . . never knowing the thrill of hitting a home run or even taking a swing at one.

Aim higher.

My all-time Champion of Enthusiasm is a 93-year-old lady I heard about in 2010. She's Rocky Plus. When the press asked her for her secret to a long and zesty life, she couldn't stop bubbling about the power of enthusiasm. "Furthermore," she wound up with a twinkle, "even at my age I still have four boyfriends I spend part of every single day with. I get out of bed each day with Will Power, and after breakfast I go for a stroll with Arthur Ritis. Charley Horse almost always visits me in the afternoon, and I spend the evening with Ben Gay."

Need I say more?

Mackay's Moral: Enthusiasm is the spark
that will ignite your life.

Chapter 31

Enthusiasm: An Encore

When I had the opportunity to see Billy Crystal's *700 Sundays* for a second time, this incredible one-man show really stuck with me. Billy Crystal was beyond sensational.

How can a person put on a challenging show, night in and night out, and keep it fresh and interesting? How can an entertainer like Tony Bennett sing the same songs for 50-plus years and still make every performance seem like he's more thrilled and excited about it than anyone in the audience? They're pros. They give it everything they've got, every time, just as if it were their first . . . or last performance. Their focus and enthusiasm are obvious.

When I played golf for the University of Minnesota my sophomore year, I represented my school at the NCAA Championship at Purdue University. To prepare, I played so much golf, I was certain my optic nerves had locked and could register only the color green. My game began to show signs I had decided to withdraw by taking up residence in the rough.

Our legendary coach, Les Bolstad, gave me some of the best advice I've ever received. When it comes to achieving results, it was a lesson in life that has probably helped me as much as anything else. "Harvey," he said, "every drive you hit . . . every approach shot you make . . . every putt you stroke . . . you say to yourself, 'This is the last drive I will ever hit. This is the last approach shot I will ever make. This is the last putt I will ever stroke. Therefore, it better be my best.'" I've carried that philosophy over to my sales career.

For most of my life, before I make a sales call, I've practiced saying to myself, "This is the last sales call I am ever going to make in my entire life . . . Therefore, it better be good."

I learned that when you put that kind of emphasis on your performance, your concentration will intensify, and you'll be amazed at how successful you can be. I continue to use this philosophy in a lot of what I do. For example, when I make a speech, I always tell myself, "This is the last speech I am ever going to give. I am never going to make another speech as long as I live." I put pressure on myself to always do my best.

Entertainers use this same mental trick the instant they sense they're getting stale. The late screen actor Eddie Albert (of *Green Acres* fame) was a great friend whom I loved dearly. He once told me, "If I don't treat every performance as if it will be my farewell appearance, there's a good chance it may be."

> **Enthusiasm is the juice that puts focus into overdrive. You must have it to excel.**

In his classic work *The Law of Success in Sixteen Lessons*, Napoleon Hill says that enthusiasm is an essential ingredient for success in life. Enthusiasm energizes, refreshes and motivates the person endowed with it. Hill, one of my all-time favorite writers, says some people are born with a natural enthusiasm while others have to develop it. How? Simple, he says. Work at something you love.

The late Zig Ziglar, a master motivator and one of the most enthusiastic people I ever knew, told the story of the top salesperson in his company— the best out of 1,200 people! When she broke all the sales records, Zig asked her how she did it. She replied, "God didn't make me with an off switch." Tigers don't *have* off switches.

Remember, if you aren't getting excited about hitting the pavement every day, it will show. And that generates a lack of enthusiasm among your customers for whatever you're selling. You'll get what you give—nothing. Flip your switch to *on* and see what you can achieve!

Mackay's Moral: Enthusiasm is infectious. Start an epidemic.

Chapter 32

Your Attitude Determines Your Altitude

Is your outlook partly sunny or partly cloudy?

When you wake up every day, you have two choices. You can be positive or negative . . . an optimist or a pessimist.

I choose to be an optimist. I see the glass as half full, not half empty. I realize that after every storm the sun shines, that there is a solution to every problem.

It's like the two traveling salesmen who fell on hard times and ended up broke and stranded in a small town in Montana. They needed money to move on and learned that the town paid $20 each for wolf pelts. They sensed the opportunity. That night they set out with a couple of clubs and some borrowed supplies and made camp in the distant hills. They were no sooner asleep than one was startled by an eerie howl. He crawled outside the tent to find himself surrounded by hundreds of snarling wolves. Back into the tent he crawled and shook his buddy.

"Wake up!" he cried. "Wake up! We're rich!"

It's all a matter of perspective.

You can whine because you have to go to work or you can be grateful that you have a good job.

You can complain about learning new software—again—or be excited about having a new challenge.

You can grumble about your incompetent boss or do everything in your power to make your department successful.

You get the idea.

A terrible tornado swept through Minnesota a few summers back. There was massive damage. An entire town was wiped out. People were distraught. In the aftermath, a photojournalist for a local TV station captured a slightly different slant when he shot footage of a man standing by his car, which had been crushed by a fallen tree. He was smiling, waving at people driving by and holding a sign that read, "new-style compact car."

Pop quiz: What is the most common sentiment expressed by victims of disasters like this? "At least we're all okay." A few hours earlier they wouldn't have given that a second thought. Strange how a little wind can change your perspective.

How many sales books have celebrated this chestnut? The shoe company sent a salesperson to a newly developing country to check the potential market there. He came home and reported, "There is no market there. Nobody wears shoes."

The company decided to test it again, this time with a more positive salesperson. Within a few hours an e-mail came in: "Start shipping shoes immediately . . . No competition!"

The pessimists don't grow your business or even maintain the status quo. They make the job harder for everyone around them. And the worst part is that their surliness rubs off on others. It's a no-win situation from any perspective. Encourage your employees to look at each business challenge as an opportunity rather than a problem.

> **"I am an optimist. It doesn't seem too much use being anything else."—Sir Winston Churchill**

There is a monastery in Montserrat, Spain, that is a certain test of attitude. Set halfway up a 4,000-foot mountain, the monastery offers inspiration from every view. But the monks there must maintain silence, as the story goes, except for once every two years, when they may utter exactly two words.

After his first two years, one young initiate was invited to speak to the abbot. "Bed lumpy," he said. Two years later, the same young man again met with the abbot. This time, his two words were, "Food awful." Another two years went by, and the young monk went to the abbot and said simply, "I quit."

The abbot, shaking his head, said, "I was somewhat expecting this. All you've done since you've been here is complain, complain, complain."

Don't wait for divine inspiration to improve your outlook. Some people see the positive in every situation, while others go through life waiting for their induction into the negative attitude hall of fame. Life is a matter of perspective. You choose.

Mackay's Moral: Keep your eye on the doughnut and not on the hole.

Quickie #9
The Plus of Minor-League Play

When I got my wife, Carol Ann, to say "I do" ages ago, we entered serious negotiations to nail down the ground rules for our marriage.

Then we hit on it.

I would make all the major decisions, and she would make all the minor decisions!

Many of my friends have asked me, "Harvey, how on earth could that ever work out?"

My answer: "Very simple . . . There have never been any major decisions."

Chapter 33

Change Your Thoughts, Change Your Life

If what you see is what you get, what will you get?

That all depends on what you see.

A guy pulled into a small restaurant on the outskirts of town. He told his server, "I was just transferred to your town, and I've never been to this part of the country. What are people like here?"

"What are people like where you come from?" the server asked.

"Not so nice," the man replied. "In fact, they can be quite rude."

The server shook her head and said, "Well, I'm afraid you'll find the people in this town to be the same way."

A second fellow came in and sat at a nearby table. He called out to the server, "I'm just moving to your area. Is it nice here?"

"Was it nice where you came from?" inquired the server.

"Oh, yes! I came from a great place. The people were friendly, and I hated to leave."

"Well, you'll find the same to be true of this town."

At hearing this, the first customer was irritated and asked his server, "So tell me, what is this town really like?"

She just shrugged her shoulders and said, "It's all a matter of perception. You'll find things to be just the way you think they are."

Is your glass half full or half empty? What do you see? Do you love your job even though there are a few things that bug you? Or do you let the little annoyances drive you crazy and complain to your coworkers nonstop?

As radio commentator Paul Harvey once said, "I have never seen a monument erected to a pessimist."

A pessimist makes difficulties out of opportunities. When something is utterly uncommon, Arabs say it is as rare as bird's milk. So it is with successful pessimists. You need to be able to look on the bright side of tough situations in order to take risks and to survive both successes and failures. The sooner you accept that you will have both successes and failures, the easier it will be to get your business and personal life headed in the right direction.

An optimist, on the other hand, understands that life can be a bumpy road, but at least it is leading somewhere. Optimists learn from mistakes and failures, and are not afraid to fail again. They know that as long as you get up after you're knocked down, you are not defeated.

The annals of business are full of very successful people who have gone bankrupt, lost companies, faced public humiliation and still came out on top. The only difference was their attitude.

People that overcame severe setbacks believed in themselves and the others around them. Hard work, discipline and occasionally a little bit of luck kept them going. There's no reason it can't work for all of us too.

In his book *How to Stop Worrying and Start Living* (which I highly recommend), Dale Carnegie tells the story of a young man who worried himself into a nervous breakdown. He worried about everything: his weight, his hair, his money, losing the girl he wanted to marry and what others thought about him. He worried that he had ulcers. Eventually, his worry made it impossible for him to work. Something had to give, and that was when he had his breakdown.

The young man avoided everyone and cried a lot. He decided to go to Florida to see if a change in scenery would help him. When he got on the train, his father handed him a letter and told him not to open it until he reached his destination. He was even more miserable in Florida than he had been at home.

Finally, he opened the letter from his father: "Son, you are 1,500 miles from home, and you don't feel any different, do you? I knew you wouldn't, because you took with you the one thing that is the cause of all your trouble, that is, yourself. There is nothing wrong with either your body or your mind. It is not the situations you have met that have thrown you; it is what you think of these situations. 'As a man thinketh in his heart, so he is.' When you realize that, son, come home, for you will be cured." After some reflection he realized his father was right. It was not the world that needed to change; it was merely the lens of his mind that needed adjustment.

Attitude is paramount in sales. If you're trying to entice a prospect or close a sale, it's mighty hard to do either when your world is a dismal gray. Customers x-ray right through a glum attitude. They'll find little comfort in you if you have scant confidence in yourself.

Mackay's Moral: If seeing is believing,
it pays to see the bright side.

120

Quickie #10
Without a Goal,
You'll Never Score One

I once heard a math teacher announce an unusual dream at a school assembly: "I hope you all fail," he said to an audience of high school seniors eager to go out and conquer the world. "Because if you don't, you haven't set your goals high enough."

Getting by without setting goals is the ultimate way to shortchange your life. It's not a way to failure. It's the definition of nonstarting.

Evangelist Robert H. Schuller describes four kinds of people:

- **First come the cop-outs.** These people set no goals and make no decisions.
- **Second are the hold-outs.** They have a beautiful dream, but uncertainty makes them afraid to respond to its challenge.
- **The dropouts are third.** They start to make their dream come true, but when the going gets tough, they quit.
- **Finally, there are the all-outs.** These brave souls know where they're headed and do what it takes to get there.

It all starts with goals: Winners make goals. Losers make excuses.

Chapter 34

Your Positive Self— Right Underneath Your Fingers

When comedian and actor Jamie Foxx first met with Ray Charles, Jamie was sitting on a piano bench alongside his childhood hero preparing for his role in the movie *Ray*. It would earn him an Academy Award. They were playing the blues, Ray laying down a riff, Jamie answering with one of his own. Then the music legend started to play something much more difficult, and Jamie froze. Ray Charles broke the silence by saying, "It's right underneath your fingers, baby. That's all you have to understand, everything is right underneath your fingers."

That's now the metaphor Jamie uses for his life. He knows he has all the tools he needs "right underneath his fingers."

It's a natural reaction to be timid about trying new things for fear of making a fool of yourself. We're afraid of exposing our weaknesses for all to see. I'm here today to tell you, you would be a bigger fool not to try.

A psychologist at the University of Pennsylvania showed that optimists are more successful than equally talented pessimists in business, education, sports and politics. Based on his research, the insurance and financial services corporation Met Life developed a test to distinguish between the optimists and pessimists when hiring salespeople. The results of that experiment were phenomenal! The optimists outsold the pessimists by 20 percent the first year. During the second year, the difference jumped to 50 percent. Find me a salesperson—or company—that wouldn't beg for those numbers. I know we would find office space for those optimists at MackayMitchell Envelope Company!

The right attitude, coupled with the courage to reach for opportunity, is the defining factor for success. For example, Patrick O'Malley started as a truck driver, but ended his career as chairman of Canteen, a big vending machine service company. His philosophy: "I think it is absolutely essential that you have PMA (positive mental attitude) in every aspect of life and that you start early."

I would add this to Mr. O'Malley's advice: It's never too late to start early. Don't get discouraged just because you haven't yet been practicing what he's preaching. If you are still breathing air and taking nourishment, now is a fine time to improve your attitude and look for—or create—opportunities.

> **Life is a series of opportunities. The often neglected fact of life is that opportunities multiply as you take advantage of them.**

Opportunities shrivel up and die if you ignore them. I don't have much of a green thumb, but I do know that if you nourish and encourage a rosebush, it will provide bouquets. Neglect it, and all you have left is thorns. Which do you want underneath your fingers?

If finding opportunities sounds like hard work, let me reassure you: It is. Someone once told me life is hard. But I say, compared to what?

We live in a time when everything, quite literally, is underneath our fingers. The Internet presents us with opportunities that no other generation before has known, an explosion unparalleled in the history of business development. We can now expand our customer base to the entire globe. And online classes have redefined learning.

Google is a common verb now, putting information on every imaginable topic underneath our fingers. I am continually amazed at the instant availability of facts and figures that just a few years ago took a team of researchers days or weeks to uncover.

I am an eternal optimist. I firmly believe that there is virtually nothing we can't do if we set our minds to it. It helps to be realistic—I know I am never going to pitch in the World Series, but I could be a player/manager of a top-notch company. I took a big gamble getting my company off the ground, but I've never looked back.

Ray Charles started his life dirt poor and lost his eyesight as a child. If he could adopt the attitude that everything is "right underneath your fingers," there is really no excuse for the rest of us. We who have so few challenges to overcome should not be any less optimistic.

John Gardner, a chief engineer of Lyndon Johnson's Great Society, summed it up well: "We need to believe in ourselves, but not to believe that life is easy."

Mackay's Moral: Every accomplishment
begins with the decision to try.

Chapter 35

Worrying Makes You Cross the Bridge Before You Come to It

Recently I saw a survey showing that 40 percent of the things we worry about never happen, 30 percent are in the past and can't be helped, 12 percent concern the affairs of others that aren't our business, 10 percent are about sickness—real or imagined—and 8 percent are worth worrying about. I would submit that even those 8 percent aren't usually worth the energy of worry.

Did you know that the English word "worry" is derived from an Old English word that means to strangle or to choke? That's easy to believe. People do literally worry themselves to death . . . or to heart disease, high blood pressure, ulcers, nervous disorders and all sorts of other nasty conditions. Is it worth it?

Some folks seem to think this is a recent phenomenon, but I've got news for you: Advice about worry goes back as far as the Bible. We didn't invent it. We just need to find a way to keep it from ruling our lives. I have a couple of favorite books to recommend.

First, an oldie: Dale Carnegie's *How to Stop Worrying and Start Living*. It was first published in 1948, but the advice is just as fresh and valuable as it was then. In fact, it's right-on for our times. Being a chronic list maker, I found two sections that really knocked my socks off. Both are about businesspeople trying to solve problems without the added burden of worrying.

Carnegie credits Willis H. Carrier, whose name appears on many air conditioners, with these silver bullets:

1.   Analyze the situation honestly and figure out what is the worst possible thing that could happen.
2.   Prepare yourself mentally to accept the worst, if necessary.
3.   Then calmly try to improve upon the worst, which you have already agreed mentally to accept.

Bingo! You can handle anything now. You know what you have to do; it's just a matter of doing it. Without worrying.

The other approach of Carnegie's that I like is a system once put into practice at a large publishing company by an executive named Leon. He was sick and tired of boring and unproductive meetings marked by excessive hand-wringing. He enforced a rule that everyone who wished to present a problem to him first had to submit a memo answering these four questions:

1.   What's the problem?
2.   What's the cause of the problem?
3.   What are all possible solutions to the problem?
4.   Which solution do you suggest?

Leon rarely had to deal with problems after that, nor did he worry about them. He found that his associates used the system to find workable solutions without tying up hours in useless meetings. He estimated that he'd eliminated three-fourths of his meeting time and improved his productivity, health and happiness. Was he just passing the buck? Of course not! He was paying those folks to do their jobs, *and* he was giving them great training at decision making.

> **You can't saw sawdust. A day of worry is more exhausting than a day of work.**

Another little gem that's made its way to a #1 *New York Times* bestseller is the late Richard Carlson's *Don't Sweat the Small Stuff . . . and it's all small stuff.* This book can improve perspective in 100 small doses. I love the chapter titles, helpful in themselves: "Repeat to Yourself, 'Life Isn't an Emergency,'" "Practice Ignoring Negative Thoughts," and my favorite, "Let Go of the Idea that Gentle, Relaxed People Can't Be Superachievers."

People get so busy worrying about yesterday or tomorrow that they forget about today. And today is what you have to work with.

Take the story of the fighter who, after taking the full count in a late round of a brawl, finally came to in the dressing room. As his head cleared and he realized what had happened, he said to his manager, "Boy, did I have him worried. He thought he killed me."

Now that's putting the worry where it belongs.

Mackay's Moral: Today is the tomorrow you
worried about yesterday.

POSITIVE ENERGY—The Fortune Cookies

There's no business that isn't like show business.

_____

Never say no for the other guy.

_____

A great salesperson inspires buyers to see the product's benefits as traits they have discovered or identified.

_____

When you are good to others, you are best to yourself.

_____

Make it your business to be happy and your business will be happy.

_____

No one ever invented a good substitute for a good nature.

_____

If you don't climb the mountain, you can't see the view.

_____

The world always looks brighter from behind a smile.

_____

Your day usually goes the way the corners of your mouth turn.

_____

People do not live by bread alone. They need buttering up once in a while.

_____

Nothing will improve a person's hearing more than sincere praise.

_____

Work isn't work if you like it.

_____

SETBACKS

Chapter 36

There's No Education Like Adversity

Life is not a steady ascent. It doesn't go straight up . . . a lot of lumps and a lot of bumps . . . a lot of throttling up and a lot of throttling down. I have never yet met a single successful person who has not had to overcome either a little or a lot of adversity in his or her life. (And I think most readers of this book would agree.)

One school of business studied 400 executives who had made it to the top and compared them to 400 who fell by the wayside during their careers. The idea was to discover how those who became successful differed from those who didn't.

Education was not the key factor, because some high school dropouts were running companies while some MBAs were slamming into dead ends. Experience? Then those at the top should have been older, but that wasn't the case. Technical skills, social skills and dozens of other career-related variables were examined as well. Those factors didn't provide the explanation either.

What was the only quality that consistently distinguished those who made it from those who did not? They persevered.

Adversity will come to every person at some time. How you meet it, what you make of it, what you allow it to take from you and give to you, is determined by your mental habits. In short, you have to take the cards that are dealt to you in life—and make something of them.

You can train your mind to face life's toughest challenges, and it is especially important to develop this habit before you actually need it. Little children get their first lesson with *The Little Engine That Could*. Faced with pulling many train cars up an enormous hill, larger engines refused to attempt it. Finally, a small engine agrees to try, repeating the mantra "I-think-I-can, I-think-I-can." After reaching the crest, the little engine triumphantly chugs, "I-thought-I-could, I-thought-I-could."

I'd like to alter the story a bit for the grown-up crowd. Change the chant to "I-know-I-can, I-know-I-can!"

Adversity can actually be a positive thing, even though it certainly doesn't feel that way when we are facing it. Adversity is what defines us. It is easy to have a great attitude, a strong work ethic and a positive outlook when things are going great. But how do we stand up during tough times?

Consider the following phenomenal achievements of famous people who experienced severe adversity:

- When Bob Dylan performed at his high school talent show, classmates booed him off the stage.
- Walt Disney experienced both bankruptcy and a tragic nervous breakdown, but still made it to the top of the mountain.
- Sir Walter Raleigh wrote the *Historie of the World* during a 13-year imprisonment.
- Martin Luther translated the Bible while enduring confinement in the Wartburg Castle.
- Dante wrote the *Divine Comedy* while under a sentence of death and during 20 years in exile.
- Handicapped by a crippling disease as a baby, Helen Keller was not able to see or hear during her long life, yet she became a famous author and activist known for her charm and wisdom.

We must push through the adversity we face. If we don't, we will be poorly prepared for winning. People are successful because they face adversity head-on to gain strength and skill. They don't take the path of least resistance. Adversity is a powerful teacher.

President Abraham Lincoln said, "My great concern is not whether you have failed but whether you are content with your failure." Lincoln saw more than his fair share of failures in his early life, yet he is regarded as one of our greatest presidents.

When you get discouraged, when you cannot seem to make it, there is one thing you cannot do without. It is that priceless ingredient of success called relentless effort. You must never give up. Remind yourself that success cannot be achieved without adversity.

> **When fate throws a dagger at you, there are only two ways to catch it: either by the blade or by the handle.**

There was an old farmer who had suffered through a lifetime of troubles and afflictions that would have leveled any other ordinary mortal. But through it all he never lost his sense of humor.

"How have you managed to keep so happy and serene?" asked a friend.

"It ain't hard," said the old fellow, with a twinkle in his eye. "I've just learned to cooperate with the inevitable."

"Cooperating with the inevitable" enables us to catch adversity by the handle, thereby using it as the tool that it was intended to be.

Mackay's Moral: Adversity causes some people
to break and others to break records.

"*No, the computers are up.* <u>*We're*</u> *down.*"

Chapter 37

Overcoming the Fear of No

Rejection is a part of life. You can't avoid it, whether you're a salesperson with a tough quota or a shy nerd hoping for a date with a supermodel. You can't let the fear of rejection paralyze you from the start, or you'll never get any sales—or any dates.

Like many of us, Jonathan Robinson, now a professional speaker and author, was shy as a young man—painfully so, especially when it came to women. One day in college he decided to do something drastic about it. He handed a friend $50 and told him, "Don't give this back to me unless I get rejected by 10 different women by the end of today."

The idea was to push through his fear of rejection, with money as a motivator. Robinson headed through the campus, looking for women to ask out. The first time, he barely stammered through his question. The woman he approached thought he was babbling and blew him off. After a while he grew calmer and the prospects warmer.

Then something unexpected happened: His seventh target agreed to go out with him. Robinson was so shocked he was tongue-tied, but he managed to get the woman's phone number. Number eight also said yes to him.

In all, he collected six more phone numbers, and had to resort to consciously chilling his charm to reach his quota of 10 rejections in order to get his $50 back. Not only did he get his money and plenty of dates, he vanquished his fear of rejection. I'm not recommending the Robinson gambit to beat rejection, but it pays to know your worst fears are usually trumped-up traumas.

Early in my career, when I was struggling to start my company, I made a list of all the accounts I wanted to sell. Some were immediately attainable, while others were far out of my reach. That list was the impetus for my eventual success. It made me really listen to my potential customers and find out what I needed to do to change "No, thanks" to "Where do I sign?"

You can't escape rejection, I learned. But you can let it go. That requires reprogramming your mind-set. Here are some exercises that paid big dividends for me:

- **Dissect thoughts under the microscope.** When faced with a challenge, what do you tell yourself? "I'm no good . . ." "This is too hard . . ." "I'll never make it . . ." Don't let negative self-talk sabotage your attitude. Size up the evidence objectively. Chances are you'll realize your worries aren't accurate or realistic. Drain the power out of irrational fears.
- **Identify realistic fears.** Whom do you fear? What might go wrong? Knowledge is power, so clarify the facts: Who has the power to reject you? Why would that person say no? The answers will help you prepare your best offer, and facing them will help you keep your composure.
- **Focus on the moment.** Keep your perspective. Rejection lasts only a moment, and once it's over you'll be able to move on to the next opportunity. Overcoming your fears can be an exhilarating experience, so savor your triumph. Great athletes and ace competitors of all sorts are masters of deftly moving through both ups and downs . . . and not wallowing in either.
- **Be more assertive.** Most fears of rejection rest on the desire for approval from other people. Don't base your self-esteem on others'

opinions. Learn to express your own needs—appropriately—and say no to requests when you genuinely can't help. People respect peers who stand up for themselves.

Mackay's Moral: Don't regard rejection as failure—think of it as the dress rehearsal for your next glowing success.

138

Quickie #11
Arrogance: The 7 Deadly Signs

Here is my watch list for the seven deadly signs of salesperson arrogance:

1. "Our product sells itself."
2. "The only people on our sales team who matter to me are my superiors or at least my equals."
3. "Who cares that our competitor's accounting manager is afraid they'll be taken over and is out looking for a job? I listen to input only from vice presidents and above."
4. "I don't need to walk our plant. Leave that to those grunts in manufacturing."
5. "You'll never learn a thing from a competitor weaker than you."
6. "We can always rely on X for a reference. I may not have talked with him for a few months, but he will never forget how we saved his bacon two years ago."
7. "Customer complaints don't matter. Those e-mails are just written by oddball cranks."

Chapter 38

Beat Rejection Before It Beats You

Whatever you do, don't take rejection personally. It may have nothing at all to do with you.

A board member from a charitable organization went to call on a very wealthy man who hadn't given the organization a contribution in five years. As the visitor was talking to him about his social responsibilities and obligations, the millionaire interrupted, "Wait a minute! Do your records show my father is 90 years old and at his doctor's office once a week? My son has been out of work for two years. I have a widowed sister with five kids struggling to make ends meet. Now . . . if I don't help them, why should I help you?"

The millionaire wasn't blasting the fund-raiser. He was flat-out rejecting the notion of giving at all! When you collide with a stone wall, don't lose a lot of sleep—or a lot of time—over it.

When life turns negative, act positive.

Warren Spahn was a battler. In a career that spanned 21 seasons, he won more games than any left-handed pitcher in the history of major-league baseball. But he had to overcome a rocky start to do it. In 1942, he was sent down to the minor leagues. Then he lost four years while serving in the army in WWII. Incidentally, he was decorated for his part in the Battle of the Bulge. In mid-career, when he lost his fastball, he developed such a diverse repertoire of pitches that he outfoxed batters for another dozen years. He always adapted. He never gave up.

We live in an age of instant gratification. When it comes to having a can-do attitude and taking the bull by the horns, this approach to life can't be beaten. But when you hit setbacks, it can land you in trouble. Then you need to have an attitude of persistence. You need to have resilience. Not only do you have to bounce, you have to keep bouncing back.

Looking for a sales job? Don't be discouraged. Get out there now and move. Work the phone. Browse the Net. Check the want ads. Circulate that résumé. And use your Rolodex or computerized contact management system to the hilt. Think countercyclical. Most people think the perfect job-hunting season is spring. But the job market always has many openings in the beginning of the year because people tend to change jobs after they've collected their year-end bonuses.

Don't be discouraged when you don't get the storybook start, going straight from receiving your diploma to collecting the big salary while occupying the corner office. That kind of facile success is more the exception than the rule. And because success like that is untested, it is always fragile. Far better to struggle a bit and pay your dues.

Tone up your positive reflexes.

And don't forget this aspect of getting a career foothold. Sometimes the thing you most desire will not turn out to be your ticket to triumph. How about the Rocky *before* Sylvester Stallone's Rocky—Rocky Marciano, the only heavyweight champion of the world to retire undefeated. As a boy in Brockton, Massachusetts, Rocky was an outstanding athlete, excelling in many sports. He was especially gifted in football and baseball. Because his idol was the great Joe DiMaggio, he dreamed of a career in major-league baseball. If that had worked out, he might well have had the unenviable task of batting against the great Warren Spahn.

But baseball didn't pan out for Rocky. He had a tryout at Wrigley Field with the Cubs, but he failed it. He kicked around as a young man after that, working various jobs and playing amateur sports until he took up boxing. He trained hard but did not turn pro until he was 25. This is absurdly late for a boxer and almost a guarantee of failure.

Red Smith wrote of him: "Fear was not in his vocabulary and pain had no meaning." Rocky kept winning bout after bout, working his way from prelims to windups. Finally, at age 29, he got his title shot. After twelve rounds against Jersey Joe Walcott, Rocky was behind on all three cards. Then, in the thirteenth, he knocked Walcott out and won the title.

You can't ever let early obstacles derail you.

John Gielgud was arguably one of the greatest actors in the English-speaking world. Yet after watching him on the stage for the first time, his first acting teacher told him to forget his ambitions as an actor.

"You walk like a cat with rickets," the teacher told him. Gielgud, like any winner, ignored this early setback. And so should you.

Mackay's Moral: Failure is not falling down, but staying down.

"Have you ever considered another line of work?"

Chapter 39

Those Who Don't Know Don't Know They Don't Know

A while back, I found myself waiting in the dentist's office, so I picked up a copy of *People* magazine. I read a short article about two psychologists who'd conducted a study on arrogance and uncovered the hideous truth that I've been preaching for years: "People don't know that they don't know."

Psychologists David Dunning and Justin Kruger tested students at Cornell University on a range of subjects from logical reasoning to grammar to the ability to spot a funny joke. They compared how well people thought they did versus how well they actually did. "Overall, people overestimated themselves," explained Dunning, a professor at Cornell. "And those who did worst were most likely to think they had outperformed everyone else. Incompetent people don't know they're incompetent."

Arrogance is one of the deadliest of all the human failings that can destroy a business. It is the easiest to rationalize and the hardest to recognize in ourselves.

Herb Kelleher, cofounder and chairman emeritus of Southwest Airlines, preaches that arrogance is the greatest danger to a successful company. "A company is never more vulnerable to complacency than when it's at the height of its success," he's said. Kelleher once wrote in his annual letter to all employees that "the #1 threat is us." He continued: "We must not let success breed complacency; cockiness; greediness; laziness; indifference; preoccupation with nonessentials; bureaucracy; hierarchy; quarrelsomeness; or obliviousness to threats posed by the outside world."

The creators of the *Titanic* could have used a similar warning. They spared no expense to make sure it would be unsinkable. But the ship's officers were unconcerned by their inability to get accurate information on possible hazards lying in its course. The ship had two lookouts on her masts, but the lookouts had no binoculars. The crew couldn't see far enough ahead to react to danger, and they had no way to get their information to the captain if they did see a problem approaching.

And we all know what happened. The unsinkable ocean liner went to her death, along with most of her passengers, on her maiden voyage from Europe to New York, the victim of a disastrous collision with an iceberg. Disasters like this can happen all too easily in business too, if we aren't careful. Pay attention to the competition.

Peter Drucker, the late management consultant and author, made this point: "The most charismatic leaders in history were Hitler, Stalin and Mao. What matters is leadership. Charisma is almost always misleadership, partly because it covers up the lack of substance, partly because it creates arrogance, and partly because it creates paranoia if you're not successful."

Don't confuse this type of arrogance with the inner confidence that you find in all true champions—be it in sports, business or life. These people have a self-assured manner that says, "I have the edge over you" or "You don't have a chance against me." Inner confidence allows you to perform up to the level of your capabilities, not beyond. It takes a lot of work and experience to go to the next level. When you gamble foolishly, you make mistakes.

A classic story illustrates this point. A minister, a Boy Scout and a computer executive were flying to a meeting in a small private plane. About halfway to their destination, the pilot came back and announced that the plane was going to crash and that there were only three parachutes for four people.

The pilot said, "I am going to use one of the parachutes because I have a wife and four small children." He jumped.

The computer executive said, "I should have one of the parachutes because I am the smartest man in the world and my company needs me." And he jumped.

The minister turned to the Boy Scout and, smiling sadly, said, "You are young and I have lived a good, long life, so you take the last parachute and I'll go down with the plane."

The Boy Scout said, "Relax, Reverend. The smartest man in the world just strapped on my backpack and jumped out of the plane!"

Mackay's Moral: I know that you don't know, but you don't know that you don't know.

Quickie #12
Overcoming Rejection:
Tried & True Tips

- Take the criticism, but don't take it to heart.
- Realize 10 setbacks are the admission price for any major win.
- Analyze every failure, but never wallow in it.
- Don't break stride and let this loss cost you your focus on the next race.
- Recognize no one person can please everybody.
- Don't rationalize the hurt by saying you didn't want to succeed that much anyway.
- Tally up what you've learned and how you will use it not to make the same mistake again.
- Let the setback motivate you to try that fresh new approach you have had stuffed in your back pocket for months.
- Don't assume you are branded with failure and walk around as if you're wearing a scarlet letter.
- Don't worry when you lose. Worry when you stop being a contender.

Chapter 40

Comeback Kids
Don't Kid Around

The great jazz vocalist Billie Holiday used to quip, "I'm always making a comeback, but nobody ever tells me where I've been." Today celebrities have a tougher time coming back. That's especially true when they're rebounding from scuffles with the law. People may forget, but the Internet has one heck of a memory. Blemishes are forever. Or are they? Two mega-celebrities have shaken up the rules.

Michael Milken, the king of junk bonds, and Martha Stewart, the queen of julienned beans, have crafted earthshaking turnarounds. You may never expect to be sent up the river. Still, there's plenty to learn from how these two tackled adversity. Both have proven to be masters of selling their new identities to a skeptical and often cynical public.

Rudy Giuliani—then U.S. Attorney in New York—prosecuted Milken on a slew of securities-related violations. Milken pleaded guilty and was sentenced to prison for 10 years but was released after 22 months. He was ordered to pay $600 million in settlements and fines.

After prison, the real lightning hit. Within weeks of being released, Milken was diagnosed with prostate cancer. He underwent treatments and radically changed his lifestyle. He beat the disease, but Milken didn't stop there.

Mike Milken reorganized the war on cancer. He founded the Prostate Cancer Foundation. It's the world's biggest source of prostate cancer research funding. His management savvy at the helm of this foundation has accelerated the pace of prostate cancer research. Experts say he's a force in cutting cancer fatalities. *Fortune* magazine even put him on its cover, dubbing him "The Man Who Changed Medicine."

Martha Stewart's tapestry has a different weave. In Martha's kitchen, her sticky stock deal couldn't have been smaller potatoes. It was the arrogance people saw in her that fried the public. After a testy trial, some were happy to see Martha hauled off to the slammer.

Martha Stewart could have stewed away her time in stir. Instead she foraged for dandelions and other salad fixings in the prison yards. Martha took up crocheting. She read books and practiced yoga. While she was briefly out of circulation, Sears and Kmart sealed a merger that would put Martha's merchandise in front of millions more eyeballs. Not bad for an alumna of a lockup cleaning crew.

Comebacks don't just happen. They require thoughtful planning and a keen eye for learning and changing how you're regarded.

- **Take your medicine.** In many people's judgment, Martha Stewart did plenty of stupid things. But she did one smart one. She served her time quickly and got the ordeal behind her. She read the handwriting on the wall. She knew every day she wasted fighting the verdict would deteriorate her credibility and her assets.

- **Win over your worst enemy.** Take a guess: Which one person would never be a Milken booster? If you bet on Rudy Giuliani, you should have folded. Giuliani is also a fellow prostate cancer survivor, as am I. Giuliani has written that Milken's assault on prostate cancer has made him "an extremely effective advocate . . . Milken not only faced up to a deadly disease but is doing a great deal to help others do the same." Do good, and the world will come around.

- **Respect the public will.** Milken bonded with prostate cancer victims. Martha Stewart brought attention to the plight of female inmates. When the tide turns against you, go with the flow. That holds for small things as much as big ones. Let's say there's a plan to increase the dues in your club. You're the only member to oppose the hike. The dues are raised. Be the first to pay the increase. People won't remember you as a curmudgeon. They'll peg you as a team player.

- **Change what you'll be remembered for.** Mike Milken could have embedded himself in history as a Wall Street rogue. Instead, he looks like he's working overtime to become the next Alfred Nobel. And who knows—Milken may just reach his goal.

Mackay's Moral: When you stumble,
nothing beats being humble.

"*You don't scare me. I come from a long line of salesmen.*"

Chapter 41

Watch Out for These Four-Letter Words

There are certain four-letter words that have no business in business. Many, in fact, are bad for business—so bad that using them may determine whether you stay in business.

No, we're not talking about profanity here—that's a given. These are everyday words that really smart people eliminated from their vocabularies early on. Let me share some of the most offensive. I've even used them in sentences so you can see how to avoid some common mistakes.

Can't: As in "We can't do that" or "You can't expect us to meet that deadline." Your customers come to you because they think you can do what they ask. If you truly cannot produce what they're asking for, be honest but then help them find someone who can, even if it's your competition. They'll remember that you went the extra mile to make them happy.

Busy: "I'm too busy to do that now" or "I'll call you when I'm not so busy." The last thing your customers want to know is that they rank at the bottom of the food chain. It is acceptable to say that you will need a few days to do the job right, or that you'll knock off a few bucks in exchange for their patience. It is never okay to imply that they aren't as important as all your other customers.

Bore: "This project is such a bore" or "Don't bore me with the details." Unemployment is boring. Try to find something to love about every customer account you serve. An ingenious salesperson always will. Life is too short to be bored or boring.

Same: "We've done it the same way for years" or "Same old, same old." If you've been doing something the same way for years, it's a good sign you're doing it the wrong way. Maybe it's time to find a new and better way to do it. People change. Technologies change. Your customers aren't asking you to dye your hair purple and wear your kid's jeans. But their businesses change and they're looking to you to follow—or to lead. You should question why you're still doing things the same old way.

Safe: "Let's play it safe." Safe is important in baseball, but in business you must be prepared to take some risks. The scary part about taking risks is that they don't always work. That said, I'll take a good calculated risk any day of the week over the boring, same, safe way. Sometimes it's risky *not* to take a risk. To triple your success ratio, sometimes you have to triple your failure ratio. Smart customers know this too.

Rude: No example sentence needed here. There is never, ever, *ever* an excuse to be rude to a customer, coworker or stranger on the street. You're staking your name on your behavior, and you don't want your name to become a four-letter word.

Mean: Your lawyer should be mean. Your tennis serve might be mean. You can't afford to be mean. You are dealing with customers whose business and referrals will determine where your kids go to college and what kind of retirement you can look forward to. If that doesn't make you nice, I don't know what will.

Isn't: "That isn't our job." A salesperson's job description always includes every last chore that's required to satisfy the customer. You need to take your turn. That's how you become invaluable to customers. Never pass up the chance to do something new, just because you think you're too good. The farther up the ladder you climb, the farther down you can fall. It's important for your firm to have secure footing on each rung.

Fear: "I fear we may be moving too fast" or "My biggest fear is that we can't do this" only demonstrate one fact: you haven't done your homework. Common sense, thorough research and sound advice should allay your fears to a reasonable level. Knowing what is acceptable risk should help too. If your biggest fear is that rain will ruin an outdoor promotion, plan something inside. If you fear your suppliers will keep you from meeting a production deadline, find a more reliable supplier. Take charge.

Last: "Nice guys finish last." I consider myself a nice guy, and I hate to finish last. But I've had to lose a few times in order to win the next round. I've learned something from every last-place finish.

Mackay's Moral: Sticks and stones can break your bones, but these four-letter words will hurt your business.

Chapter 42

Race to the Top

The film *Seabiscuit* depicts loyalty every bit as much as it spotlights reality. In 2003, the year the movie came out, the public was hysterical about another horse, Smarty Jones. This horse—with indifferent breeding from a second-tier racetrack—nearly won the Triple Crown. Smarty Jones electrified the world of horse racing and excited people who rarely watch the sport of kings.

Smarty Jones and Seabiscuit had a lot in common, besides being slightly undersized and the products of mediocre bloodlines. Each had an unknown jockey and a trainer unfamiliar with the top-shelf racing circuit. Each had an owner who had been successful in business but was new to horse racing. Seabiscuit had a jockey blind in one eye while Smarty Jones as a two-year-old had smacked his head so hard on a starting gate he nearly knocked his own eye out. He'd only narrowly escaped brain damage from the blow.

Yet little Smarty Jones from ticky-tacky Philadelphia Park lost the Triple Crown by a mere ten feet. He was nipped in the stretch at the mile-and-a-half Belmont "Test of the Champion" by a long shot named Birdstone. The crowd that day was record-setting for a New York sporting event, and the television audience for Smarty's Cinderella quest nearly went off the charts.

Success may not always be predictable, but its achievement nearly always relies on a spirit of positive thinking.

As the 2004 NBA Finals began, TV broadcaster Al Michaels opened his telecast by declaring that, according to most experts, the Detroit Pistons had less of a chance of upsetting the mighty Los Angeles Lakers to win the championship than Birdstone had of beating Smarty Jones. The Lakers had four future Hall of Famers on their team.

Detroit promptly called upon team cohesion, superior defense, better effort, unselfish play, relentless hustle and superb coaching strategy to close out the Lakers in five games. Having not a single All-Star on an NBA champion team is almost as rare as a left-handed catcher in baseball. I named six positives illustrated by the Pistons. Believe me, I could name lots more.

A month before these two triumphs of positive thinking broke into the headlines, Phil Mickelson walked off with the green jacket, symbol of the Masters championship. This marked Phil's first win in a major golf championship, something his detractors said he would never do. They'd put the classic sports monkey on his back: "He can't win the big one." Well, he won the big one. Then, in the next two majors, the U.S. Open and the British Open, Phil was in the hunt until the end. Who couldn't love the picture of Phil wearing his green jacket and hoisting his Masters trophy with one arm while hugging his young daughter in the other?

Need a business story to pick you up? Not long ago, the footwear manufacturer Puma was in serious financial difficulty. For eight years they had losses. They had a warehouse with a million and a half pairs of sneakers no one wanted. They hired Jochen Zeitz, 29 at the time, and named him CEO at 30. He morphed the company from selling sports equipment to vending designer athletic wear and rebranded it as a worldwide trendsetter in sports fashion apparel. By the spring of 2007, Puma was valued at more than $7 billion and was the target of a friendly takeover by PPR, the French luxury goods company and owner of Gucci.

Here's another stirring comeback to feel positive about. Look at the late Jack LaLanne, who was 96 when he died in 2011. He was the prototype of all fitness gurus, with a TV exercise show that ran for four decades, from the '50s through the '80s. Years later, his show reached a new generation on the tube in the first decade of this century, compliments of ESPN Classic.

Mackay's Moral: Positives abound if you just look around.

Chapter 43

Wrestle Self-Confidence from Self-Doubt

The successful salesperson is almost always depicted as supremely self-assured, confident beyond the shadow of a doubt. As with most stereotypes, the portrait is misleading. For one thing, salespeople, without a doubt, tend to do a poor job of recognizing and empathizing with their customers' doubts. Doubt—grueling, hard-chiseled skepticism—is the toughest customer's middle name.

The issue isn't eliminating doubt. It's managing doubt into an advantage.

Will Smith is a success by any Hollywood standard. He is a Grammy Award–winning rapper. He starred in a hit television sitcom. He's been nominated for two Best Actor Academy Awards. He's had eight consecutive films that grossed more than $100 million. He's also a film and television producer. And you may not know that he was accepted at, but did not attend, MIT—yes, the Massachusetts Institute of Technology.

> One of the secrets to success might surprise you—it's constructive self-doubt.

Smith refuses to run away from his fears and applies doubt in a positive way. Whenever he feels fear, he faces it head-on. He tells a story about being in Jamaica as a young man, where he watched people jump off a high cliff into the water below. He was fascinated, but also terrified, because he didn't know how to swim. He wasn't going to let that stop him, however. So he walked to the edge of the cliff. Several minutes later, he jumped. Obviously, he lived to tell the tale.

Much of his early behavior was in response to a fear that he couldn't live up to the high esteem in which he was held by his mother and grandmother. He concentrated his efforts on trying to meet their expectations. Smith still has some self-doubts, especially in terms of fulfilling the expectations of those he loves.

Of his fear, Smith said in an interview, "I've learned to use it, to flip that negative energy around and make it a challenge. I keep going because I doubt myself. It drives me to do better. I've learned that the mastery of self-doubt is the key to success."

I'll admit there have been times when I've questioned a decision or approached a problem and responded more out of fear than reason. I maintained a pretty calm façade, but, truth be told, I had all my fingers and toes crossed for good luck. Most of the time, the result was exactly what I had hoped for. A few times, I got fooled.

Those less-than-desirable outcomes serve as a vivid reminder that arrogance is costly. A measure of self-doubt is a healthy part of a strong selling psyche. In fact, it's a necessary ingredient. Effective self-doubt is essential for dealing with rejection, especially when it comes face-to-face with the minefield of high-risk, high-reward sales. As French author Jules Renard said, "There are moments when everything goes well; don't be frightened, it won't last." How true!

Reasonable doubt is the balance wheel that prevents unchecked confidence from spinning into lethal arrogance. Confidence allows you to proceed with the belief you will succeed. Arrogance prevents you from intelligently reality-testing your decisions, and is almost always a recipe for disaster.

"You gain strength, courage and confidence by every experience in which you really stop to look fear in the face," former First Lady Eleanor Roosevelt once remarked. "You are able to say to yourself, 'I have lived through this horror. I can take the next thing that comes along.' You must do the thing you think you cannot do."

That's how every effective seller tests the "water temperature" of customer receptivity to gradually build the scope of deals and contracts. Each time you decide to push the pricing envelope an inch further, or to propose a new line of products, or, picking up on a customer's comment, you decide it's time to tighten the terms of a deal; you're reassessing what was considered to be rock-ribbed certainty.

Mackay's Moral: Without a doubt, question your decisions.

Quickie #13
Hands-On Beats All Else

In the National Hockey League, there's a saying: "You can't ride the boards to glory." In other words, you'll never win the Hart Trophy—recognition for being the League's most valuable player—with your fanny glued to the bench.

For sales—as with everything else in life—there is no substitute for hands-on experience, day in and day out. If you're in the majors, you can bat a thousand in the batting cage, but there is no replacement for going up against an ace reliever with a nasty change-up while 40,000 riveted fans in the stands hold their breath.

When I was 19, I played for Minnesota in the NCAA golf championships at Purdue, confident I would be the next Ben Hogan. Competitors from the South like Don January and Ken Venturi banished my dreams to the rough forever.

My mother sat me down and explained the facts of life: "Harvey, you started playing golf at age 7. That's probably the same age as these other guys. But weather makes it impossible for you to practice much of the year. So you've been playing 6 months for 12 years. They've been playing 12 months for 12 years. And 72 months of live experience will never beat 144 months. You better find another dream."

Same goes for sales. Hawking lemonade and Girl Scout cookies can teach you a lot about rejection and renewal while your sales bones are still growing and resilient. Get in the ring early . . . and often.

Chapter 44

Lose the Right Battles to Win the War

New York Yankee great Mickey Mantle had a response for critics who pointed out that he had struck out a whopping 1,710 times in the course of his career:

"They may be just strikeouts to some people, but to me every one of them was nearly a home run."

Our most popular sports are very forgiving of failure. In football, you get four tries to make 10 yards. Who cares about the first three failures if the fourth try nets you a first down? In baseball, even if you swing at three pitches and miss each time, you can still make it to first base if the catcher drops the ball.

If you're in sales, you know what rejection is.

Every parent has faced the situation where a child becomes discouraged and wants to quit while trying to achieve some objective, like learning to ride a bike. We are torn between wanting to insulate our children from pain and knowing that we must encourage them to overcome their fears if they are to grow.

So what do we do? We do both. We dry their tears, put them back on the bike and encourage them to keep trying. Over and over and over until they learn. As kids cease to be kids, and Mom and Dad aren't there to bandage the banged-up knees, we hope that those early experiences carry over into tougher situations.

I recall a time early in my sales career when I'd been turned down by six prospects in a row. By the time I was heading out door six, it was late afternoon and it had been raining all day. I was tired, wet and annoyed with myself. It was one of those days where I had pushed all the wrong buttons.

If I had made one tiny sale, I would have called it quits. But I didn't want to have to spend the evening thinking about the day's misadventures and the blank order pad that would be staring at me the next morning. One more call. Just one more call. Just one more try to ride the bike. The result was the biggest sale I had ever made up to that time. Every career salesperson has a story similar to mine.

It's easy to give up. One of the lessons of failure is not always just "Try, try again," but "Try something different."

I've yet to meet a salesperson who sells everyone.

John was a pastor who hadn't had much success. He received a call to a church in a declining inner-city area. Most of the members had moved to the suburbs, leaving a skeleton crew that made up the Sunday congregation. John had tried everything he could think of to boost attendance, but nothing worked.

The young people in the neighborhood didn't attend church, but John always knew they were around because he could hear their music blasting from boom boxes.

"How can I reach these people?" John wondered. He could hear the answer: music. Loud music. Music that most church people hate but that the neighborhood kids would embrace.

John started having concerts on Saturday nights, and after a lot of promotion, they caught on. Before long, he had a full house. He didn't publicize it to his regular church members, but he knew the word would get out. He wasn't surprised when one Saturday night he spotted Elsworth, a crusty old member of the church's power structure, in the congregation. The louder the music grew, the more pained the expression on Elsworth's face became. After the service, Elsworth asked John to meet with him in John's office.

"Pastor, I hate that music. I can't see how anyone can like it, but evidently some do. We haven't had a crowd like this for 20 years. You let me know how much it's going to cost to continue this program of yours and I'll see to it that it's taken care of."

Elsworth was as good as his word, and although he never rocked and never rolled, when he died, his pallbearers included some of the formerly unwashed youth who were first introduced to the church through the music programs. John's church is now considered a model of how a dying inner-city institution can be transformed into a large, vibrant church.

Life is not always fair when it passes out the natural gifts, like looks and talent. But no one was ever born with determination and character. You have to develop those yourself and if you do, all the rewards life has to offer can be yours.

Mackay's Moral: "Try till you die" doesn't
mean riding a dead horse.

Quickie #14
The "Weaker Sex" Isn't Anymore

Our society is changing. Women represent:

- 65 percent of all pharmacy graduates.
- 62 percent of auditing and accounting students in college.
- 44 percent of law school students.
- 46 percent of medical school students.
- 41 percent of recent MBAs.

In 2010, women represented 49 percent of the total enrollment in the MD programs at the Yale School of Medicine, and they were also 49 percent of Yale Law School's student body.

The number of female business travelers will equal male business travelers in the next five years.

The number of women entrepreneurs is multiplying 2–3 times faster than men, depending on which market in the country you are studying. And I call this next one "Woman bites dog": Female entrepreneurs employ more than all the Fortune 500 companies combined... And within the last five years, women business owners have outnumbered their male counterparts.

Sales has often been branded a sexist refuge. Smart selling strategies respect and reflect the changing stats.

Chapter 45

Neutralize Firing Before It Burns You

Getting fired remains a fearsome experience for most people. Because sales is a higher-risk career than most, the peril of getting fired is often very real. Eight years ago, I wrote a book titled *We Got Fired! . . . And It's the Best Thing That Ever Happened to Us*. It recaps the experience of prominent figures who were fired early in their careers. Each of them overcame the setback to become incredible success stories.

Having been fired may not have been one's proudest moment, but it's no blemish to hide. In my youth, I was fired as a salesman at a St. Paul haberdasher for presuming privileges to which I certainly wasn't entitled. In *We Got Fired*, I tell the whole story and how the experience became an indelible learning experience for me.

One of life's most valuable lessons is always to be prepared for the next pink slip you might be dealt. That might include:

- losing your job
- having your bankers snip their financing strings for your business
- being dealt a dreaded cancer verdict

I've waded through each of the above and swear I'm a better person for each experience. I've been fired, and I've fired people to be sure. Sometimes, and for a multitude of reasons, a person just isn't right for the job. As an employer, I've learned one cherished lesson over the years: It's not the people you fire who make your life miserable. It's the people you don't fire.

When an impasse is reached, both parties better find a way to move on. For those on the receiving end of the bad news, the real time to start worrying about what you'll do when you're fired is the day you get hired. Make a contingency plan, file it away and get down to business.

For a salesperson, I re-emphasize, firing goes with the landscape of any high-risk profession. This is totally different from resigning yourself to failure. I also subscribe to wisdom uttered by former Secretary of State George Shultz: "The minute you start talking about what you're going to do if you lose, you've lost."

Look at things this way: What happens if you're forced out for whatever reason—fairly or unfairly? Only a dummy doesn't know where the emergency exit is. Have a plan. File it away. Then concentrate on winning.

You can always let your future cast doubt on a firing employer's decision. In 2011 *Forbes* pegged J. K. Rowling's net worth at a billion dollars. Though their estimate for 2012 is lower, her Harry Potter books have still sold 400 million copies. According to *Inc.com*, Rowling was "a former secretary who was once fired for writing short stories at her computer [and] used her severance pay to help finance the first Harry Potter" book.

The famous last words of Rowling's former boss are reported on the Web as being: "We made the right decision to sack her, and I wouldn't be surprised to see her come crawling back here for her old job once this Harry Potter thing blows over." As the Rowling case readily proves, termination notices sometimes don't pan out exactly as expected.

Are you in an industry vulnerable to downsizing? Is your company going through a rough patch? There's one piece of regular maintenance I recommend every salesperson attend to at least every couple of months. It would have been unknown just five years ago. Check out and always keep fresh your professional image on social media sites. Above all, do so with LinkedIn and Facebook.

- Are your professional achievements up-to-the-minute?
- Have you described your specialized skills and cutting-edge knowledge?

- Can site visitors link to articles you might have written or talks you have given, including thoughtful pieces for community organizations and fundraising campaigns?
- Have you purged your own postings of a totally blotto you at your frat's toga bash?

Social media have become a mandatory checkpoint in more and more employment searches. The stats are both overwhelming and sobering:

- According to *Forbes*, nearly 90 percent of companies used social media networks for recruiting in 2011.
- About a third of employers rejected candidates based on something they found about them online.

A last word about firing is about last words. They, too, stick around forever. Never utter them in the heat of anger or with the sting of rejection. Last words can both seal and open new doors in unexpected ways.

When any person or organization is fired, they are wise to consider a practice we have followed for years. And that is the first thing we say to a lost customer at MackayMitchell Envelope: "Thank you for giving us your business all these years." And we say it with sincerity and mean it. The next offer we make is: "What can we do to make it an easy transition for you?" And finally: "If things don't work out, we're ready, willing and able to consider stepping right back in. We sure would love to keep in touch with you from time to time." And we do.

That message has, in time, earned us platinum recommendations . . . and has reopened doors to accounts we feared were irretrievably lost.

Mackay's Moral: He who burns bridges had better be a pretty good swimmer.

Chapter 46

Refuse to Lose

"This is the worst day of my life. I must have been nuts to think I could do this."

Those were the words of my assistant, Greg Bailey, as he climbed Mount of the Holy Cross in the Vail area one summer not long ago. Holy Cross is one of Colorado's famous 14,000-foot peaks commonly referred to as the "Fourteeners." He took his two sons on a mountain climbing expedition as part of an extended-family father/son bonding in what he thought sounded like a fun hike or adventure.

Once Greg got down from more than eight hours on the mountain and recovered, he had a completely different perspective. He wanted to climb another Fourteener . . . of course, at a later date after he'd trained better.

He told me climbing that mountain was the hardest thing he had ever done in his life. He had never tested himself like that . . . never pushed himself to that level.

Nothing, including me, could stop him from going the next year. The guys climbed two Fourteeners, Mount Sherman and Mount Massive, the largest mountain in Colorado and the second tallest, respectively.

In preparation for his second climb, Greg trained a lot more at a local ski resort in the Minneapolis/St. Paul area. He trekked up and down the slopes relentlessly. Greg is convinced that training helped a great deal, but success still boiled down to how bad he wanted to do it. Being physically fit, he believes, is only half the battle. The rest is mental. After nearly seven miles and at 14,000 feet elevation, he had to convince his body to go on to the summit. He did it, but said there wasn't one person in their group who didn't question his own ability or desire to make it to the top and complete the 14-mile trek.

Why do people push themselves to another level? What makes them attempt things that others think are unattainable, or even crazy to try? Is it the excitement, adventure, stimulation or just plain challenge? And what makes people successful? Is it sheer determination? The thrill of accomplishment? The desire to achieve? The will to persevere?

> **Long ago I learned that there are three kinds of people in the world:**
>
> - **the wills**
> - **the won'ts**
> - **and the can'ts.**
>
> **The first accomplish everything. The second oppose everything. The third fail in everything.**

Remember the Jack Nicklaus quote: "I never missed a putt in my mind." The same holds true for tennis. Perry Jones, former U.S. Davis Cup coach, said, "It is not how you hold your racket, it's how you hold your mind."

Every game, every job or, in Greg's case, every mountain is a battle of mental toughness. Support and encouragement from your companions help, but ultimately it's up to you. It's you against the mountain. And sometimes you have to perform at your best when you're feeling your worst. Champions block out the hurt and do what's necessary to win or get the job done. Excuses are easy. Anyone can make them up. You either do it or you don't. It's that simple.

The *Los Angeles Times* has published a report regarding a five-year study of 120 of America's top artists, athletes and scholars. Benjamin Bloom, a University of Chicago education professor, who led the team of researchers, said, "We expected to find tales of great natural gifts. We didn't find that at all. Their mothers often said it was their other child who had the greater gift."

The study concluded that the key element common to all these successful people was, surprisingly, not talent, but an extraordinary drive and determination. They had mental toughness. They decided they would achieve, and they did!

My friend Joe Theismann quarterbacked the Washington Redskins to two consecutive Super Bowl appearances in the 1980s. His team won in 1983, but lost the following year. Today, he wears both his winner's ring and his loser's ring as reminders concerning his attitude and effort.

During the first championship game, Joe was thrilled to be there and gave his very best effort. A year later things were different. "I was griping about the weather, my shoes, practice times, everything," he stated. His focus was more on convenience and comfort than unbridled effort. He wasn't as mentally tough the second year. Theismann says, "The difference in those two rings lies in applying oneself and not accepting anything but the best."

Keep your eye on the prize. If you focus on the struggle, you lose sight of the purpose.

There will always be a mountain to climb.

Consider the mountain that factored in a war between two tribes. One of the tribes lived in the lowlands while the other lived high in the mountains. One day the mountain people conducted a raid on the lowlanders and plundered a village. During the raid, they kidnapped a baby and took it with them back up into the mountains.

Enraged at the loss, the lowlanders resolved to recover the kidnapped baby no matter what the cost. But they didn't know how to climb the mountain. They didn't know any of the trails the mountain people used, nor did they know where to find the mountain people or how to track them in the steep terrain. Even so, the lowlanders sent out a rescue party of their best fighting men to climb the mountain and bring the baby home.

The men tried first one method of climbing and then another, all to no avail. After several days of effort, they had succeeded in climbing only several hundred feet up the mountain. Thoroughly discouraged, the lowlander men decided that the cause was lost, and they reluctantly prepared to return to their village below.

As they were packing their gear for the descent, they suddenly saw the baby's mother walking toward them. They stood silent, gazing at her with the realization that she was coming down the mountain they had totally failed to climb.

Then they saw that she had the kidnapped baby strapped to her back. They all stared in amazement. How was that possible? The first man to greet her said, "We couldn't climb this mountain. How did you do so when we, the strongest and most able men in the village, couldn't do it?"

She shrugged her shoulders and replied, "It wasn't your baby."

Mackay's Moral: The only thing that matters
is if you say you can't do it.

"Well, Stoddard, I think I've bounced enough ideas off you for one day."

Quickie #15
The Confidence Game

For about six weeks every year, beginning in late December and continuing through early February, football fans get the ultimate fix: the college bowl games, the NFL play-offs and, finally, the Super Bowl. It's also an annual refresher course in winning and losing that separates the champs from the also-rans.

For a moment, consider the losers in these annual contests. The also-rans work mighty hard to get to those games in the first place. What causes these exceptional teams to be eliminated? Much of the reason can be traced to split-second breakdowns in what you might call the confidence game.

Legendary Alabama football coach Paul Bryant retired with 323 wins over 38 seasons. "Bear" Bryant used to say that members of a winning team needed five things:

1. Tell me what you expect from me.
2. Give me an opportunity to perform.
3. Let me know how I'm doing.
4. Give me guidance when I need it.
5. Reward me according to my contributions.

Winners need straight information. Too often, you'll hear salespeople complain they're not getting a constant flow of confident support. Confidence is surely important. So is exact and clear direction at critical moments. When everything is on the line, make sure you're listening for the right signals.

BOUNCING BACK—The Fortune Cookies

Make the second effort your second nature.

Success has no rules, but you can learn a lot from failure.

Knockdowns are not knockouts.

Failure is no more fatal than success is permanent.

Believe in yourself, even when no one else does.

Don't get dejected if you're rejected.

Rough water is no place to check to see if you packed your life preserver.

Success is to be measured not so much by the position one has reached in life as the obstacles one has overcome while trying to succeed.

Past failure often furnishes the finest material from which to build future success.

I would never have amounted to anything had I not been forced to come up the hard way. —*J. C. Penney*

People stumble over pebbles, never over mountains.

The difference between failure and success is doing a thing nearly right and doing it exactly right.

When you're pinned to the mat, the only place to look is up.

How people play the game shows something of their character. How they lose shows all of it.

If you walk backward, you'll never stub your toe.

Don't let ups and downs leave you down and out.

THE
CHAMPIONSHIP
STRIDE

Chapter 47

Never Look a Gift Mule
in the Mouth

The real pros know how to motivate themselves before they start having bad days. They look at work differently, not just as a means of making a living, but as a significant part of a quality life. Their particular mix of attitude, responsibility, cooperation and accomplishment make them a valuable commodity in any organization.

Joan is a busy realtor with an active family who also manages to organize a sizable silent auction for her church and spends time helping at her kids' school as well. Joan's willingness to get the job done, no matter what the job happens to be, has earned her the respect and awe of everyone who has ever worked with her. Does she have boundless energy? No. She's not even a morning person. Her secret? "I have exactly 24 hours to make life better than it was yesterday," she says. Joan would probably laugh if I told her she was a mule.

> **The quiet asset of determination can be as awesome as it is invisible.**

Mules, by the way, like their jobs and perform well as a result. If they find themselves getting in a rut, they stubbornly haul themselves out. That quiet determination is a huge asset in business. The ability to get over the bumps is frequently the difference between success and Chapter 11.

Mules are often hard to miss because of their size and stature—especially the strain known as Mammoth Jack. That's why their contributions are routinely taken for granted. One thinks of the 6-foot-3 Detroit Red Wings center Johan Franzén. Dubbed "The Mule" by his teammates, Franzén can also catch fire. He has, for example, surpassed super-star Gordie Howe's number of game-winning goals in a month, a remarkable five.

Rationality may be another enviable mule trait. "My favorite animal is the mule. He has more horse sense than a horse. He knows when to stop eating—and he knows when to stop working," President Harry S. Truman once remarked. Being a Democrat, Truman's bias for the son-of-a-donkey mule comes as no surprise.

The mules—the steady, willing, get-the-job-done employees—are worth their weight in gold. Don't confuse the reliable, day-in, day-out dependability with a lack of creativity. It's usually the mules, the folks who are *there*, who find creative solutions to everyday problems. They know how things work. Mules know what Woody Allen meant when he said, "80 percent of life is showing up."

Mackay's Moral: Being a mule beats being an ass any day.

Quickie #16
The Magic of Teamwork

A salesman was driving on a two-lane country road in a rainstorm and got stuck in a ditch. He asked a farmer for help. The farmer hitched up Elmo, his blind mule, to the salesman's car and hollered out, "Pull, Sam, pull!" Nothing happened. He again yelled, "Pull, Bessie, pull!" Still nothing. "Pull, Jackson, pull!" Still nothing.

Finally he hollered, "Pull, Elmo, pull!" And Elmo ripped the car right out of the ditch.

The driver was perplexed and said, "I don't understand. Why did you have to call out all those different names?"

"Look, if he didn't think he had any help, he wouldn't even try!"

Chapter 48

Your Best Captive Audience

How many people talk to themselves? As you're reading this, you might even be saying to yourself, "Who, me? I don't talk to myself."

There are those who think people who talk to themselves are crazy, but nothing could be further from the truth. People who talk to themselves are competitive, and they are often trying to better themselves.

I'm constantly talking to myself. When you do, you are coaching yourself. It's an opportunity to give yourself some constant, immediate, unfiltered feedback. You have access to yourself 24 hours a day. And the price is right.

Years ago, when I was building Mackay Envelope Company, I had a lot of pep talks with myself. I had to, in order to keep alive my dream of owning my own company. I had plenty of ups, many downs, and needed all the encouragement I could get. And it wasn't always coming from other sources! So I kept telling myself that things would work out . . . that I could pull this off . . . that I was the right person for the job . . . 40-plus years and a few zillion envelopes later, I'm glad I listened.

In doing some research on this subject, I discovered that "private speech," as psychologists call it, starts as soon as kids learn to talk, typically between 18 and 24 months. It serves two purposes: 1) it helps kids practice language skills, and 2) it allows them to reflect on daytime experiences. (And let's not forget how it entertains eavesdropping parents.) In elementary school kids begin to transition from self-talk to interpersonal communication.

"A lot of parents think that it's socially unacceptable or weird if a child talks to himself," says Laura Berk, professor of psychology at Illinois State University and author of *Awakening Children's Minds*. "But in fact it's normal and typical, and we find that children who engage in task-relevant private speech generally perform better over time."

I agree 1,000 percent. Unfortunately, as kids become adults, they grow out of talking to themselves. Maybe it's because society frowns on it. But the self-talk I'm referring to is not a sign of insecurity or insanity.

> **Listening is crucial. When you talk to yourself, that's no exception.**

I talk to myself to help me think and map out my thoughts, to provide feedback and, probably most important of all, to motivate myself.

Jack Canfield, cocreator of the wildly successful *Chicken Soup for the Soul* books, tells us that research shows that the average person talks to himself thousands of times a day!

There's a downside to this research, however: It is 80 percent negative—things like what you should have done or said instead of what actually happened, your shortcomings, your fears and so on. Those negative thoughts have tremendous influence over our behavior. But you can change them.

I advise every one of you to continue to talk to yourself throughout your life. I want you to ask yourself: How am I doing? Am I living up to my commitments? I want you to evaluate yourself after a presentation or after a one-on-one with a potential customer. Tell yourself what you could have done better, what you absolutely aced, what you will do on the next call or with the next customer. You have to ignite your own passion.

As with a lot of things, you have two choices. You can talk yourself into success or failure, into feeling good or bad, thinking positively or negatively. The choice is yours, but you can train yourself to use self-talk as a positive tool. It is up to you to decide whether the conversation in your head is helpful or hurtful. Remember, you can talk yourself out of negative thoughts.

Attitude is everything. You must build up your confidence and positive energy. Focus on the best thing that can happen, not the worst. Too many people talk themselves out of good ideas. Let your thoughts take you where you want to go.

Mackay's Moral: Listen to your inner voice—it has a lot to say.

Chapter 49

Get in the Zone

We often hear athletes say they were "in the zone" after fantastic performances. Finding the zone is that magical moment when performance seems inspired and effortless.

Basketball players say that when they are in the zone the basket seems larger than a bushel basket and the shots come easier. The late Ted Williams, the legendary Boston Red Sox hitter, said that when he was in the zone, everything was so clear to him that he could see the seams on a pitched ball.

Rod Laver, the former Australian tennis star, said, "You get a great feeling when you're hitting the ball really well. The ball comes over the net looking as big as a soccer ball, and everything seems to be moving in slow motion. You feel as if there's nothing you can't do with the ball. You get confidence. You're loose, relaxed. Everything is working for you."

You don't have to be an athlete to get in the zone. Jazz musicians say they're in the zone when they're in their groove and the instrument almost plays itself. Sometimes opera singers suddenly experience a remarkable phenomenon, hitting high and low notes they could never reach before.

Writing in the *New York Times*, author Lawrence Shainberg explained, "Being 'in the zone' is that moment in which performance 'transcends the normal or usual' . . . 'In the zone' can be a onetime phenomenon—or it can be an incredible breakthrough that continues year after year."

Businesses and employees can also get in the zone. You can just feel it. Everything clicks. Everything seems like a piece of cake, with extra frosting. The billion-dollar question is: How do you get yourself in the zone? If we could figure that out, the world would be a far different place. All we can do is try to do the things that give us the best chance to get in the zone. Consider these suggestions:

- **Commit yourself to excellence.** You must want to be the best. Good enough to get by doesn't hack it. People who want to get in the zone crave coaching and mentoring. They want to learn more. They look for tougher competition. There are no easy ways to be the best.
- **Work hard.** To become better, you must be willing to put in the time and energy and make the necessary sacrifices. Look at the greatest athletes—they are the hardest workers—Roger Federer, Serena and Venus Williams, Jerry Rice, LeBron James, Michelle Kwan, Derek Jeter, Ichiro Suzuki, Mia Hamm . . . they are constantly working to improve themselves.
- **Practice perfect.** As I have said, perfect practice makes perfect. Practice alone does not make perfect—you have to add that one word: *perfect*. If you practice the wrong concepts, all you're doing is practicing a flaw. You're putting a ceiling on how good you can become. Study the best and learn from them. Then go out and do the same. You must prepare to win.
- **Radiate confidence.** Confidence is a combination of mental and physical skills learned from practicing the right concepts. Confidence enables you to perform to the best of your abilities. It allows you to perform without the fear of failure. A coach can't tell a player to have confidence; it has to come from within.
- **Concentrate.** If you have total concentration, you will have total control of yourself. Great athletes maintain their poise and concentration when they're staring defeat in the face. Never lose your composure.
- **Stay in condition.** Fatigue makes cowards of us all. It robs you of your skills. When you're tired, your problems seem bigger. It's the best-conditioned athlete, not the most talented, who generally wins when the going gets tough.

- **Thrive on pressure.** To be a champion, you have to learn to handle stress and pressure. But if you've prepared mentally and physically, you don't have to worry. Winners look forward to pressure.
- **Love what you do.** And you'll never have to work a day in your life. That's the subtitle of one of my books. Enthusiasm and the love of what you're doing are necessary to put in all the effort we've discussed. When you're in the zone, you're unstoppable.

Mackay's Moral: When you're in the zone,
you're on the throne. You rule!

Quickie #17
Unload Your Stress

A lecturer, when explaining stress management to an audience, raised a glass of water and asked, "How heavy is this glass of water?"

Answers ranged from 20 grams to 500 grams.

The lecturer replied, "The absolute weight doesn't matter. It depends on how long you try to hold it. If I hold it for a minute, that's not a problem. If I hold it for an hour, I'll have an ache in my right arm. If I hold it for a day, you'll have to call an ambulance. In each case, it's the same weight, but the longer I hold it, the heavier it becomes."

He continued, "And that's the way it is with stress management. If we carry our burdens all the time, sooner or later, as the burden becomes increasingly heavy, we won't be able to carry on. As with the glass of water, you have to put it down for a while and rest before holding it again. When we're refreshed, we can carry on with the burden."

You can relieve a lot of stress if you just accept that some days you're the pigeon and some days you're the statue.

Chapter 50

Give Yourself a Break

When I was a young salesman, among the many lessons I learned from an old dog was when to call a time out. Inexperienced salespeople have a tendency to celebrate a victory by goofing off for a while, which was exactly what I was doing one afternoon. Coming off the golf course, I ran into an old-timer who was a competitor of mine from the envelope wars.

"Charlie, I only hope the big order you just landed wasn't one of my customers," I said.

"Hell, no. I couldn't sell a box of #10 envelopes to a chain-letter freak."

"Then why are you out here beating the daylights out of the ball instead of beating the bushes?"

"Because when you're cold, you're cold, and when you're hot, you're hot. I need to loosen up a little. I need to get that win streak going again. You still think you've got a hot putter?"

Thus challenged, we took a couple of spins around the putting green, where he relieved me of about $35.

"Thanks, Harvey. I'm rejuvenated. Now, if you can just give me the name of that customer you were so worried about, I'll be back in the trenches tomorrow."

"No way, Charlie. The rehab program ends here. Thanks for the putting lesson."

I thought he was nuts not to be out calling on customers, but the more I thought about it, the more I realized I was the one who had his priorities wrong. In sales, athletics, gambling and the stock market, we calculate success by the percentages.

But by focusing on the percentages, we lose sight of how those percentages are achieved: not in an orderly way but in streaks, in stretches and in bursts.

Spot your streaks and master running them.

A tremendous baseball player will hit .300, which means he gets three hits every 10 times at bat, or seven or eight hits a week. Many weeks, however, that great hitter won't get his seven or eight hits. He'll get two or three. He's in a slump. Other weeks, he's on a hot streak and everything seems to fall in for a base hit. The ball has eyes, eluding every fielder. He's able to count the stitches on the ball as each pitch comes to the plate. That's the week he gets 12, 13 or 15 hits and becomes a .300 hitter.

The great athletes can't explain their hot streaks any more than they can explain their slumps. But one thing is for sure: The smart ones never take themselves out of the lineup when they're in the zone.

I'll never forget the story of Wally Pipp, the Yankee first baseman who one day told the manager, "I've got a cold. Let the kid play." The kid was Lou Gehrig, and he was not about to make Pipp's mistake. That was the first day of Gehrig's run of 2,130 consecutive games played. He didn't take himself out of the lineup until he was dying.

When a manager goes to the mound, it isn't to congratulate his pitcher on a job well done. It's to determine whether he's losing it and if it's time for a change. Streaks are not confined to individuals.

Streaks can also occur when groups of people act collectively, even when those people do not necessarily agree among themselves. The price of a stock represents the conflicting opinions of thousands of buyers and sellers. Yet the major moves in the stock will be concentrated over a handful of days. Don't hold me to the numbers, but I recollect reading somewhere that the famous 80/20 rule applies here too. The significant action—80 percent of the stock's price movement—will take place during only 20 percent of the trading days.

If you're in sales, think back to the best streak you've ever had. What did you do differently that week? I don't know if ballplayers or salespeople are more superstitious than the average person, but the successful ones in each field tend to look at the conditions that were present when they were on a hot streak and try, try, try to re-create them.

Unlike what the ballplayers do, however, if you're in sales and you're on a hot streak, I recommend you change your socks.

Mackay's Moral: A streak of luck is no stroke of luck.

Chapter 51

The Psychology of a Slump

Read the sports pages on any given day and you'll likely find a hard-luck story about some player or team experiencing the worst slump in years. But slumps aren't confined to sports—they're news on the front page and in the business section too.

There are housing slumps and retail sales slumps. A slump on Wall Street is bad news for a lot of businesses. Hollywood media analysts will bewail a box office slump.

Politicians know their electability diminishes with a slump in approval ratings, and a slump in voter turnout usually indicates an apathetic or disgusted electorate. Dejected singles bemoan their dating slumps.

Despite their hitting droughts and TD famines, I still have a soft spot for even the most overpaid pro athletes. How exactly do they cope with their extended failures getting splashed across the papers and blogs? Does that inspire them to do better?

Slugger Hank Aaron said, "My motto was always to keep swinging. Whether I was in a slump or feeling bad or having trouble off the field, the only thing to do was keep swinging."

Actor Frank Langella credits his slumps for some of his successes: "What helped me most were my failures and slumps—when I couldn't get work, people weren't interested in me or had written me off."

Legendary Boston Celtics coach Red Auerbach has shared the story of how he coaxed Bill Walton out of a slump in the 1985–86 season. Walton, usually a team leader, wasn't scoring. Auerbach told Walton it didn't matter how much he scored; all he cared about was Walton's contribution to the team. Remarkably, after that conversation Walton got back in the groove and his performance improved significantly.

"He became loose," Auerbach said, "and he never looked to see what he scored. All he looked at was: 'Did we win?'"

If you're in a sales slump, get back to the basics. Look at your goals and see if you have been really following your plan to achieve them. If you haven't been completely true to plan, fix that. If you have, then you need a new action plan. Have you been prospecting enough? Are you delivering what your customers need and want? Are you overpromising and disappointing?

Slumps are usually caused by not doing the simple things well. Look at your own performance before you place the blame elsewhere.

Any slump is *your* slump, not something you stumbled into. You may have to work a little harder—or a lot harder—until you figure out how to turn things around.

If you can't reach a solution on your own, ask some trusted colleagues for advice. Check your ego and be prepared for brutal honesty. You want good results, don't you?

Stay focused on the desired outcome and don't let distractions clutter your thinking. Start simply and work your way up. Unless you have been doing everything wrong, there's no need to start from scratch.

Keep a positive outlook. If you were successful before, there's no reason you can't be successful again. Your confidence is an important component of your recovery. Your skill set is still intact. You may have to use it differently, or develop it further, but you really never forget it.

The eternal optimist Yogi Berra should inspire you: "I ain't in no slump . . . I just ain't hitting!"

Mackay's Moral: A slump may bring you down,
but you have nowhere to go but up.

Chapter 52

Coming Through in the Clutch

At the age of 26, I walked into the General Mills boardroom and faced off against four competitors in a bid to get their business for Mackay Envelope. I knew all the things I wanted to say, but I got a little confused. Then I stumbled more and hemmed and hawed. I had not prepared myself to perform . . . under pressure.

In the last five years, the literature that's popped up on choking—and I'm not talking Heimlich maneuver—could gag a herd of hippos. Experts of every stripe have taken a different slant on how choking happens on the gridiron or at the conference table.

Google your way to a 2010 article in the technology magazine *Wired* titled "The Tight Collar: The New Science of Choking Under Pressure," by David Dobbs. It's all about "what generates or destroys performance under pressure" and nails what misfires in an athlete's "skull to make [a] feared major-leaguer bat like an amateur."

Short circuits in the clutch have tripped many a sure-footed salesperson to blow a routine close in a million-dollar deal.

Scientists like Sian Beilock, a psychology professor at the University of Chicago, are subjecting choking to hard-fisted scientific analysis, Dobbs explains in the article. Classic chokes "appear to rise from the process known colloquially as 'thinking too much' or 'paralysis through analysis.'"

"This is the micromanaged putt, the aimed pitch, the overdirected free throw." When Beilock tasked soccer aces "to keep track of which side of which foot was contacting the ball as they dribbled," speed slowed and errors rose. Beilock regularly "gets similar results when she asks good golfers to monitor, say, how far back they take their backswings." "You can jump off the physical track by overmonitoring," says Dobbs, "and fall off the cognitive track through inattention." The chokeless manage "the tension between when to think and when not to . . . [It's in] a gray area between groove and gag."

Engaged in an all-or-nothing presentation or the closing paces of a hard-fisted negotiation? Try visualizing the smooth, effortless momentum of follow-through in a letter-perfect golf swing . . . and smother any little voices in your inner gallery trying to chatter you into micromanaging.

Surely excess nervousness is a contributor, though it's not the whole story. You can sweat bullets and still do everything right, provided, of course, you keep your focus and make the right moves. A PGA champ can miss an 8-foot putt in the U.S. Open. Did he choke or make a mental error of playing it right to left? The pro could have putted the ball exactly as he wanted, but it wasn't the right read.

Two truths stand out:

- You have to be conscious of what you're doing, but you can't be obsessed with the technique of doing it.
- When the pressure is really on, you've got to be yourself. It has to be the best you can possibly be, but it has to be you. As many a great coach has observed time and again: *You can't play outside your range.* At the Super Bowl, you have to play the same game that got you there. You can't be obsessed with the prestige forum and play a different game from the one you excel in and expect to win.

Mackay's Moral: Under pressure, if you obsess over something that's hard for you to swallow, a choke is sure to follow.

Chapter 53

Don't Coast
to an Apathy Crash

Comfortable in your job? Things look rosy? Tempted to ease up on the throttle and coast a little? Pinch yourself!

Jane Goodall, the trailblazing naturalist and chimpanzee champion, relayed a fable about competition that her mother used to read to her and her sister when they were little:

> *The mighty eagle is sure he will win, and majestically with those great, strong wings he flies higher and higher, and gradually the other birds get tired and start drifting back to the ground. Finally, even the eagle can go no higher, but that's all right, because he looks down and sees all the other birds below him.*
>
> *That's what he thinks, but hiding in the feathers on his back is a little wren, and she takes off and flies highest of all.*

That's the danger of coasting, of not giving it your all. It's the tortoise and the hare all over again. Everyone knew that the rabbit was faster, but he coasted—took things for granted—and lost to the plodding reptile.

Even in winning, people can coast. For example, at the 2008 Olympic Games in Beijing I remember watching the men's 100-yard dash final, when Usain Bolt from Jamaica blew away the field and won with a world-record time. However, I couldn't help but think how fast he actually could have run it had he not coasted at the end and looked around at his competitors. That's surely not his style meet after meet. You don't have to tell Usain Bolt that competition is always against tomorrow, not yesterday.

Writing in the *Economist* in 2010, Bolt remarked, "In 2009 I became the fastest man in the world after I clocked 9.58 seconds in the 100 meters at the World Track and Field Championships in Berlin . . . But the science of track and field suggests that the times should get even quicker."

Several years ago, at one of Lockheed Martin's electronics facilities in Orlando, Fla., complacency from past successes started to infect one of its manufacturing processes. Occasionally, parts were omitted from component kits prepared for assembly and inspection at another factory. Each missing part disrupted the assembly process and frustrated the workers constructing the products.

Norman Augustine, retired chairman of Lockheed Martin, explained, "I borrowed an idea from an automobile dealer in Dallas I had heard about. The dealer received few complaints from customers because he gave them the home telephone numbers of the mechanics who worked on their cars. I arranged for workers to include their names, work phone numbers and self-addressed postcards in the kits they prepared. Complaints dropped precipitously."

From personal experience, I can tell you that Mr. Augustine is 100 percent correct. When you put your name on a business, as I did, you have nothing to hide behind. The buck stops here. Maybe I'll squeeze in a round of golf or a short vacation, but that's as far as I let myself go.

It's easier to stay motivated than to get motivated again.

An elderly carpenter was ready to retire. He told his employer of his plans to leave the house building business and live a more leisurely life so he and his wife could enjoy their extended family. He would miss the paycheck, but he needed to retire. They could get by.

The contractor was sorry to see his good worker go and asked if he would build just one more house as a personal favor. The carpenter said yes, but in time it was easy to see that his heart wasn't in his work anymore. He resorted to shoddy workmanship and used inferior materials. An unfortunate end to a dedicated career.

When the carpenter finished his work, his employer came to inspect the house. He asked, "Are you satisfied with the house?" When the carpenter said that he was, his employer replied, "Good, because the house is yours. My gift to you."

Talk about coming home to roost! So it is with us. We build our lives a day at a time, until some 2 × 4, ill placed during a lapse of attention, smacks us right between the eyes.

Mackay's Moral: Coasting is a breeze. It's the downhill collisions that are costly.

Quickie #18
The Power Rx of Attitude

The late Norman Cousins was a famous magazine editor of the *Saturday Review* and an acclaimed book author when, at midlife, he came down with what doctors believed was an incurable illness. Undiscouraged, Cousins began an exhaustive study of the illness on his own. In the process, he proved to himself and others that laughter can be a major contributor to healing, since the flow of endorphins increases every time you laugh or feel good. To keep his endorphins flowing, Cousins watched every Marx Brothers movie he could put his hands on—anything to keep him in a positive frame of mind. It worked.

Cured miraculously, Cousins spent the last part of his life as a lecturer at the UCLA medical school. He was fond of telling his students that "the control center of your life is your attitude. Negative attitudes lead to illness, low self-esteem and depression. Positive attitudes lead to hope, love, caring, fun and endorphin flow."

Chapter 54

Courage—What Sets You Apart from the Crowd

In his final broadcast as anchor of the *CBS Evening News* a few years ago, Dan Rather paid homage to people around the world who daily struggle with danger, sickness, death, disease, poverty and other challenges. Rather concluded his broadcast with the same memorable ending he used 24 years earlier when he took over from Walter Cronkite. He often used to end his broadcasts this way—he'd look at the camera and say one word: "Courage."

That sign-off intrigued me. Courage is regarded as a major human virtue. Courage is bravery, valor, standing up to danger, guts and nerve all rolled into one. I'm not a soldier, a policeman, a doctor or a relief worker. I'm a businessman. So what does courage have to do with running a business?

Plenty. I admit that most folks' daily lives are not filled with such dramatic challenges. We all face situations that require us to reach down deep within ourselves to do what is right and brave and occasionally difficult. Courage can involve making decisions that are unpopular or time-consuming or even expensive.

> **It's easy to be ordinary. Courage is what sets you apart from the crowd . . . especially when the crowd checks out.**

In his book *The Edge*, Howard Ferguson says, "It takes courage to sacrifice; to work long, hard hours when you could be relaxing; to work out when you're tired or sick; to focus on being the best you can be when there are so many distractions; to seek out tough competition when you know you will probably get beaten. It's easy to be average, but it's hard to be the best."

He goes on to say, "Most people are completely unaware that they possess this type of courage. Why? Because if they were aware of it, they'd have to test it—and that's risky. So most people play it safe and don't risk 'going for it.' They're afraid of going into the unknown. There are no guarantees."

Designer Laurel Burch, who created the popular Spirit of Womankind jewelry and accessories, had the courage to be different and follow her dream. Her path to prosperity inspires those who might otherwise give up. Burch told of meeting a man in the jungles of Bali: "We didn't have more than two or three words in common, but when he saw my drawings, he threw his head back and his eyes sparkled. His delight was universal. Now he carves mythical menageries that cluster like shrines in my house, my shops and my displays. All ways of life increase one's sense of spirit. All offerings come back in such ways."

Determined people like Laurel Burch possess the stamina and courage to pursue their ambitions despite criticism, ridicule or unfavorable circumstances. In fact, discouragement often spurs them on to greater things.

"Whatever you do, you need courage," wrote essayist Ralph Waldo Emerson. "Whatever course you decide upon, there is always someone to tell you, you are wrong. There are always difficulties arising which tempt you to believe that your critics are right. To map out a course of action and follow it to an end requires some of the same courage which a soldier needs. Peace has its victories, but it takes brave men to win them."

During the darkest days of World War II in Britain, one of Winston Churchill's friends thanked him for his inspiring speeches. The friend told him the speeches were giving courage to the people. "You are mistaken," Churchill responded. "They already have the courage. I only focus on it."

In one of my all-time favorite movies, *The Wizard of Oz*, the Cowardly Lion is looking for, of course, courage. When he finally meets the Wizard, he has some questions (and answers):

What makes a King out of a slave? Courage.
What makes the elephant charge his tusk in the misty mist or the dusky dusk? Courage.

What makes the muskrat guard his musk? Courage.
What makes the Sphinx the Seventh Wonder? Courage.
What makes the dawn come up like thunder? Courage.
What makes the Hottentot so hot? Courage.
What puts the ape in ape-ricot? Courage.
Whatta they got that I ain't got? Courage.

And you know what comes next: the Wizard awards the Cowardly Lion the Medal of Courage so he would always be brave. That's something we could all use.

Mackay's Moral: Courage is ordinary people
doing extraordinary things.

Quickie #19
Be Resourceful or Be Remorseful

One night a girl gets home quite late, after her midnight curfew. The next morning at breakfast her mother says, "Didn't I hear the clock strike two as you came in last night?"

"Yes, Mother," the daughter replies. "The clock started to strike twelve, but I stopped it as soon as I could to keep it from waking you."

Parents can return the favor, though. A young mother is worried about her nine-year-old son. No matter how much she scolds him, he keeps running around with his shirttail out. Her neighbor has four boys, and each of them always wears his shirt neatly tucked in. Finally, in desperation the young mother asks her neighbor to tell her the secret.

"Oh, it's all very simple," she says. "I just take all their shirts and sew an edging of lace on the bottom."

Chapter 55

Think Big to Sell Big

If you want to sell big, think creatively. I love creativity. You can learn a lot by studying creative companies and creative people. When I deliver motivational speeches to corporations, I'm constantly looking for examples of creativity. I've learned some remarkably unique sales techniques by talking to various members of my audiences.

I always ask people how many sales reps their companies have. Then I tell them that we have 500 employees at MackayMitchell Envelope Company . . . and when I'm asked how many sales reps we have, I say 500. Everyone sells in our company. Everyone is in touch with customers.

Here's just a sample of the creative ideas audience members have shared with me after recent talks.

- Lynn endeared herself to the sellers of a 200,000-square-foot industrial building. She was one of several real estate brokers trying to get the listing, so Lynn drove out to the building and took smashing photos of a billboard she had installed. It read, "We're ready to go!" She put this in her presentation and the clients loved it. Lynn got the listing.
- Rod had a sheet metal customer who couldn't take delivery on a $1 million order because he didn't have a place to put it. Rod leased a building for his customer for three months and paid for it . . . and got a customer for life out of the deal.

- Barbara, who has a plumbing and heating business, told me that word of mouth is the best advertising. Her company installed a furnace that was constantly needing service—circuit board, blower and so on. So her company decided to install a new furnace at their expense. The customer was so happy that she told 10 people, which resulted in a lot of new business.
- Steve and his commercial real estate brokerage were invited—along with five competitors—to present to a large company, with only two days' notice. He went up in a plane and took some aerial photos and put them in a brochure for the meeting. They were the first company to present—at 8:30 a.m., the worst position. At 10 a.m., Steve got a call to say that the client canceled all the other appointments. "You showed us what proactive means!"
- Jay told me that once he was on a sales call in Sun City, Arizona. The customer fancied himself a screenwriter and asked him to read the part of Ben Franklin's son in one of his scripts. Although it had nothing to do with their business, he complied. Twenty minutes later they wrote up the order.
- School Nights, where a percentage of sales from a given night are donated to a local school, increased sales on those nights between 75 and 100 percent at a local restaurant. Reading programs are another hit. Teachers can reward students with a free sandwich at the restaurant for reading five books. The successful students also get their photos put up on the Wall of Fame at the restaurant—which their parents love to come in and see.
- For a highly competitive account, Ben discovered the client loved classical music. So he burned a Mozart CD and personally delivered it. He got the business.
- Lance is a big believer in what I call "clip and ship"—sharing news items from the Web or photos with others. These little touches build a human bond that breaks the ice for any sales situation. Lance was recently at a father/daughter dance where he recognized a lot of the other dads—people he's done business with or would like to do business with. He'd brought along a

camera, so he took photos of them with their daughters and sent prints to them. They loved the photos and remembered who sent them. Great PR!

- Mary Anne, a power company manager, makes herself available 24 hours a day, 7 days a week. During a service outage, she received a call from a customer at 2 a.m. She was at the location with a technician in the middle of the night to correct the problem. After every appointment with a prospective customer, she handwrites a thank-you note and mails it the same day.

By updating and examining information in the Mackay 66 Customer Profile®, you will find countless creative ways to nurture customer relations. Just visit my website (harveymackay.com), and you can get the form for free.

Mackay's Moral: Creativity creates business.

Chapter 56

Trust Your Hunches

My favorite *Peanuts* character, Charlie Brown, is on the pitcher's mound psyching himself up: "It's the last of the ninth. The bases are loaded. There are two out, and the count is three and two on the batter. If I get him out, we win!" At this point, Charlie is surrounded by his friends and teammates, who are shouting, "Throw him a fastball! Throw him a curve!" And so on.

All alone on the pitcher's mound, Charlie thinks to himself, "The world is filled with people who are anxious to serve in an advisory capacity."

Decision making is jungle warfare at its worst. Choose well, and you are a hero. Make a bad choice, and your career could be over. Sometimes the choices are so dicey, the options all look alike. Or as Yogi Berra said, "When you come to a fork in the road, take it."

After you've done all your homework, when making decisions, I've found that you have to trust your gut. Deep down, your gut is likely to know what's right. Keep track of what instinct tells you to do.

> **It's amazing how often expert advice sides with your gut.**

Psychologist Joyce Brothers advises, "Trust your hunches . . . They are usually based on facts filed away just below the conscious level."

Sigmund Freud was once asked why it was so difficult for some people to make decisions. He shocked the questioner when he said he asked people to toss a coin. He went on to explain: "I did not say you should follow blindly what the coin tells you. What I want you to do is to note what the coin indicates. Then look into your own reactions. Ask yourself: Am I pleased? Am I disappointed? That will help you to recognize how you really feel about the matter, deep down inside. With that as a basis, you'll then be ready to make up your mind and come to the right decision."

Andrew Carnegie felt that making decisions was a measure of success. He said, "It has been my experience that a man who cannot reach a decision promptly once he has all the necessary facts for the decision at hand, cannot be depended upon to carry through any decision he may make. I have also discovered that men who reach decisions promptly usually have the capacity to move with definiteness of purpose in other circumstances."

Strong leaders are forceful about making decisions. They're confident that their decisions reflect the best thinking around them. Warren Buffett, CEO of Berkshire Hathaway, said, "My idea of a group decision is to look in the mirror."

Presiding over a nation split down the middle over the issue of slavery, Abraham Lincoln faced some of the most difficult decisions any president has encountered. In 1863, worried about the future of a nation breaking apart at the seams, Lincoln made a bold decision to take charge, take risks and move ahead. He wrote one of the most profound statements about human rights of all time, the Emancipation Proclamation.

Lincoln took these ideas to his cabinet, which then numbered only six. After reading the proclamation to them, he asked for their consensus and support. The vote, including Lincoln's, was two ayes and five nays. Lincoln announced the vote as recorded: two ayes, five nays. And then he said, "The ayes have it."

Few of us will ever have to make a decision that monumental, but as managers we will have to make plenty of smaller decisions that affect the lives and careers of our employees.

James Barksdale, former CEO of Netscape, was a charismatic manager whose maxims endeared him to his employees. Like other legendary managers before him, he was fond of "snake" homilies, but I particularly like the 1-2-3 of Barksdale's package. It was formulated at a management retreat soon after he took over Netscape. It's known as his three-snake rule:

- The first rule: If you see a snake, kill it. Don't set up a snake committee. Don't set up a snake user group. Don't write snake memos. Kill it.
- The second rule: Don't play with dead snakes. (Don't revisit decisions.)
- The paradoxical third: All opportunities start out looking like snakes.

Mackay's Moral: Don't be afraid to make a decision.
Be afraid not to make a decision.

"Thank God! A panel of experts!"

Chapter 57

Obscure to Awesome

When my supervisor at Quality Park Envelope dragged me along into the sales department, he knew I wasn't just deadwood pushing a broom. I'd done everything in my power to convince him I was a player. A player without many plays, sure, but he needed me.

Long-haul players pay their dues and prove their value long before they get a chance to shine.

College football legend Lou Holtz wanted to play football when he was in high school. There was only one problem. He was as skinny as a rail and wore Coke-bottle glasses. Holtz didn't get much playing time. He was a fourth-string guard. The coach put him in the game only when the other three guards went down or the game was hopelessly out of reach. So Holtz learned all the other positions, which dramatically increased his chances of playing in case someone got hurt.

Bring plenty to the party.

That's exactly what Google has done too. For years, I used to urge people to research background on customers and contacts at their public or local college libraries. Since the computer search engine Google hit the scene, my advice has been "Go Google them." The results are instant—not to mention what you'll save on gas and parking. Want to "Google" Google? Check out *The Google Story* by David Vise and Mark Malseed (Delacorte, 2005), which traces the formative Google saga, the rise of the hottest meteor in business history.

In just a few short years, to "Google"—to search for something on the Internet—has become a new word in everyone's vocabulary. The term "Google" comes from "googol," which in math is a colossal number—one with a hundred zeros strung out after it! Two Stanford graduate students, Sergey Brin and Larry Page, forgot about their next sheepskins. Instead, they turned dorm digs into a data center and penny-pinched together a patchwork of modest computers. They transformed their research project into a business with an enterprise value of $195 billion in January 2013. Today it's one of the largest media companies on the planet. In 2011, Google earned more than $11 billion on revenues of nearly $38 billion. (No wonder its stock was selling at $704 a share in January 2013.) Brin and Page are worth over $20 billion each.

You may not bring the next Google to market, but there are lessons to be learned from this company that are sage advice for any businessperson:

- **Disregard the impossible.** Larry Page says, "I got this crazy idea that I was going to download the entire Web onto my computer." He credits the concept to "having a healthy disregard for the impossible . . . You should try to do things that most people would not." From the telephone to the television, people have said the great innovations in history were either impossible or unusable. If you have the technical background, what star would you chase and possibly parlay into the next blockbuster?

- **Do the unexpected.** Some people still think that Google runs off a single computer the size of Cincinnati with a memory chip bigger than Mount Rushmore. In fact, Google is a network of "100,000 inexpensive PCs." The ingenuity is in how Google has wired them together to operate its breakthrough search program. One mammoth Google data center, worth an estimated $600 million, sits on the Columbia River in Oregon. One reason: cheap hydroelectricity.

- **Remember what they taught you at home.** Brin and Page might have been Ph.D. dropouts, but they had computer programs in their blood and probably in their bassinets. Brin's father was a math professor; Page's parents were computer science professors.

If a special expertise is in your genes or if it's the topic hashed out over the kitchen table nightly, you may be smarter than you think—and you can apply that knowledge in very different ways.

- **Use modern motivators.** As Google got off the ground, the company attracted top employees by offering everything from free food to laundry on the premises. They landed a blue-ribbon chef who had cooked for the Grateful Dead and whipped up irresistible buttermilk-fried chicken. Another hot ticket: Google software engineers get to spend 20 percent of their time "working on whatever project that interests them." *Fortune* magazine has rated Google right up there with the consulting firm McKinsey as the very top employers of freshly minted MBAs.

- **What you know now may not be what you become.** Brin and Page started out on the trail of a computer science feat. But Google doesn't make its money by being a search engine. Google's oodles of dough are racked up by ad revenues from online advertising linked to its website. Who would have expected two computer nerds to redefine the world of Madison Avenue?

- **Rewrite the rules.** Google's home page—the one most visited and the one clicked on first—doesn't have a single ad. And when you own the most memorable logo of your time, who would think of having fun with the way it's displayed? But the page is spruced up with increasingly complex and interactive Google Doodles. With pop-ups hammering your eyeballs everywhere on the Web, the Google doormat says welcome with homespun simplicity. A policy of having no ads on the home page is calculated defiance of everyone's inclination to cash in fast. And Brin and Page know how to give back: "Google is in the process of digitizing millions of books" from the world's great libraries. For coming generations, Google could be their gateway to the A-to-Z textbook from cradle to grave.

Who can imagine life without Google today? It all seems so obvious. The real breakthrough is that 20 years ago no one could have even imagined what Google could or would do. Today it's a fact of life. Make the impossible routine, and you can skip, laugh (anything but yawn) all the way to the bank.

Surely Google is a marvel of technology, but it also represents a milestone for sales. It has ushered in the next era beyond the hard sell . . . beyond the soft sell . . . to the transparent sell. Study the style well.

Mackay's Moral: It's hard saying no to someone or something that's everywhere!

Quickie #20
That Slippery Slope

You can't know enough about your customers, suppliers, employees, competitors and audiences. Incomplete information can sometimes be riskier than none at all. Here's an example: Harold got a phone call from Al who asked if he was going to Rotary the next night.

Harold said, "Yes."

Al said, "I have a big problem. My guest speaker just canceled. Would you be able to speak?"

Harold said, "Sure."

Al said, "What might you talk about?"

Harold said, "Sex."

The next day Harold delivered a 45-minute speech and got a standing ovation. He came home and his wife asked him, "What did you talk about?"

Now Harold was smart enough to know that his wife thought he didn't know anything about sex, so he said, "Skiing."

The next day Harold's wife was at the supermarket, and she saw Al's wife one aisle away.

Al's wife hollered out, "I spoke to my husband, and he said your husband gave a great speech at Rotary. He must be terrific."

Harold's wife hollered back, "I don't understand. He's only done it once and his hat blew off."

Chapter 58

Passion: The Prime Mover

I recently came across a terrific description of a salesperson . . . and it's from the 1940s. Aside from the sexist language, a sign of those times, I think it's still right on.

During a convention of Chrysler sales managers in Los Angeles—back when Chrysler was an auto superpower—Harry G. Moock, a company vice president, issued this description of a salesman:

"He has the curiosity of a cat, the tenacity of a bulldog, the friendship of a little child, the diplomacy of a wayward husband, the patience of a self-sacrificing wife, the passion of a Sinatra fan, the assurance of a Harvard man, the good humor of a comedian, the simplicity of a jackass, and the tireless energy of a bill collector."

What can I say . . . ? I've always been a Sinatra fan.

Passion is at the top of the list of skills you need to excel whether you're in sales or any other profession.

A salesperson without passion is just an order taker.

If you're in sales, you can have a great product, a tremendous territory and a fabulous marketing campaign, but if you don't have passion, it's hard to make a sale. When you have passion, you speak with conviction, act with authority and present with zeal. When you are excited and passionate about a product—or anything for that matter—people notice. They want in on the action. They want to know what can be so good.

There is no substitute for passion. If you don't have an intense, burning desire for what you're doing, there's no way you'll be able to endure the long, hard hours it takes to become successful.

"Make sure that the career you choose is one you enjoy," said Kathy Whitworth, who won 88 LPGA tournaments, more than anyone on either the men's or women's professional circuit. I was lucky enough to be in the gallery when she won four of them. "If you don't enjoy what you are doing, it will be difficult to give the extra time, effort and devotion it takes to be a success. If it is a career that you find fun and enjoyable, then you will do whatever it takes. You will give freely of your time and effort, and you will not feel that you are making sacrifices in order to be a success."

President Harry Truman once said, "Good work is never done in cold blood; heat is needed to forge anything. Every great achievement is the story of a flaming heart."

J. Paul Getty, the wealthy oil tycoon, actually ranked passion ahead of imagination, business acumen and ambition in listing the necessary ingredients of business success.

Mark Twain was once asked the reason for his success. He said, "I was born excited."

My readers have heard me say many times, "When you love what you do, you will never have to work another day in your life." In fact, the subtitle to one of my books is this: *Do What You Love, Love What You Do, and Deliver More Than You Promise.*

An exceptional salesperson almost always has a passion for details. The mastery comes from surfacing those details effortlessly in a conversation or during a negotiation. Without a passion to learn, you will never build that reservoir of vital facts.

An ancient sage was approached by a man who asked the great teacher to help him learn. The master took the would-be student into the water and suddenly pushed him under and held him there. Surging to the surface, out of breath, the young man gasped, "Why did you do that?"

The wise man answered, "When you want to learn as bad as you wanted to breathe, you will."

Hopefully you're happy and passionate about your work every day. If you aren't, think back to the times when you were and what you can do or need to do to get that feeling back.

Surround yourself with people who are passionate about their jobs. You'll catch their passion. And remember that you can't just be passionate when you feel like it. You have to be passionate about your job, product or cause all the time.

Sam Walton, the founder of Walmart, had 10 "Rules for Success." Rule #1 was "Commit to your business. Believe in it more than anything else. If you love your work, you'll be out there every day trying to do the best you can, and pretty soon everybody around will catch the passion from you—like a fever."

Mackay's Moral: The biggest challenge is not to add years to your life—but passion to your years.

"*Most successful suit sale we ever had, I should say.*"

Chapter 59

Be a *Successful* Maverick

Bill Gove was a legend as a salesman at 3M and one of my favorite heroes. He used to tell this story in his motivational talks to the troops:

> *I was just starting out in sales when my boss called me in and said, "Bill, I want you to go to New Orleans and see our fieldman, Harry. You've never met anyone like him. He's about 60 pounds overweight, his clothes look like a buffet line of whatever he ate for lunch, he garbles his words and he writes his orders on the back of a napkin."*
>
> *So I said, "Sure, I'll go down there. What do you want me to do? Buy him a copy of* Dress for Success? *Put him on a diet? Fire him?"*
>
> *"Hell, no. Find out what this guy is eating and make sure he gets all he wants. He's our biggest producer. And while you're down there, you'd better get some for yourself."*

A remarkable maverick is often cut considerable slack.

General Ulysses S. Grant may have bent his elbow to raise jiggers of Old Crow—his favorite brand—as often as he did to salute the troops. But President Lincoln, as I have said, still found him indispensable as a general.

Could a curmudgeon like Harry or a boozer like Grant be successful today? Of course. You see it all the time in sports. The basketball player who averages 20 points a game is on a longer leash than the backup guard. It isn't fair, it isn't right, but it's the way of the world in a world where results often matter more than how you get them.

Bill Gove and I used to tell young salespeople, "If you can sell, don't worry about the paperwork. We'll get someone to take care of it." All kinds of people can fill out forms . . . few can really sell.

These days, with everything so tech-centered, there's less tolerance for the klutz, even a mad demon of a salesperson klutz, because a screwup online can cost the company zillions. Today Harry's mustard-stained napkins might not pass muster, no matter how big the order. That said, I wouldn't be too quick to ax Harry if there's a way to keep him safely on board.

Earl is the opposite of Harry. The word that fits him is "bearing." He struts like he's on his way to chair a board meeting. Earl's paperwork is perfect; his desk is neat. He's on time for every sales meeting, and without having to be begged, he automatically takes a seat in the front row. Earl would be the perfect salesperson except for one thing: He couldn't give away envelopes to Publishers Clearing House.

Customers just don't warm up to him.

Most salespeople fit somewhere in between Harry and Earl, not daring to be as nonconformist as Harry, but able to avoid setting people's teeth on edge à la Earl.

Smart companies have come to realize that salespeople need to be rid of duties that have nothing to do with sales.

Dumb companies remain enmeshed in structure, processes and politics. They tend to be internally focused on the company culture, the company rule book, the company dress code and the company haircut. They have meetings to see if they should have meetings.

The most productive time salespeople have is the time they spend with their customers, not with their fellow employees. Great sales managers and their teams are externally focused. Totally.

Company committees? Internal planning projects? There's Earl in the front row again, his hand raised, volunteering for the job. Earl knows his future isn't in sales; it's in getting into the bureaucracy. When the Earls of the world get promoted as their reward for doing the grunt work that many successful salespeople hate, the regimen of regular sales meetings, new forms to fill out and mandatory attendance takes a big leap skyward.

If you ask an Earl to groom a Harry, Harry may make less noise when he eats. Will Harry's output rise? Are you kidding? You have to be careful what you ask for.

Mackay's Moral: If you're going to be different, you better produce. Most managers hate mavericks, but all managers love results.

ATTITUDE—The Fortune Cookies

Ability is what you're capable of doing. Motivation determines what you do. Attitude determines how well you do it.

———————

Attitudes are every bit as important as aptitudes.

———————

Remember the 10 most powerful two-letter words in the English language: If it is to be, it is up to me.

———————

Optimists are right. So are pessimists. It's up to you to choose which you will be.

———————

If you think you can or you think you can't, you're right.

———————

Live—and work—like your mother is watching.

———————

It's not my net worth. It's my self-worth. —*Jamie Dimon, CEO, JPMorgan Chase*

———————

People have to saddle their dreams before they can ride them.

———————

What sets you apart is what gets you ahead.

———————

An obstacle is something you see when you take your eyes off the goal.

———————

Courage is not the absence of fear; it is the mastery of it.

———————

Definition of a spoiled brat: Someone born on third base who thinks he hit a triple to get there.

———————

Negativity makes a person look at the land of milk and honey and see only calories and cholesterol.

———————

Triumph is just *umph* added to try.

———————

Positive thinking turns obstacles into opportunities.

———————

How bad a day can it be when you are looking at the right side of the grass? —*Michael Bloomberg*

CONNECT

Chapter 60

Make the Internet
Your Sales Scalpel

Alex Mandossian is a whiz in electronic marketing and has generated $233 million in sales for clients and partners using the latest Web techniques. Alex uses the Internet to make prospecting scalpel-sharp and to dramatically reduce both the rate and the demoralizing impact of rejection. His signature tool is the teleseminar, which informs prospects about a product or service. He has trained more than 14,000 students in teleseminar techniques since 2002. Recently he and I talked about the nuts and bolts of adding these remarkable advances to the skill set of the traditional salesperson.

Some salespeople say, "The Internet Is a fine tool for some folks, especially the younger ones. Me? I'm of the old school." Is that realistic? Can anyone in sales these days afford not to sell over the Internet?

It's possible to sell without the help of the Internet, but it makes the salesperson's job a lot tougher and less rewarding. The Internet is a selling adjunct to "old-school" methods, not a replacement . . . It's a reliable, low-cost prospecting tool to prequalify prospects.

Prequalifying prospects the old-school, human-to-human way reduces productivity and invites personal rejection. The 21st-century selling pro puts the burden of prequalifying on the Internet.

Online prequalification tools such as assessments, surveys and tutorials dramatically reduce customer acquisition costs and practically eliminate personal

222   The Mackay MBA of Selling in the Real World

rejection. Sales professionals should have online prequalification systems in place. This screening lets them deal only with educated prospects during their initial human interaction.

You distinguish between prospects and educated prospects. Why is the difference so important?

Educated prospects are more likely to be motivated buyers. Sales pros with online prequalification systems are more productive. They close more deals faster, easier and with less rejection.

For the salesperson who feels unsure about using the Internet or modern high-tech methods, how about some tips that would dramatically change both a person's computer skills and confidence levels?

Any salesperson, no matter how "techphobic," can quickly and easily utilize the Internet to prequalify prospects. The only requirements are a computer, online access and a basic understanding of human persuasion.

Here are three tips to make the Internet a reliable prequalification tool.

I call the first the "Online Intake Survey."

Here's a simple case where it worked wonders. A chiropractor in Mahwah, New Jersey, was struggling to convert initial consultations into long-term patients. His low conversion rate not only reduced his personal productivity, but it also threatened his confidence. He was having a classic sales problem in building his long-term customer base.

His solution was to create an online survey, and he made it a prerequisite for initial office consultations. The payoff: His prospect-to-patient conversion quintupled!

The online survey asked for three simple pieces of information: a brief recap of the patient's history with chiropractic care, if any; whether the person was in pain; and how soon they wanted to come in for treatment. The answers were submitted online, and the chiropractor created two different initial consultation presentations tailored around answers to the online survey.

Within a few days after putting his simple intake survey online, the chiropractor's conversion rate catapulted from a dismal 15 percent to a remarkable 77 percent. As a result, his productivity increased and his patient acquisition costs decreased.

That's amazing! And so fundamental: Designing two different pitches based on a simple database both streamlined his selling and made it far more reliable. Tell us about this second technique—I think it's an Online Referral Survey?

A financial services adviser in Chicago felt awkward asking for more business. Specifically, he had a tough time approaching clients for referrals. So he published an online referral follow-up survey. Originally developed by Fred Reichheld, it's called "The Ultimate Question."

He essentially asked two things: How likely is it that you would recommend us? And what would you say? Evaluating the answers, he was able to group his customers into three categories: promoters, passives and detractors.

The payoff was threefold: First, the survey unearthed clients who were most likely to "promote" and those most likely to "detract" the firm. Second, it produced a "scorecard" for referrals. And third, it revealed which clients were delighted with their services and, more important, which ones were dissatisfied.

This focused questioning simply harnesses the Internet as an efficient new tool to support selling practices that have been known for decades.

Is there some way to team up the Internet with conventional sales promotion techniques?

Harvey, that's exactly where my third tip is targeted. I call it the "Private Invitation Sale."

An independent cosmetics retailer in Manhattan saw his sales evaporate after his peak selling season. So he put a big fishbowl near the checkout register with a sign that read, "Drop in your e-mail address to get a 50 percent discount on every item you can buy (in 3 hours) during our upcoming Private Invitation Sale."

Once this retailer acquired about a thousand e-mail addresses, he set the date for the 3-hour Private Invitation Sale. He hired the biggest bodyguard he could find to man the door. He bought a red carpet runner that would lead into the front door. He even got red velvet rope (like the kind you see at the front of night clubs to corral customers standing in line).

A week before the 3-hour sale, he dripped a sequence of three e-mail messages with links to print online tickets—only two per customer—that were print-friendly and numbered for first-come, first-served access.

On the day of the sale, passersby were stunned at the long line at the door, along with the security guard letting customers in 20 at a time by ticket number.

In just 3 hours, the retailer did more business than he did during the entire same month one year prior. Once again, the evidence speaks volumes. The Internet is not a tool that replaces old-school selling methods, but a powerful, influential adjunct to capture more profits, faster, better and easier.

Do you motivate people over the Internet in the same way you do one-on-one?

Motivating and influencing on the Internet is faster, easier and costs significantly less than the traditional one-to-one methods. The most reliable way to motivate and educate prospects online is to provide an "ethical bribe" in exchange for an e-mail address.

Ethical bribes—the enticements you give the prospect—might include video, audio, white papers, e-books, free subscriptions, free podcasts or special reports. What makes an ethical bribe effective? Relevance ranks first. Your giveaway must be relevant to your prospects and must not just satisfy but exceed their expectations.

Here are two examples of ethical enticements that really paid off:

A cosmetic dentist in Pasadena offered an online Consumer Awareness Guide titled "The 9 Critical Questions You Must Ask Your Dentist Before You Climb into the Dental Chair."

A BMW auto dealer in Los Angeles put a surprise $500 gift certificate in each car sold, which could only be redeemed online toward BMW accessories. As soon as customers redeemed their gift certificates online, they were invited for a private one-on-one car maintenance consultation before picking up their complimentary accessories. About two months after the Internet sales campaign started, the dealer's accessory sales had increased by 83 percent.

People want to be educated. That can be your most powerful giveaway, can't it?

Enter the teleseminar. A teleseminar is a virtual event in which participants call in to a bridge line and listen and learn from an authority, the keynote speaker. You can conduct a teleseminar from anywhere in the world. The most significant advantage of teleseminar marketing is repurposing. Once you record and transcribe your teleseminar's audio content, you can transform it into blog posts, online articles, workshops, e-books, e-courses and practically any other information product imaginable!

Let's step back and take a look at the big picture. It's not simply a case of turning the whole sales process over to the Internet. Isn't it a matter of using the Internet in very specific ways and at particular points in time during each sales situation?

World-class salesmanship in the 21st century demands multiple channels of communication—both online and offline—to prequalify and follow up with new customers. The old-school method of one-on-one interaction is still critical at the moment of truth—when the sale is closed.

Closing sales simply using the Internet is very hard. Salespeople who attempt to use the Internet to close sales suffer from what I call "creative avoidance." When prospects face buying decisions, the one-on-one interaction is not only more personal, but necessary to complete the sale. As Foster Hibbard, an associate of sales guru Napoleon Hill, used to say, "Doing is easy. It's deciding that's difficult."

The ideal scenario utilizes the Internet to prequalify prospects before the close and to follow up after the close. When done right, the majority of the sales pro's time is spent closing prequalified prospects with little resistance.

Is "virtual + physical"—Web presence + physical follow-up—the new one-two punch in sales? Before, prospects would validate customers by sizing up the leave-with packages. Do prospects now do this on the Web?

It's the context, not the content, of a sales process that's decisive. And the single most important contextual element of sales flow is sequencing.

Imagine the Internet's roles in the sales process are like two slices of bread surrounding a juicy entrée in a gourmet sandwich—that is, the presale qualification process and the postsale follow-up touches. The heart of the sale "sandwich" is the close. This is the point when human intervention by the sales pro is required most to shepherd the prospect gently and convincingly to become a customer.

So the ideal and most productive sales sequence that blends virtual and physical methods looks something like this:

Internet (Pre-Qualify) → Sales Professional (Close) → Internet (Follow-Up)

This sequence brings new meaning to the age-old sales acronym A-B-C, which stands for Always Be Closing. There's one productivity element that marks the difference between "national-class" salespeople from world-class salespeople. World-class sales pros spend 80 percent of their time in the closing sales phase, because the prequalification is done for them with little human effort!

A salesperson may feel he or she has a strong, recognizable face-to-face personality. What do people generally need to project more strongly about themselves to come across with an effective Internet presence?

Sales pros with strong and recognizable face-to-face personalities are the ideal candidates to add Internet prospecting and follow-up to their marketing mix. You see, Internet screening and focusing supplement these kinds of salespeople in exactly those areas where most are weak. Sales professionals who are strong personality types are typically horrible at prequalification and follow-up.

It's true that sales pros with strong personalities may have thick skin. They typically don't flinch when facing push-back or resistance from prospects when the tension builds to close a sale, because closing sales is their strength. And that's why they should spend 80 percent of their time in closing sessions and 20 percent of their time prequalifying and following up.

It doesn't matter if you're a top producer or a newbie salesperson wet behind the ears. The Internet is your passport to taking on the repetitive, mundane tasks that don't require human intervention.

You see the Internet as a psychological and motivational edge for sellers. How exactly does that work?

What makes the Internet powerful is the ability to sift and sort quality leads so the sales pro interacts only with motivated buyers. This not only saves time, it also protects the confidence of the sales pro.

Building trust is about being predictable. If you've put your prospect in the position to anticipate your next move, then you have rapport. The prospect may know you, like you, but trusting requires one-on-one interaction. For some top producers, this trust can spell the beginning of a lifelong customer relationship. Prospects who convert into customers are like caterpillars turning into butterflies.

In the game of sales and the Internet, the quality of prospects almost always trumps the quantity of prospects. Real estate agents know the three words that determine wild success are "location, location, location." Top-producing sales professionals know that the three most important words to close more sales are "prequalification, prequalification, prequalification."

How do smart salespeople use social networks to read the psychology of the market?

Social networking is driven by the principles of appreciation and belonging. The pioneering psychologist William James once said, "The deepest principle of human nature is the craving to be appreciated." That's exactly what social networks and online communities provide. When salespeople join social networks, they're smartest if they add value to the discussion rather than promoting or selling products directly.

Mackay's Moral: Take a lesson from the old fishermen.
It pays to cast a wide net.

Quickie #21
What a Web!

The Internet is the single most powerful force shaping our world. It has also been the fastest-growing source of information in history:

- Radio took 38 years to reach 50 million listeners.
- Television took 13 years to reach 50 million households.
- The Internet took only 4 years to reach 50 million users in the United States.
- By the year 2012, there were 2.4 billion Internet users worldwide. That's more than a third of all the people on the planet—a staggering increase from 361 million at the end of 2000.

Chapter 61

Social Media—
The New Sales Megacenter

Nothing is more preposterous than the idea of an antisocial salesperson. But I'm amazed at how many salespeople are either unaware of the power of social media . . . or opposed to it as yet another newfangled interference to press-the-flesh selling.

"Is social media a fad or is it the biggest shift since the Industrial Revolution?" asks Erik Qualman, author of *Socialnomics*. When you digest the stats, the conclusion becomes inescapable and overpowering.

As of 2010, Generation Y—those born between 1980 and 2000—outnumbers baby boomers. And 96 percent of them have joined a social network! There was no initiation, no dues, no recommendations. Just a few taps on the keyboard and—*voilà!*—instant connection to friends and family, immediate information sharing, finding the kid who smeared peanut butter on you in kindergarten story time . . .

As technology improves and changes, it also changes the way we live . . . and sell.

Perhaps the star of the social media show is Facebook, which added 100 million users in just nine months and had a billion active users as of October 2012. Not bad for a company born in a dorm room.

If Facebook were a country, it would have the third largest population behind only China and India. The fastest-growing segment of Facebook is women ages 55-65. (The jury is still out on how many of those women's children have accepted a friend request from their mothers.)

We no longer search for the news; the news finds us. More than 1.5 million pieces of content—Web links, news stories, blog posts, notes, photos, etc.—are shared on Facebook daily. In the near future we will no longer need to search for products and services. They will find us via social media.

So will our dreamboats. One out of eight couples married in the United States last year met via social media.

Generations Y and Z—the youngest techies, born after 1995—consider e-mail passé. In 2009, Boston College stopped distributing e-mail addresses to incoming freshmen.

For those who prefer their communications in 140 characters or less, a Twitter account is a must. Ashton Kutcher and Ellen DeGeneres have more Twitter followers than the entire populations of Ireland, Norway and Panama. Approximately 60 percent of Twitter usage is on mobile devices people update anywhere and anytime. Twitter and phone apps for Black Friday after Thanksgiving changed the way shoppers planned their retail strategies. (Knowing this, smart merchants use the very same info to shape how they pitch their goods.) On the downside, imagine what an unfavorable Tweet means for bad customer experiences.

How did we ever function before LinkedIn? One of the most remarkable employment statistics I discovered while researching my last book, *Use Your Head to Get Your Foot in the Door*, is that 80 percent of companies are using LinkedIn as their primary tool to find employees.

Remember the advertising slogan "What happens in Vegas stays in Vegas"? That's a little misleading, because what happens in Vegas also pops up on Twitter, Flickr, Facebook, YouTube or any other social media you might use.

Wikipedia—an open-source, collaboratively edited encyclopedia with 100,000 contributors—contains 24 million articles in 285 languages. YouTube, owned by Google, is an enormous video-sharing website. It contains more than 120 million video files and streams more than 4 billion of them each day. A whopping 70 percent of people 18 to 34 years old have watched TV on the Web, while only 33 percent have ever viewed a show on DVR or

TiVo. And 25 percent have watched a video on their phone in the last month. There are also a growing number of e-readers available—35 percent of book sales on Amazon are for the Kindle reader. Some publishers estimate that e-books will make up 50 percent of book sales in the next five years. *The Christian Science Monitor* reported that in the first quarter of 2012 e-book sales surpassed hardcover book sales for the first time.

There are more than 200 million blogs, and 54 percent of bloggers post content or Tweet daily. Here are some facts to consider:

- 34 percent of bloggers post opinions about products or brands.
- 78 percent of consumers trust peer recommendations.
- Only 14 percent of consumers trust advertising.

Perhaps the most astonishing fact of all is that social media have overtaken porn as the #1 activity on the Web.

Successful companies using social media have learned the importance of listening first and selling second. Erik Qualman says, "They act more like party planners, aggregators, and content providers than traditional advertisers."

This is an unprecedented change in the way the world is putting a face on how we know each other. What does this new digitized world mean for salespeople?

- **Learn the basic social media networks, their language and how they work.** This means learning what the little emoticons mean. And, OMG, if you can't manage your way around a basic chat room conversation, you'll soon be saying "smithwaws"—smack me in the head with a wooden spoon—an awful lot!
- **Track the buzz on your business.** Google regularly to find out who's praising you and dissing you on Twitter and blogs. Entire organizations, such as Google Analytics, have sprung up overnight to help businesses interpret social network attitudes and other traffic trends on the Web. Spot these trends and the patterns. Once you have a grounding in how your business is regarded, go find out what the take is on your competition.

- **Spend trench time.** Find a pal you're comfortable with on Linked-In or Twitter and learn to dialogue—preferably with someone who knows a little or a lot more about social networks than you do. You don't have to go high risk, but you need to know how this world works, because that's how people will spend time talking with each other in the future.

The world is being inhaled in an entirely new way. New generations of salespeople "get" this because that's the way they live, though it has little to do with the way many others of us grew up. Mike DiLorenzo, social media marketing director for the National Hockey League, sums it up with one sizzling slap shot: "Social networks aren't about websites. They're about experiences."

Social media represent a fundamental shift in the way we communicate. To stay current—and competitive—in business, don't be a *twit*. Put on your best *face* and *link* into these tremendous opportunities.

Mackay's Moral: If you want to have the world at your fingertips, brush up on your social media skills.

Chapter 62

Be an Affinity Groupie

Earlier I emphasized the astounding power of the Internet as a life-changing force. It is also changing the way networks are created and used, especially by young people.

Affinity groups are springing up every nanosecond thanks to the Internet. What *is* an affinity group? Definitions range all over the landscape. Affinity groups can be as serious as wheelchair-confined citizens seeking barrier-free access to a city's municipal buildings . . . or as lighthearted as the International Buster Keaton Society reminiscing about the Great Stone Face of comedy. (Did you know, for example, that Buster learned card tricks from the legendary magician Harry Houdini?)

Some large companies now encourage affinity groups of minority segments in their employee workforce. It can be a magnetic way to assimilate such groups into the larger company population.

I identified the following collection of affinity groups in just five minutes of surfing:

- the Nephrology Journal Club—devoted to the study of kidney disease
- aircraft buffs of planes flown in the Spanish Civil War
- a CareerBuilder site searching for computer-information-technology sales staff.

Why would you want to spend your very precious time tinkering with such very special interests?

- More and more, networking will be built around special-interest contacts.
- Like it or not, the Internet will be the center for these contacts.
- Affinity groups pride themselves on having little hierarchy, which can be a great way to access key sales contacts. Let's say a contemplated freeway interchange endangers a landmark 19th-century mill. Dig in, and you could find yourself forming ranks with the chairwoman of the town's biggest pharmaceutical manufacturer. Better yet, find out what the affinities of your top ten "need-to-knows" are and zero in on *where* to dig.

You may have plenty of good reasons for not sharing personal data about yourself on these sites, but at least learn how they work. Tune in, even if you are just a "ghost" in a chat room. Remember: The Save the Boxwood Clarinet Society may not rate a hoot to you. But a zest for woodwinds could be your ace customer's #1 after-hours passion. Take careful notes.

Mackay's Moral: Tuning in to people's affinities guarantees you the strongest signal to get your own message heard.

Chapter 63

Don't Make 50 Your Psychological Speed Limit

"Use it or lose it" is one of my favorite adages. Are you over 50 and regularly selling to prospects between 25 and 45? How can you hope to land winning punches without a handle on where these younger minds live? Just as you tone up your abs in the gym or clock time on the treadmill, check out where young people get their information and their entertainment.

- Stream a top-rated TV show on your notebook. Pick something you might otherwise not watch, like *The Big Bang Theory* or *So You Think You Can Dance*. Invest as much attention in the ads as the content.
- You may not agree with Jon Stewart's politics, but an amazing number of young people get their news from Comedy Central's *The Daily Show*, according to Pew Research Center and other authorities. So vary your routine viewing and check Stewart out if you want to know what page your younger clients are on.
- Does your competitor's crew across town have a favorite postwork watering hole? Drop in and take heed of the young people who seem to be attracting the largest social crowds. As a bonus, you might overhear a shred of the most astonishing gossip.
- It's quite possible your bosses are younger than you, and their reflexes may be a tad more agile too. If they're into extreme

snowboarding, for instance, you don't have to jib or free carve your way into the orthopedic ward, but it pays to learn a term or two . . . and their slope performance goals.

- If your waistline has become something of a battleground and you're at a departmental lunch, nix ordering a trans fat bombshell. Stay in touch with food trends. Don't know *gejang* from *kimchi*? You've not likely been tipped off that Korean cuisine is now huge (which it apparently is).

- Have you read a book with a Kindle yet? Do you regularly scroll through the *Wired* website for the latest phalanx of apps and techno-innovations? Have you played (and graciously lost) Xbox games with your kids or grandkids?

Sales mastery doesn't just entail closing a series of deals. You have to keep growing and modernizing your mind-set. It isn't just the experience. It's often the attitudes and the vocabulary that go with it. These send signals to customers that are as memorable as the duds you sport or your manners in a white-tablecloth restaurant.

Mackay's Moral: If you want to stay in the game, you'd better know the standings.

"I'll have someone from my generation get in touch
with someone from your generation."

Chapter 64

Putting the Byte on Techies

If you're scouring the Web for advice on selling to techies, finding surefire tips may be harder than you think. (By techie, I mean anyone who is seriously into the tech realm. You know the type. They touch and feel the world through the lens of technology.)

You and I might find selling and buying the very juice of life. For others, the world is packed in a different box. Your challenge is to enter their universe and chat in terms that excite their imagination and stimulate their desires while being painstakingly careful not to talk through your hat.

The following tips may help you capture techie attention:

1. **Know your stuff.** Let's say you're selling goods to general consumers that are only somewhat technical (like gourmet cookware) or not technical in the slightest (such as designer fragrances). You don't have to know all that much, but say what you do know with resounding accuracy and confidence. The trick is not trying to impress a techie with just a tiny bit of background . . . because you won't.

2. **If you don't have a clue, don't go there.** Never dish up baloney to a techie. A simple "I don't know"—especially if you think you know, but don't—will likely earn you respect and trust. The implications are serious. Unlike most areas of sales, you may really need to learn the technology to sell the product. Short of this, the other common solution for big-ticket industrial items is

to have a thoroughly grounded technical expert as part of the sales team.

3. **Don't spout features randomly.** You're probably trading sound bites with someone who has three sizes of needle-nose pliers in her tool kit and who sorts search algorithms apart from string algorithms (whatever that means). Talk orderly-mind-to-orderly-mind and don't flit randomly from one kind of trait to characteristics of a whole different order.

4. **Don't gender gaffe.** Just because you're pitching a woman, don't assume you're not selling a techie. Nearly half of the undergraduate student body of MIT is female.

5. **Wheel out authorities.** Know the highest level of testing agency, trade publication, sponsored competition or revered practitioner that endorses quality for whatever goods or services you are selling. These are shorthand—often decisive benchmarks—techies rely on religiously in making complex decisions.

6. **Unleash customer ingenuity.** Techies prize applying their own creative intelligence. Show them a feature that seems to ignite an interest, and they will often—sometimes aloud—argue the trait into an overwhelming virtue. Stand back and nod admiringly.

7. **Realize newness is an appeal, not a threat.** Techies thrive on it. The average layman is intimidated by a barrage of technical data. Your typical nerd would rather snack on stats than an energy bar. Just be sure to know your stuff before you even dream of pitching a propeller head.

8. **Steer technical chat.** If you're not deeply versed in technical aspects of the product and are acting as a coordinator, be a ready resource with the manufacturing, engineering or product design specialists who can answer questions. That means phone contact and e-mail addresses just a click away. Develop reliable liaisons with these support resources and follow up to make sure questions are answered pronto.

9. **Supplement and satisfy insecurities.** It's possible the techie customer is already fully convinced the gizmo of the moment is an engineering marvel. Your work may be to create a sense of security

for techies about nontech issues. Their concerns may be: Is it styled right? Will management think it's too ostentatious? Will my nontechie peers (or friends) feel I've done something outrageously self-centered?

10. **Sell services neatly.** Many techies flail and lurch in buying services because they are packaged in what seems to be a sloppy, random or arbitrary way. A touch of tidy, rational organization—especially a neat grid of the various features—can work wonders.

11. **Fortify the courtship.** Techie buyers often need time to romance themselves on the merits of the merchandise. Premature pressure to close can undermine all the careful legwork you've done to make the sale enticing.

Mackay's Moral: Don't short the circuit board
wired to a true techie's heart.

Chapter 65

Selling on Candid Camera

In the shower and in front of mirrors, sellers have practiced their pitches for decades, if not centuries. In my books and columns, I've long recommended that job applicants polish their interviewing skills using home videocams. These days, webcams of incredible quality are built into most laptops and have become a fixture of everyday life.

> **Videocams were once crucial as practice tools for sales. Increasingly, they create the actual venue of sales calls.**

Slowly but surely the sales setting is itself changing. Bob Dilenschneider, head of the Dilenschneider Group, was CEO of the huge PR firm Hill & Knowlton before he founded his current business. He regularly prepares a compendium of key trends for his clients, and I've been fortunate to be on his exclusive mailing list for a quarter century.

Many of the stats Bob captures jump off the page. The following ones should wrestle future-focused salespeople to the ground to rethink what their core pitch is all about:

- Emerging "technology may undermine the term 'face-to-face meeting,' as telepresence is technically face-to-face. As the technology becomes more widespread, more and more businesses will opt to use telepresence."

- "Conversing 'face-to-face' with people is becoming cheaper. Over time, videoconferencing may do to in-person meetings what e-mails did to letters."
- "Phone calls over Wi-Fi will become more convenient and secure . . . Videoconferencing on iPods has become possible. Front- and rear-facing cameras are rumored to be on the fourth-generation iPod Touch."

This doesn't mean preparation is *less* important. It will be vastly more important now, because sales meetings and presentations are far likelier to be handheld and on-the-go as the technology for mobile teleconferencing evolves.

Mackay's Moral: The old saying that salespeople hold their future in their hands has never been truer.

Chapter 66

Customer Service: The Digital Retread

One of the exciting things about the Internet is you can sometimes find provocative ideas coming from unfamiliar information sources. At MyCustomer .com, one such posting appeared in October 2010. The author is Guy Stephens, founder of the LinkedIn group Where Social Media Meets Customer Service. Beyond this identification, I have no idea who Guy Stephens is, but his observations certainly make sense. The title of this posting: "All Change: The Four Trends Reshaping Customer Service."

Stephens' signal message tells the huge scope of the story: "The emergence in 2009 of social media as a real catalyst of change signaled for the first time the possibility that customer service had a vital role to play in winning the hearts and minds of customers."

Here are the four broad trends pinpointed by Stephens, along with my interpretation as to why they are Richter-scale earthshaking.

1. **"The rise of help networks."** Before social media really took off, people had to rely on the companies that make the products and services for help. Now customers rely on each other, using "social platforms where the sharing of information between trusted 'friends' is paramount." This makes customers more self-sufficient and authoritative advice more decentralized. The rise of "the Twitterverse" has prompted firms like Best Buy to launch their own

networks like Twelpforce, an innovative new channel that allows customers to "Tweet their way directly into Best Buy's most powerful knowledge base: their people." Study what's happening. Help networks are making many customers product-smarter than salespeople, and maybe even a few design engineers! This trend will revolutionize the world of after-sale support in the decade to come.

2. **"Customer service 'on the go.'"** Smartphones like the iPhone and the Motorola Droid have redefined the accessibility of the customer. "Customer service agents are no longer bound by having to be in one fixed place for a particular period of time to help customers or indeed people." Both dispensers and receivers of information have the full technical palette at their fingertips, and it doesn't matter where on the planet they might be.

3. **"The decentralization of trust."** Networking plus mobility are repositioning the center of gravity for trust away from the originator of the product and services. In a way, it's now up to a firm to earn its way back into the picture as being the credible authority on its own goods. Stephens points out that YouTube is becoming a "video knowledge base." (WikiHow is another.) I would liken this development to the growing reliance on Wikipedia as a general reference tool. Stephens sensibly finds these new aggregators to be overwhelming "proof that knowledge also has the capacity to be viral"—that is, instantly transmitted by word of mouth with nearly no intervention.

4. **"The intermediation of business processes."** This last point is not only a mouthful, it's a mind-full! "Business processes themselves are moving into the hands of intermediaries." The white-hot evidence: Complaints are "no longer the exclusive domain of a company, limited to their e-mail or a phone call."

Mackay's Moral: When you cast out your help line, anchor it well, or your company's reputation might sink in the drink.

Quickie #22
Manicure the Pitch

In many business-to-business transactions, the chief information officer (CIO) has become an incredibly important partner in top-management purchasing decisions.

According to Jerry Gregoire, editor of *CIO* magazine, "One of the most important reasons why CIO-level executives don't trust information technology salespeople is because salespeople consistently use sales techniques that are designed for the insurance, car and real estate industries—not for the technology space." Always remember exactly to whom your pitch is directed. That includes how that person has been trained to think and make decisions. You don't grab gray matter the same way you grab soil.

The big diff? "CIOs come from a technical and advanced educational background, where life is based on scientific notation and a structured thought process."

This book is dedicated to selling skills and attitudes designed for success in almost every industry. The tips I offer create a reliable launching pad for outstanding sales performance. But you can't enter the fray with this wisdom alone, especially when selling high-tech products to space-age minds. That demands technical knowledge—often at a very sophisticated level—as well as day-to-day experience with techies, folks whose minds tick a little differently and more analytically than the norm.

A major-league manager knows exactly which reliever he'll call in from the bull pen to duel it out with a particular slugger. Similarly, a salesperson may need either to hone specialized skills or to draft knowledgeable experts before sealing a deal with a high-tech prospect.

Chapter 67

Customer Service in the Internet Age

For years, we believed that if customers received bad service, they would pass the word along to 20 or so people. Conversely, if they were on the receiving end of great service, they might tell a few folks, but not in numbers anywhere near the bad-news story.

Enter the Internet. Bad reports can span the globe instantly. Good reports can too, but they are not shared as frequently.

One company that learned this lesson the hard way is United Airlines. In March 2008, Dave Carroll and his band, Sons of Maxwell, were flying on United Airlines from Halifax to Omaha with a stopover in Chicago. At that first stop, as Carroll tells the story, a woman seated near the band members looked out the window and exclaimed, "They're throwing guitars out there!"

Band members then witnessed their expensive instruments being handled roughly. Carroll's guitar alone was a $3,500 Taylor model. Concerned, he approached the flight attendant and was sent to an agent outside the plane. That person claimed to have no authority and walked away. A third employee at the gate dismissed his complaint, explaining, "That's why we make you sign the waiver." Problem: Carroll and his band had neither been offered nor signed such a waiver.

When he finally got to check out his guitar in Omaha, he discovered the base of the guitar had been smashed. Even a $1,200 repair didn't restore it to its original condition. And Carroll's experience with United as he sought restitution is a horror story that spanned nine months of phone calls, e-mails, faxes, buck-passing and a final "Sorry, but we're not paying." Most of us would have given up at that point, but then most of us aren't as creative as Dave Carroll. He turned it into a career opportunity.

"At that moment it occurred to me that I had been fighting a losing battle," Carroll wrote. "The system is designed to frustrate affected customers into giving up their claims, and United is very good at it. But I realized then that as a songwriter and traveling musician I wasn't without options. In my final reply to (the United rep), I told her that I would be writing three songs about United and my experience in the whole matter. I would then make videos for these songs and offer them for free download on YouTube. My goal: to get 1 million hits in one year."

Dave Carroll got his 1 million hits—and 9 million more. Two years later, he passed the 10 million mark, and the videos are still enormously popular.

United did take notice. CNN reported that after 50,000 views the company admitted it was a "unique learning opportunity" and incorporated the incident into some of its training programs. United finally offered Carroll reimbursement, but he refused, encouraging the airline to give it to another deserving passenger. United's reputation was tarnished.

Can any company afford this kind of publicity?

Many airlines were confronted with weather-related cancellations and other service problems galore in the winter of 2010–2011. Suddenly the lightbulb glowed. Airlines began to turn to Twitter and other social media to alert themselves to problems and to implement solutions for their customers.

Social media sites are rapidly becoming the customer service desks of the 21st century.

Customer service has taken on a whole new meaning with the rise of websites like Angie's List and Yelp, which provide unfiltered reviews of services and products. Some require subscriptions; others are free. Google your company and see if you appear in the blogosphere. And never underestimate the power of YouTube and Facebook groups.

No one in a company should understand the return policies better than the sales staff. That includes the authority given to representatives who deal with the public and the follow-up after a sale. And, even more important, after an issue has been resolved, it should be up to the sales rep to make sure the customer is satisfied with the outcome.

Make certain policies reinforce the attitude that the customer may not always be right, but they are always the customer. Message: Excellent customer service is paramount to your company's success.

Advocate professional surveying of your customers. Give them the opportunity to rate your service. It's a chance to improve your company without having to hire a consultant. Then incorporate the changes that you can.

How companies serve their customers should never be debatable. When there are unrealistic expectations from a customer, honesty is the only acceptable answer. Help customers understand your product-line focus and, when necessary, its limitations. (You may, for example, not be able to offer your customer a full-line assortment. The drag on your cost structure might be too huge.) Some salespeople even help a customer find an alternative source for a particular need, then win back business with other products or services their company is really good at.

Never forget the cost of fighting millions of negative hits on YouTube for just one blatant and newsworthy customer service gaffe. It can dissolve all the good publicity financed by an entire year's worth of image ads . . . and sometimes even more.

Mackay's Moral: If you don't serve your customer,
they'll serve notice.

"Would you like to hear some music while you hold?"

Chapter 68

The Mackay 25
Sales Call Prep Checklist

The Mackay 66 Customer Profile has become a classic in customer/prospect meeting preparation. Over time, we have seen the need for a different kind of pre-meeting planning tool. I call it the Mackay 25.

The Mackay 25 is more streamlined—less focused on the details and identity of the individual buyer or prospect and more geared to getting an instant snapshot of the prospect or buyer's attitudes and expectations. It tries to get to the heart of what is commonly known today as relationship selling. Is being right about people important or, quite probably, more important than being right on price? If you agree with me that it is, this checklist can be your meal ticket. There is also a thrust that zeroes in on dealing with remedial issues so you can move an account to a solid footing quickly.

THE MACKAY 25
SALES CALL PREP CHECKLIST

Date: _____

By: _____

CALL PROFILE

1. Name: _____

    Nickname: _____

Title: _____

Admin. Assistant: _____

Receptionist: _____

Contact numbers: _____

E-mail addresses: _____

Company name and address: _____

_____

_____

Special driving and parking instructions:

_____

_____

2. Purpose of the call:

_____

_____

SALES HISTORY

3. New account? Lapsed? (If yes, reason.)

_____

_____

If lapsed, last account manager and date relationship ended:

_____

_____

When was a visit to this company last made and what was the result?

_____

_____

PERSON TO BE VISITED

4. How does this person function in the decision-making chain?
    (Gathers information, evaluates resource pool, makes ad hoc
    decisions, etc.)

    _____

    _____

    If call contact is not ultimate purchasing decision maker, who is
    and where is the call contact positioned in the decision-making
    chain?

    _____

    _____

5. Does the individual have preferences in the way he/she collects
    information or makes decisions?

    _____

    _____

6. What does the call contact enjoy talking about? What motivates
    this person professionally and personally?

    _____

    _____

7. Is the contact a high-tech communicator (BlackBerry, smart-
    phone, etc.), and are we expected to stay in touch this way?

    _____

    _____

    What take-with/leave-behind information is essential for this
    call?

    _____

    _____

OUR IMAGE

8. How can buying from us or expanding sales to us enhance this person's departmental performance? Career?

_____

_____

9. How does this prospect/customer expect to be sold and treated on a personal level?

_____

_____

10. Instinctively, what does this client like/dislike about us?

_____

_____

11. How does the customer/prospect perceive us (strategically, financially, in our quality and service levels)?

_____

_____

Has the customer/prospect had service or quality issues in the past? What can be done to avoid them in the future?

_____

_____

12. Is there any heads-up this company needs to be given about pending operational/service/pricing plans within our own business?

_____

_____

13. Are there any community activities or sponsorships shared by our company and the customer/prospect? Any recent news in this area that should be mentioned?

_____

_____

MARKETPLACE

14. What useful new information about the marketplace can we bring to this contact?

_____

_____

15. What useful new information can we supply about competitors? Any credible industry rumors?

_____

_____

16. What can we do to help this business achieve a strategic or tactical breakthrough in its marketing positioning?

_____

_____

17. Forthcoming industry or trade events at which we will have contact with this company:

_____

_____

INTELLIGENCE UPDATE

18. Company website (if a subsidiary, that of parent as well): Be sure to Google company for late-breaking news.

_____

_____

19. Who are our leading internal and friendly outside expert resources on this business and what are the approach recommendations?

_____

_____

20. What is the financial state of the prospect/customer company?

_____

_____

21. Any recent or pending organizational changes?

_____

_____

22. In general, what are the key driving factors in the buying decisions of this company (price, quality, innovation, etc.)?

_____

_____

COMPETITIVE POSITIONING

23. If this account represents current business served by a competitor, identify the competitor(s):

_____

_____

24. If a competitor has the account, how long? Why are they pre-
ferred?

_____

_____

25. Who is the competitor's account manager or rep? (Any important appeals or criticisms of their account personnel?)

_____

_____

MackayMitchell Envelope Company
Minneapolis, Minnesota
Harvey Mackay © 2011

Chapter 69

The Unanswered Serve

Few woes in the salesperson's life surpass the unanswered call, the ignored text message or the e-mail ricocheting in cyberspace.

You know your priorities are not their priorities. However, their attention is also your paycheck.

> **A call is a friendly serve. The goal is not to ace it, but to get it returned.**

There are all kinds of enticements you can add so that calls will be returned. Here are some of my favorites:

- Discover your target's favorite charity and pledge a $100 contribution if they return your call.
- Learn the individual's #1 not-for-profit community organization and offer 10 hours of pro bono work in exchange for an interview.
- Find out if the target's favorite charity needs some pro bono equipment or services of the sort your firm offers, and let it be known you want to make a donation.
- Read the individual's most recently published comments or trade association talk and send a letter as to why you found the speech compelling.
- If a trade or industry conference is taking place in a distant location, find out the name of the hottest restaurant in town, book

tentative reservations well in advance and send a note suggesting you meet there during the course of the event.

- Analyze the prospect company's latest new product in a brief, constructive and impactful way. Even better, send them an insightful analysis by a technical expert whose reports they would not regularly receive.

- Study a new product line introduced by a competitor and send a brief report to your target as to why it creates an unexpected opportunity for this person's company.

- Talk with your target's administrative assistant and learn about *that* person's hobbies, vacations or hometown in the hopes that building a genuine, humanized phone relationship with the gate-keeper will help open the gate.

Mackay's Moral: While the cost of dialing has dropped, the cost of answers is often up.

"I'll check and see if he's available."

Quickie #23
Ignorant, Period!

Technology is not an option . . . it is an imperative!

Sales reps and managers who pride themselves on being computer ignorant are half right . . . they are ignorant, period!

Chapter 70

Turning a Tweet Mind-Set into Sales Nest Eggs

Sam Richter is a nationally recognized authority on using the Internet to optimize sales. In the first part of this book, I included his invaluable advice on the benefits of LinkedIn and Facebook. Below is a recent conversation Sam and I had on the power of Twitter. If you don't "get" the psychology of Twitter and how it is completely revamping the world of selling, you're headed for a sales deep freeze with no known deicer.

Sam, how important has Twitter become to our understanding of how the world works, especially the business world?

Twitter has 500 million users and 140 million of them tweet daily. It is now the second most heavily trafficked social networking site. Globally, Twitter was the fourteenth most searched keyword on the Internet for the year 2012.

Twitter is presently one of the best social bookmarking, social networking as well as social marketing websites on the globe. Of those using the service, currently around 70 percent of them use it for business purposes.

We both know social networking's importance will continue to expand. Professionals in sales, business development and account management must learn to Tweet both as a research tool and as a sales technique. Give us a basic rundown of how Twitter works.

Twitter is an instant messaging tool that can be accessed from computers and mobile devices. Twitter messages go to anyone on the Internet who wants to read them. Once you have a free Twitter account (twitter.com), you can send messages using a maximum of 140 characters, including spaces and punctuation.

Tweets, as Twitter messages are known, typically include a link to a digital asset—for example, a website, video or photo. Those with Twitter accounts can "follow" other Tweeters, simply by going to the other person's Twitter account and clicking the Follow button. (You can find Tweeters using Twitter's own search engine or a specialized search engine like Tweepz.com.) You can use your Twitter account to read the messages that the people you follow are sending.

This is starting to get complicated. Suddenly Twitter creates a whole new set of tasks for me each day. I want Twitter to make my life simpler, not vice versa. Are there tools that can help?

Aggregation is the solution. Aggregation just means collecting and organizing. Once you start following many people, you may want to consider a Twitter aggregation tool like TweetDeck (tweetdeck.com) or HootSuite (hootsuite.com). These and other services—some free, some paid—help you organize those you follow as well as integrate multiple social networks or accounts, including Facebook and LinkedIn. They are also worthwhile aids for managing your own Tweets.

Our goal is to increase ease and confidence with Twitter as a tool. You also offer a shortcut that can be downloaded to help salespeople manage Twitter.

Readers will find a number of "Twitter-mining" resources at my website (knowmorecenter.com). Download and install the free "Know More!" toolbar so you can quickly and easily access my favorite sales intelligence sources directly from any Web browser.

What makes Twitter so great from a sales intelligence perspective is that, for some reason, people tend to share a lot of personal and even private business information. I've seen people Tweet about new products they are working on, upcoming meetings and even dissatisfied clients, all of which can provide a salesperson with a wealth of information.

That brings up an important distinction: Even though you don't want to be broadcasting information like this on the Web yourself, you'd be foolish not to track what other people are saying . . . especially since it's instant public knowledge these days. Again, are there shortcuts to make this easier?

I recommend a Twitter search engine called Topsy (topsy.com). Use Topsy to instantly see the real-time conversations that Tweeters are having related to your search. For example, enter a company name and you'll find people—employees, vendors, customers, the media and others—talking about the company, sharing news, discussing products and more.

You can also set up a Topsy alert. Enter a search in Topsy, and if you like the results, click the "Create an Alert" link. Then, whenever someone Tweets about your chosen topic at any point in the future, Topsy will send you an e-mail. It's a great way to stay on top of competitors, prospects and clients—and hear what people are saying about your company . . . or someone else's.

So far we've talked about Twitter as a reconnaissance tool to collect intelligence. How about Twitter as a means of publicizing products and building allegiance to your company?

Twitter has become a powerful marketing and sales support edge. Thousands of companies are using Twitter to:

- introduce products to new audiences,
- promote innovative features,
- improve service and support,
- cross-sell and up-sell offerings, and
- communicate with loyal customers.

The first Tweet was posted in March 2006, and Twitter has already revolutionized the psychology of buying and selling. I've heard that Dell, the computer systems giant, has been at the cutting edge of the Twitter explosion. Describe for us how Twitter has revolutionized how Dell tackles sales.

Dell uses Twitter to mine what customers are saying online about Dell products. They even have a dedicated Social Media Listening Command Center, where employees scour the Web for customers who've mentioned Dell products in their online conversations. In a company of Dell's size, that may mean tens of thousands of mentions in a single day!

When the conversation is positive, Dell thanks the customer. However, when the conversation is negative, that's when the real action begins. Dell has empowered its social media staff to communicate directly with the customer and solve problems. Whether it's pointing a customer to a self-help website or helping the customer locate a local retailer that has a needed part, Dell staff is able to learn about and solve issues immediately.

Small companies probably can't afford this kind of attention, but the founder or sales manager can easily create the nucleus of a Twitter campaign.

This is where the all-important difference shines through. Twitter is not a traditional marketing tool. Traditional marketing is one-way communication in which a company is telling its prospects and customers about a product or service. Print, television, radio and online advertisements are used to promote a brand and tell an audience a specific message. Twitter, on the other hand, is a conversation tool.

Twitter is meant to engage an audience and to encourage its members to become part of the conversation. The real power of Twitter is when your followers comment on your messages and Retweet them. What a powerful endorsement! A Retweet occurs when someone else shares with their followers what you have already said in a Tweet. Then, if you're lucky, a percentage of those people might Retweet the message again, sharing the information with their followers. Thus, a message that you send out to your thousand followers—if it's good enough—could theoretically be seen and read by millions.

Compared to old-time advertising, this is a pretty cost-efficient way to get the word out.

When others Retweet your information, it doesn't cost a thing. It also has a high degree of credibility, because it's a trusted individual sharing the information rather than a company pushing its own message.

Describe the downside to all of this. As is so often the case in selling, being greedy and trying to exploit an edge can backfire, can't it?

Because its potential is so large, companies often get selfish and Tweet only messages that benefit themselves. They don't attempt to add value to the message that would make it appealing and rewarding for its own sake.

Most people on Twitter (unless they're already loyal customers) don't want to read 140 characters about your products and what's new at your company. People want something interesting, educational, humorous or in some way special to them that they can share with others.

Use Twitter to relay objective information. Share a provocative article, not a puff piece that your marketing department has written. Be candid and circulate ideas that you think are relevant or interesting, preferably written by a credible third party. Let your followers know about a cool event that your firm is participating in or sponsoring. Offer your Twitter followers special discounts or coupons, and let them share the deal with *their* followers.

Twitter is really just a new-generation network that is built and nourished on the Web. It's a kind of instant Internet Rolodex, isn't it?

People who want to receive your Tweets are followers who have expressed an ongoing interest in what you have to say. Gaining followers is critical in your Twitter campaign. It's obviously the only way that the viral component of any Tweet can occur—the greater the number of followers you have, the more people are going to Retweet your message.

That's why it's so important to choose a name that's easy to remember. For example, mine is twitter.com/HarveyMackay.

Make sure you promote your Twitter user name in all your marketing materials and other communications vehicles. Choose a name that is easy to remember—using your name is best if it's available. Like yours, my Twitter name is exactly what you'd expect it to be: twitter.com/SamRichter.

Include your Twitter link in your e-mail signature. Feature it prominently on your website—most companies post the Twitter icon somewhere near the main navigation. Include a "Follow Me on Twitter" line with your Twitter link on all your marketing materials. Integrate your Twitter feed into your other social networks, including LinkedIn and Facebook.

Twitter and social networks are really the new face of selling, aren't they?

From a psychology of selling perspective, Twitter is truly a window into the future. In the past, the salesperson was the one armed with information. The salesperson was the expert who knew how his or her products could benefit the buyer. With social networks like LinkedIn, Facebook and Twitter leading the way, that is no longer necessarily true.

In the new world of selling, the buyer has a lot of information on your products. It's not just what *you* say about them. Through the Internet, a multitude of sources can offer believable insights on your products. Why are these credible? Because people always believe what others say about you more than what you say about yourself or your company, especially if you're a salesperson. Consumers are reporting if your company truly delivers on its promises every day.

The social nature of tools like Twitter allows people to easily search for product reviews, how your company handles complaints, etc. Buyers today have buyers' intelligence. That means you need to have sellers' intelligence, which isn't just its equal—it has to be even better.

Mackay's Moral: In today's selling landscape,
it's the birdbrains who don't Tweet.

CONNECTING—The Fortune Cookies

No Customer Service = No Customers.

_____

Take care of your customers, or someone else will.

_____

2 a.m. is a lousy time to try to make new friends.

_____

When advising others, "Eat your own home cooking."
—*Jamie Dimon, CEO, JPMorgan Chase*

_____

Never have coffee with another salesperson, only with a customer.

_____

Sign on my office conference table: "Our meeting will not be
interrupted . . . unless a customer calls."

_____

People, not specs, will always determine who gets the sale.

_____

It's not the sale that makes a salesperson. It's what he or she does to
ensure the next sale that makes that person a pro.

_____

Patience is the ability to let your light shine even after your fuse has blown.

_____

You can buy flattery, but envy must be earned.

_____

If you can't please everyone, please someone.

_____

Dining well at a power lunch depends on what you bring to the table.

_____

The best place to find a helping hand is at the end of your arm.

_____

Business is often sink or swim. Preparation is your life preserver.

_____

Technology should improve your life, not become your life.

_____

Why don't you meet successful hermits? Their invisible network tells all.

_____

Don't let your appearance cause your disappearance.

_____

Don't act your age; act the age you are in.

REACH OUT

Chapter 71

Country Clubbing

In Hopkins, Minnesota, outside of Minneapolis, there's a country club that was formed in 1921. According to its own website, The Oak Ridge Country Club was founded for people in the Twin Cities "who knew the difference between a golf ball and a matzo ball." So, Oak Ridge has had a bit of an ethnic slant.

After I graduated from the University of Minnesota, I couldn't afford my own apartment. My mother had just died, and I was living at home with my dad. I was scratching out a living selling envelopes for a firm named Quality Park. Seeing my frustration, my father aptly noted that "golf was the only form of human activity" I'd "taken seriously" up to that moment.

He suggested I go over to Oak Ridge and pitch the admissions committee. "Tell them you were an accomplished varsity golfer at the University of Minnesota. Propose that they let you into the club without paying the huge initiation fee. Neither of us could possibly afford it for you."

The admissions committee thought this idea was the most laughable thing they ever heard. "For nothing? You want us to admit you, a 21-year-old kid, who knows virtually no one in the entire club, for nothing? Just so you can hustle our bunch of old duffers?"

Then I promised that I would help them win the City League championship and that someday I would actually pay the initiation fee.

They answered that maybe they should defer my admission to "someday" as well. But, I could tell they were warming up. Fantasies of a City League trophy won their hearts. Ultimately they relented.

Instantly, by virtue of being admitted, I was given the opportunity to leverage a network of 300 successful business people. And those were just the Club members. That didn't begin to factor in all the contacts in the City League with whom we competed.

That membership at Oak Ridge proved my networking hole-in-one.

It created the foundations for business relationships with giant organizations, such as Fingerhut (the mail order giant—at the time, the largest single envelope user in the United States), the Minnesota Vikings, Honeywell, Pillsbury and General Mills.

In turn, these accounts gave me the contact leverage to buy my own business, the foundation of what today is the MackayMitchell Envelope Company.

Oak Ridge also introduced me to a golf partner who never bought a single envelope from me: my wife Carol Ann.

The Oak Ridge breakthrough was a life-defining networking experience for me. By the way, this story has a postscript.

Oak Ridge Country Club has always been a great place to network—for members and for friends of members. Among the notables in the broader Oak Ridge network, one fellow goes down in history as the biggest-stakes networker of recent decades. Praise of his astonishing achievements raised the rafters in the Oak Ridge clubhouse for foursome after foursome. This expert mixer was former chairman of the NASDAQ stock exchange and a member in good standing of the opulent Palm Beach Country Club in Florida—the most exclusive Jewish country club on the map.

The avid networker of whom I speak is currently enjoying a lifetime engagement at FCC Butner Medium in North Carolina. His privileges there have been extended for another 147 years.

Through his Oak Ridge contacts, starting in the 1980s, Bernie Madoff hustled at least 35 members. While he perfected his moves big-time at Oak Ridge, Madoff took a carload more to the cleaners at his home course at Palm Beach.

Mackay's Moral: What one bad apple can do to a barrel is grim. How one bad apple can spoil a network is a bottomless pit.

Quickie #24
Always Travel On The Ball

Every business trip you plan should have multiple agendas. Deals on the table may be the motive. Nourishing your network should never rank far behind.

Say you're going to Omaha or Tampa for an industry event. On your list of 100 top customers, customers #14 and #37 are there. Can you squeeze in a visit? Do you know the name of the hottest restaurant in town should lunch prove doable?

Wedge in opportunities to visit promising, though not top-of-the-list, prospects. That's often how second-tier customers morph into the first tier.

By the way, before you land at Omaha or Tampa, reach for more than that breath mint. Surf Omaha.com (with news from *The Omaha-World Herald*) or TBO.com (with stories from *The Tampa Tribune*). You'll be electrifying with the local buzz.

Chapter 72

Jaw-Dropping
Name Dropping

Robert Kiyosaki, author of *Rich Dad, Poor Dad*, hit the nail on the head when he noted: "The richest people in the world look for and build networks, everyone else looks for work."

Networks are the foundation of the New World of Business—especially of selling, more than any other business discipline.

The first rule of networking: Network in a smooth and easy manner. Forced, contrived networking shows—it won't be any fun and people will notice.

Several years ago, I attended a corporate dinner for senior executives and their guests. There must have been 150 or more people there. A bald-headed, bespectacled guy with a beard made the rounds during the pre-dinner reception. One by one, he shook hands and introduced himself to each guest.

Two-and-a-half hours later, the same scene was repeated. The same guy walked around and said "so long" to all 150. And? And, he said goodbye to each of them—99% of whom he met for the first time that evening—by name! Plus, he was 100% accurate. This memory expert's name is Benjamin Levy. I've never seen the likes of him.

You'll find his techniques in his book *Remember Every Name Every Time*. Keep three of his master principles on your front burner:

- "Our long-term memory [in our head] is, in effect, our hard-drive."
- The brain has a "constant yearning to make associations between what it already knows and what it's learning."
- And, Levy cites a Columbia University researcher who said: "'The more associations you have with something the more likely you are to remember it.'"

Apply these ideas whenever you struggle to remember anything. Most people are overcome by the seeming enormity of filing away all those little details? Wrong! It isn't the volume of information that's the problem. Social memory skills come from discipline, preparation and skillful association thinking.

Remember: What's really jaw-dropping is when you do it with effortless ease. Happen on a prospect at the supermarket that you've met only once and haven't seen in two months? Imagine the sound of their name flowing off your lips as smoothly as melted butter.

Mackay's Moral: People buy from people who remember who they are.

Quickie #25
The Spin-To-Win Habit

In sales networking, contact vitality depends on finding ways to stay in touch. For the first 25 years of my career, I would spend each Sunday night doing what I call Spin-to-Win. I'd flip through my Rolodex. I'd study all the little handwritten scribbles:

- How is the daughter of Client X doing in her first year away at college?
- How did the disk surgery fare for the wife of Client Y?
- Say, that Homecoming win must have brightened the day of Client Z, proud alumnus of Pandemonium State!

Never force this information to top billing in a phone call. Let it surface casually after you've broached a business issue. Sound contrived? If you're in sales, you better really love people. Your human concern should naturally bubble up. Whose memory doesn't need a bump or a nudge? This process just gives your tracking system reliability.

When I sold *Swim with the Sharks* to my publisher and launched my writing career, you know what was the cornerstone of my pitch? Fifty-two pounds of Rolodexes I schlepped into the meeting room in suitcases! I showed the publisher the entries and the detailed notes. I proved I was in command of the sales support network that would help launch my book.

Today Spin-to-Win is swipe and swoosh with the latest iPhone app. You build an entire library of data, and it still won't weigh more than 3.95 ounces. The Under-App, the app that makes it all happen, is one you need to implant in your head: the determination to put a fresh face on the details of the people in your sales life at the start of each and every business week.

Chapter 73

Networks Have Power Ratings

All sales networks are not created equal. Too many salespeople fail to distinguish between social acquaintances and the true, influential network they know they have.

I remember waltzing into a buyer's office, certain I had a gimme, and being told, "Just because I knew you when we were kids doesn't mean I'm going to do business with you now." Substitute "played golf," "drank beer" or "hung around together" for "knew you when we were kids," and there isn't a salesperson alive who hasn't been blown off in this same fashion.

Trade groups are happy hunting grounds for networking in all kinds of ways. If you're active in your trade club, you're in position to pick up major clues about what your competition is up to. Have a lot of the old gang from Company X dropped out recently? What's the buzz around the buffet table? Maybe Company X is on the verge of Chapter 11?

Many managers troll for executive talent at the local chapter of their industry associations. There's always a lot of gossip at these gatherings. If you're head-hunting, it's a great place to find out which frogs may be ready to jump to a new lily pad.

> **Yesterday's network is not today's network. Your social network is not your business network. Your "money" network is not your "experience" network.**

Don't assume that one network automatically flows into another.

Sure, you want to make the stretch. Any good sales rep would love to convert every relative he can trace back to Adam into a customer, and he tries to. But it isn't an automatic.

You have to lay the groundwork for network selling, the same as in any other business situation. Never presume that anyone owes you the honor of doing business with you. In this country, doing business is a privilege, not a blood debt, although a social or a family relationship certainly can ease the way. A lot of doors have been slammed in a lot of faces, including my own, of people who assumed they had a network that didn't exist.

Mackay's Moral: Don't fish for trout in a gold mine,
or pan for gold in a trout stream.

Chapter 74

Smooth the Sale?
Oil the Gate

You've got to know the gatekeeper. These are the Type B enablers of Type A-driven bosses.

To oil the gate, attend to the gatekeeper. It's usually an executive assistant or administrative aide. Sometimes it's a chief of staff. And, in the down-sized, lean-mean modern organization, it could be the telephone receptionist. Some central administrator controls the message flow in many teams. That individual may also coordinate the team calendar.

The larger the business, the bigger the role the gatekeeper will generally play. Often that includes being a crucial sounding board. Gatekeepers can control the budget. They almost always plot out the seating chart for the next dinner. Pay careful attention, therefore, to your boss' gatekeeper as much as a customer's. Many a career has shipwrecked over grousing about the boss' or key customer's gatekeeper rather than finding a way to build an effortless rapport.

An insider caution: The more harmless and low-key a gatekeeper may seem, the more power they may in fact wield. Because truly superior gatekeepers are masters of holding their own egos in check, they easily accumulate added responsibilities and decision-making power. An expert gatekeeper knows how to anticipate a boss' decision with stunning reliability. Never forget, Andrew Carnegie—one of the greatest business barons in history—first edged his way into the boardrooms of power as a $35-a-month secretary.

As every salesperson knows, the key to the sale is knowing who's got the hammer. Take time to learn a bit about the gatekeeper's hobbies, their families and their career aspirations. That makes for personally meaningful telephone small talk. While you are waiting to be connected to your main contact, make this your personal bridge to the gatekeeper.

Over time, if you build a trust bond, the gatekeeper will share valuable information about the climate and timing of your message. Is it likely to be well received or even considered on that helter-skelter, crisis-driven morning? When does your customer or prospect check e-mails? How should a message be formatted for best consideration?

Learn whether the gatekeeper is automatically copied on all of the boss' e-mails, preferably finding that out from the boss herself or himself. This is crucial info on several scores. First, when you talk with the gatekeeper you can assume that he or she is automatically in the know rather than double-briefing the aide on stuff they already know. Second, automatic e-mail copying is usually a tip-off the gatekeeper is a pivotal player in pre-making administrative decisions.

At MackayMitchell Envelope, we have 3,000 accounts. For each of them, there's no difference between the buyer and the gatekeeper when it comes to amenities. They get the same treatment, the same gifts, whatever.

Many times I've cultivated Donald Trump's assistant or Larry King's assistant or even the assistant to a key purchasing agent with some magic words: Gladys . . . or Karen . . . or whomever, "I prefer to work with you directly" than with "The Donald" or "The King."

Don't be satisfied with knowing just the A-team. Learn who the *gatekeeper's* backup is. This pinch-hitter absorbs the workflow and often the phone calls. And, remember to factor the Law of Large Numbers. Attrition applies to gatekeepers just like everyone else. Never forget that gatekeepers are promoted, fired, transferred, job hop out of companies and even die. The backup often ascends to fill the vacancy.

Mackay's Moral: The bigger the sale—nearly always—the more important the gate.

Quickie #26
NETWORKING NUANCES

Networking isn't just about handshakes. Ace networkers learn to master the navigation and the niceties that earn networkers acceptance, respect and authority. Here are four road-tested tips:

1. ***Use a light touch when thrust into the spotlight.*** Let's say you suddenly become very visible in an outside organization. Your new-found prominence will be instantly suspect and perhaps be more off-putting than advantageous. Be helpful but modest. Do your best to defer recognition to long-term leaders, ready to praise their accomplishments in giving the organization a footing.

2. ***Create timelines for your networking goals.*** Be patient. Understand that it may take 1–2 years to position yourself in a network in a credible way. Always plan the supporting network routes to business objectives far ahead. Is the CEO an opera buff or dedicated to funding a dialysis center? Are you building a network path to mesh with those passions?

3. ***Don't stall answers.*** When you acquire a serious network presence, you'll be asked for favors in no time. Don't be slow to answer calls . . . even if you can't promise your contact much help. Networks telegraph who the fast responders and who the slowpokes are. The biggest mistake you can make is not to answer a viable network member who is reaching out to you.

4. ***Act confidently and take meaningful risks.*** In networking, as in anything else, the wise person isn't the one who makes the fewest mistakes. It's the one who learns the most from them.

TICK TOCK

Chapter 75

Beat the Clock!

Management sage Peter Drucker maintained: "Until we can manage time, we can manage nothing else."

Time. We save it. We shave it. But we can't store it, speed it up or slow it down. It's the same for all of us.

We all start out in life with one thing in common—the same number of minutes and hours in each day. That remains constant whether we live 50 years or 100 years. So why is it that some people accomplish so much, and others very little? Because so few of us have learned to beat the clock.

For a salesperson, time isn't next to money in the asset column. It *is* money. That said, the majority of salespeople try to manage time in unforgivably short-sighted ways.

I learned time-management skills as a kid following my Associated Press–correspondent father around. He lived by deadlines. And aphorisms. "We've got as much time to spend every day as any Rockefeller," Jack Mackay would say. Time was his bread and butter. Or, as he put it: "Miss a deadline, miss a headline."

Time mattered to my dad as much on his days off. Maybe even more, as far as I was concerned. We would fish for largemouth bass and bluegills on Lake Harriet, smack dab in the center of Minneapolis.

Dad would say to his 10-year-old fishing partner: "Be at the dock at 2 p.m." There was no built-in fudge factor. What happened if you got there at 2:01? You were holding your fishing pole in one hand and waving bon voyage with the other. Tough love, kid . . . but it worked.

My first job after I graduated from college was with Brown & Bigelow. They made advertising and promotional novelties, like calendars and playing cards. I was in the executive training program. That meant: I pushed a broom in the factory. A realization dawned on me there. My future at B&B didn't extend far beyond the handle of that broom.

After I landed my first sales position, I asked my dad for some career advice.

"What do you want to accomplish?" he asked.

My dream was to make twice as much money as my fellow envelope salespeople. In their first year, the best had raked in $2,500.

"How many sales calls are you going to make?" Dad asked.

I scratched my head. My peers made about five calls a day. I didn't see any reason why I couldn't match them call for call. "No good," my dad said. "Do what they do and you'll make what they make. The answer's easy. Figure out how you can make ten calls a day and your income will double."

That's what I did, and it worked. In no time, I left $2,500 in the dust. How? For one thing, I learned not everyone's clock ticks to the same drumbeat.

So we did the math. We put together a game plan. It turned out to be a life plan. Everything hinged on how I would beat the clock.

I poked around and learned that 9 to 5 didn't have to be 9 to 5. It didn't matter how my clock ticked. What mattered was how my prospects' clocks ticked:

- Some buyers came in at 6 a.m.
- Some worked until 7 p.m.
- Some came in Saturday mornings.

That boiled down to an edge, if I chose to use it:

- Three hours every morning
- Two hours every afternoon
- And four hours on Saturday

This was invaluable competition-free time.

Naturally, these time slots turned out to be my most productive opportunities. They weren't the so-called normal hours when all the cookie-cutter-type salespeople were banging into each other. I called these time slots the "Golden Hours."

So, first, I had changed the playing-field clock. Then I changed my contact tactics. Cold calls were out. I called ahead to make sure the buyer was in. I made fixed appointments. Sounds basic, but the message had subtle clout: It said my product was special. It was as special as the working hours of my customers.

- First I timed my calls to match maximum customer availability.
- Then I spent time studying receptivity, not just presence.
- Was it before or after vacations?
- How much of a disruption—or sometimes an incentive—were pending quarterly meetings?
- Gradually my plans become more and more customer-centered. For example, how could I package business options and service features so that I saved or safeguarded the customer's time?

These details didn't just help me manage my own schedule more efficiently. They helped guarantee that I was up to bat when the prospects were greatest for a maximum payoff.

Mackay's Moral: The right time zone for a salesperson is always the customer's.

Quickie #27
CRUNCH TIME

We constantly watch athletes square off under "crunch time" pressure—from the bottom of the ninth, to the 2-minute drill or sudden-death overtime. There's a crunch time in sales, too. I was talking with a top-notch sales pro the other day, and he told me: "It doesn't take Zig Ziglar to write up an order that falls into your lap. I do everything pretty much the same as everyone else 99 percent of the time. I also get pretty much the same results. What I do in the other five minutes is what determines which college I can afford for our kids."

Crunch time is also "star time": Star time generally appears from nowhere. Some of it is predictable. It pays to know when your "World Series days" are going to arise each year. Former Yankee star slugger Reggie Jackson was the epitome of a crunch time star. He shone in so many World Series contests he earned the moniker Mr. October.

Many people refuel their batteries after the Big Game. Other people do better if they're rested and loose *before* crunch time. Get to know your performance chemistry. Then shuffle your calendar as best you can to match your peak performance needs. Don't fall victim to the fallacy of everyday thinking. Each day is *not* like every other. Some are more important than others. Stockpile your energy and focus on the money games.

Chapter 76

The Raja Rules

Several years ago, I learned about a young sales hotshot when I spoke to the ADT Authorized Dealers in Boca Raton. ADT, as you know, is the largest electronic security services company in North America. I try to do my homework prior to my speeches at Fortune 1000 companies. Part of my due diligence for this talk was debriefing a half dozen ADT dealers. They all sang the praises of a star ace sales rep whom I refer to by his first name—Raja.

Raja works in the Bay Area of California. He is what is known in the industry as a doorknocker. He canvases neighborhoods and goes door-to-door, much like many of the great old sales companies used to do—Encyclopaedia Britannica, Fuller Brush, Kirby Vacuums, etc.

Advertising legend David Ogilvy started out selling cooking stoves door-to-door. That's where he learned the mechanics of constructing sales appeals on the fly. I still believe door-to-door selling is one of the most effective means of reaching the public. Just ask any politician.

Selling door-to-door stacks up as an unbeatable tutorial in overcoming rejection. It can also be a brutal way to make a living. In that business, you better know how to manage time. Otherwise, you die a thousand deaths. Here are the highlights of Raja's game plan:

- **Raja is a self-starter/hungry fighter.** Raja works six days a week, sometimes seven. He says the biggest mistake people make is they don't call on enough homes or enough customers. What is it that a tiger like Raja doesn't have? That's right: an off switch.

- **Raja sets measurable goals.** He sets monthly goals broken down into weekly and daily goals. He focuses on each day because, once that day is gone, you can't recover it. His daily goal is to sell six security systems.

- **Raja translates his goals into actionable plans.** Raja does the numbers. He sells an average of 125 systems a month. To reach that level, he knows he has to make 160 presentations a month, since he closes 80–85 percent of his presentations. WOW! And he achieves this only getting into 10 percent of the homes he calls on. He regularly goes back to the same areas over and over because his first trips might just have raised awareness.

- **Raja motivates himself with tangible short- and long-term incentives.** Raja sets weekly, monthly and yearly goals and rewards himself when he reaches each goal. For example, one year he actually achieved his stretchy annual goal. He treated himself with the keys to a shiny new Mercedes.

- **Raja fishes smart.** He budgets and dedicates time to intelligent networking. Bass, as I am fond of saying, are where you find them. Raja knows that it takes time to figure out where the catch is. But once you do, the payoff can be tremendous. He's even doing some networking with property insurance agents. They're logical and credible recommenders. The agent discusses how security systems lead to reduced homeowner insurance rates. In the same breath, they mention Raja as the go-to guy.

- **Raja maximizes referrals.** He dedicates time to the systematic building of a referral business. Raja calls all his homeowners after installation of their security systems. First priority: He calls to make sure they are happy customers. If there are problems, he takes care of the situation. Once that's done, he asks for possible referrals. When I last checked, referrals amounted to 10–15 percent of his sales.

What if I were hearing about Raja today? I'm sure I would learn one other thing Raja is doing to maximize his time investment. In fact, I'd be astonished if he isn't doing it. Sure, you guessed it: Using the Internet to pre-qualify sales prospects.

Mackay's Moral: A genuine self-starter is custom-wired for ignition.

Quickie #28
In Sales, Being Late Will Be Your Own Funeral

Diana DeLonzor wrote a book titled *Never Be Late Again: 7 Cures for the Punctually Challenged*. In an article in *HR Magazine*, she canvassed human resource management "and found that 73 percent reported tardiness to be growing worse."

What motivates people to be late? Two of the reasons she offers are:

- "Some people are drawn to the adrenaline rush of that last-minute sprint to the finish line . . .
- Others receive an ego boost from over-scheduling and filling each moment with an activity."

Among DeLonzor's solutions: "Relearn to tell time. Most late people engage in 'magical thinking,' consistently underestimating the time necessary to accomplish everyday tasks.

"Magical thinking is the unshakable belief that you can drive the ten miles to work in seven minutes flat, even if day after day you fail to do so. If once five years ago you actually did make it in seven minutes, from that day forward, *seven minutes* is cemented in your mind."

You have to look life straight in the eye. De-mystify your world. Can you really afford to believe magic is for real? Not when time is concerned.

Chapter 77

Steve's Sad Bite Out of Apple

The late Steve Jobs, Apple's legendary creative powerhouse, paid the ultimate price for procrastination. Here's the technical ace of our times—the pacesetter of innovation. A mere look from him could wither a deadline at Apple HQ like a hot knife melts butter. But as to the Wizard of Cupertino's own health, here are some citations gleaned from Walter Isaacson's definitive biography *Steve Jobs*:

- Steve Jobs "kept to a strict vegan diet, with large quantities of fresh carrot and fruit juices. To that regimen he added acupuncture, a variety of herbal remedies, and occasionally a few other treatments he found on the Internet or by consulting people around the country."
- Medical authorities battled with him and warned him he was toying with a serious threat—delaying appropriate treatment. "Even the diet doctor Dean Ornish, a pioneer in alternative and nutritional methods of treating diseases, took a long walk with Jobs and insisted that sometimes traditional methods were the right option. 'You really need surgery,' Ornish told him. Jobs's obstinacy lasted for nine months after his October 2003 diagnosis."
- Still, Jobs was "one of the first twenty people in the world to have all of the genes of his cancer tumor as well as of his normal DNA sequenced. It was a process that, at the time, cost more than

$100,000." Talk about gathering data, but failing to add up the evidence soon enough.

- Former Intel CEO Andy Grove, both a mentor and a friend to Jobs, told him "he was crazy" in the way he was avoiding the problem. Grove had himself recovered from prostate cancer. And, as a fellow prostate cancer survivor myself, I would have emphatically delivered Jobs the same verdict.

The irony is inescapable: Apple invents the iPhone with its Reminder feature. And Steve Jobs *still* missed the most important wake-up call in his life!

Mackay's Moral: Despite one's best efforts, you will never be late to your own funeral.

Chapter 78

Don't Be a Time Bomb

A reader once sent me a Procrastinator's Creed—I have no idea who originated it. The Creed's most memorable tenets include:

- "I believe that if anything is worth doing right now, it would have been done already."
- "I shall never move quickly, except to avoid more work or to find excuses."
- "If at first I don't succeed, there is always next year."
- "I shall always decide not to decide, unless of course I decide to change my mind."
- "I shall never put off until tomorrow what I can forget about forever."

Old Ben Franklin had his two cents on procrastination as well: "One today is worth two tomorrows; never leave that till tomorrow which you can do today."

Procrastination is a pathology. There *are* cures for it:

- **Procrastination Tip #1: Go "public" with your commitment to do whatever you want to do.** I put pressure on myself. If I tell my friends, family and business associates about something that I'm going to do, then I'd better do it. I love salespeople who brag to cohorts, family, friends and the gang at the bowling alley. I love it when they boast they're going to be #1 or #2 on their sales team this coming year. Of course, not everyone will. But I find that the people who are #1 or #2 probably boasted they would be.

- **Procrastination Tip #2: Create a time-and-action calendar.** I've got a little contract with myself. I have a time-and-action calendar for everything that I do and accomplish. I'm kind of a nanosecond guy. I learned it from my deadline-focused news-paperman dad.

- **Procrastination Tip #3: Penalize your pocketbook.** Dick Bolen, my Florida realtor, has a cell phone message that says: "Today is _____ (*insert day, date and time*). If you leave your name and number you will be called back today. I guarantee I will call you back today and if I fail to do so, I will make a $100 contribution to your favorite charity . . . as long as it's not you."

- **Procrastination Tip #4: Keystroke it into memory or write it down.** A lot of us procrastinate because we forget. Take those things that you are procrastinating about and write them down and force yourself to do them. When I really need to do something, I put little reminders everywhere. I put a note on the floor so when I get up in the morning, I have to walk over it. I put a Post-it™ note on the mirror where I shave. I also put notes on the refrigerator, in my car, on my phone and so on. All this helps me stay focused and on track.

Of course, my methods are very old school. What if we all had smart-phones with the iPhone "Reminder" feature 20 years ago? I'll tell you this. 3M wouldn't be selling an estimated 6 billion-plus Post-it™ notes a year.

Procrastination is a sucker's game. And, do you know the vicious way pro-crastination saves the most labor? It ends up costing people their jobs.

Mackay's Moral: Contrary to popular belief, today's greatest labor-saving invention is NOT tomorrow.

Quickie #29
Dragging Out Bad News Can Pull You Under

Disciplined, routine scheduling is one of the best ways to lick procrastination. Nothing is easier to postpone than being the bearer of bad news. Make your very own "most-hated" list. Make it a practice to do at least one early in the day . . . every day. Here's a list of 11 of the most unpleasant customer phone calls facing a typical envelope (or any sort of) salesperson:

- "The price of raw materials has gone up."
- "The shipment won't be on time."
- "Our sales rep—the one who spilled cappuccino on your lap a year ago—is back on your account."
- "We did what you asked, but it cost an arm and a leg in overtime."
- "I can't get you the tickets you wanted for the big game."
- "All the original documents and artwork you sent to us were lost."
- "We can't supply you because the products you want aren't profitable for us to make."
- "We can no longer provide you with the products you want because we are getting out of those business lines altogether."
- "Your account is more than 90 days overdue."
- "We need further references for your credit check."
- "Our sales rep—the one you love—is going to a competitor."

Making these unpleasant calls tells your customer you are part of the solution.

EXCEL

Chapter 79

Strive for Excellence

A friend sent me an amusing story about working for the "Average Company," which she'd read in *Simple Tools* and thought was worth passing on. Now I'm doing you the same favor, because if you are getting bored with striving for excellence or settling for just doing a pretty good job, you may want to apply for a job there.

At the Average Company, the corporate vision is: "To be no worse than any other company." The value statement: "The greatest labor-saving device of all is tomorrow." It gets better. The corporate motto: "You don't have to be really good to get by." And the sales goal: "To match last year's sales goals, if it works out." My favorite is the management philosophy: "To not make a decision is to make a decision." I'm betting you've encountered that situation a few times.

The law of averages tells us that, eventually, everything evens out. You have a few good years, you'll probably have a bad year here and there. Most companies, if well managed, can weather the storm and come back strong and healthy. Those that don't survive probably just got a little lucky in the good years.

If you work for the Average Company, you know that sometimes things work out better than others. You try, but occasionally circumstances are out of your control . . . or are they? I'm of the opinion that you make your own luck.

The harder I work, the luckier I get. —Dave Thomas, founder of Wendy's

I study companies with reputations for excellence—I want to know what core values, corporate culture and philosophy underpin them. One that stands out is Chubb, the insurance giant. Chubb gets rave reviews from friends of mine who are independent insurance agents and brokers selling its products. Every day policyholders sing its praises and recommend Chubb to others. CEOs extol the service they receive with Chubb's corporate policies.

Chubb's commitment to integrity, promptness, courtesy and empathy has come a long way. What began in 1882 as a small marine underwriter is today an international insurance titan with assets of $50 billion. Chubb is known for its low employee turnover. Its employees tend to stay with the company for years, often for their entire careers. That's a remarkable feat, considering Chubb has more than 10,400 employees in 120 offices in 29 countries. It has a Quarter Century Club for employees, and it's crowded.

Chubb's corporate recruiting philosophy is to find and retain the best and the brightest. The company preaches personal accountability to all employees, no matter where they rank in the organization, and it prides itself on its high level of employee compensation. It also constantly, thoroughly monitors the performance of the independent agents and brokers who sell its products.

Chubb instills in all its employees and independent agents and brokers the core belief that insurance is more than a policy. Since its earliest years, Chubb has underscored the importance of providing superior service at all times. The company is legendary for the speed with which it processes and pays valid claims.

All Chubb people have the company's culture impressed on them. They are trained to embrace innovation and to value risk-taking. They are constantly reminded that each and every contact with a customer could be the last if their service does not exceed the customer's expectations. Chubb's goal is not to be the biggest insurance company in the world. Its greatest emphasis is on striving always to be the best at what it does. It wants to be the pre-eminent specialty global property and casualty insurer.

Nobody will ever confuse Chubb with the Average Company.

Mackay's Moral: The largest room in the world is the room for improvement.

Quickie #30
Big Cats: Rarely in the Bag

Oil magnate John D. Rockefeller once opined, "I do not think there is any other quality so essential to success of any kind as the quality of perseverance. It overcomes almost everything, even nature."

I'll never forget watching a broadcast of *The David Susskind Show* some years ago. He had three guests who were self-made millionaires, in their mid-30s. Each had averaged being in a dozen different businesses before hitting it big.

History abounds with such tales of perseverance. Theodore Geisel died in 1991 at the age of 87. Before he died, he wrote 47 books that have sold more than 100 million copies in 18 languages. What most people don't know about Dr. *Cat-in-the-Hat* Seuss is that he didn't write his first book until he was 33 and it was rejected by 28 publishers before Vanguard Press picked it up.

The line between failure and success is so fine that we scarcely know when we pass it—so fine that we are often on the line itself and do not know it. How many people have thrown up their hands at a time when a little more effort, a little more patience would have achieved success?

Chapter 80

Sell Yourself into
Your Dream Job

Several years ago, a longtime friend from California called from out of the blue and asked me if I would advise him on getting his dream job, for which he was applying and thought he was a viable candidate. The post was the athletic directorship at a medium-sized university that wanted to take its athletic program to the next level. The bad news was they were interviewing six people for the spot!

Within 60 minutes I gave him the game plan, assuring him that if he followed through on these ideas, he would automatically leapfrog over the competition. Worst-case scenario, it would be a photo finish. Here's what I urged him to do:

- Write up a 3–5-year business plan with strategies and tactics describing how he intended to implement the plan.
- Go back and interview the school's last five athletic directors, or however many were still alive. Ask them what they would do differently if they had it to do all over again.
- Lay out a fund-raising campaign, because most athletic programs are financially under siege.
- Get a list of the search committee members and Google each of them, adding to the research he'd done about his own personal network.

- Travel incognito to the university. Walk the campus and talk to students about what they were looking for in their athletic director.
- Discreetly contact the conference commissioner and inhale any feedback he could get.
- Describe substantively how he intended to handle the media, as the prior athletic director's losing program had been unsuccessful in this area.
- Appraise the assistant athletic director. If he intended to replace him or her, tell the search committee whom he planned to hire.
- Assemble a stable of current well-known or successful athletic directors who could offer advice when he needed it. Let the search committee members know their names and how well connected they were in this circle, as well as in the professional network he had developed over the years.

Of course, my friend got the job, and it was the start of a phenomenal career. Each successive step was built on doing the same sort of preparation that had landed him this opening. And doing the preparation better and better each time.

The point of all the preparation is this: If you really want a job, there is no such thing as a cold call. If you do your homework, you should be able to anticipate every tough interview question thrown at you. If you want to convince people you are the perfect fit for a particular job, you have to persuade them you know just what it takes to get the job done.

Mackay's Moral: You'll never pass the test without doing the homework.

"*Today's lesson is about targets of opportunity.*"

Chapter 81

Fall in Love with Your Job

My best friend on the East Coast is sporting goods maven Mitchell Modell, who owns more than 150 stores in the Northeast. Virtually everyone in New York is familiar with the slogan "Gotta go to Mo's." Mitchell knows sports inside out and has learned that networking is the most challenging "contact sport" of all. First he did it on a Rolodex. Then on a BlackBerry. Now he does it on an iPad. He's like me—afraid to go to sleep at night, afraid of what he might miss while he's out. In short, Mitchell loves his job. His tombstone will probably read, "He couldn't sleep fast enough."

But surveys show that there are countless Americans who hate their jobs. They dread going to work. Sunday nights some become ill because they have to go back to the grind the next day. I feel for these people, and I wish I had some magic formula for them.

If you can't switch jobs, switch attitudes.

Next to an unhappy marriage, there is no more miserable human condition than being unhappy in your job. Fifty percent of all marriages fail, but how many of us bail out from our jobs because the boss is driving us nuts or the company cafeteria serves lousy coffee?

A few years ago, I would have just said, "Quit." But in today's wonderful world of downsizing, you can't just walk out the door and down the street to your next position. Kids in college, a huge mortgage and piles of credit card debt chain more people to their desks than Planters has peanuts or Intel has chips.

It isn't just lower-level employees who have the problem. I've known many executives whose ulcers have acted up every time they left for the office.

Pauline was in senior management with a large East Coast company. She had all the trappings: the big house, the fancy cars, the right club memberships. But the pressure to perform, to top last year's numbers, and then last quarter's numbers, and then last month's numbers—month after month—got to be more than she could take. She never lost her determination to hang in there. But she lost her health. Pauline mistook her job for her life, and ended up losing both.

If you're stuck in a job that you hate and you can't bring yourself to quit, the only solution is to try to change your mental attitude. It can't all be intolerable. Start by thinking of the part you find least objectionable, and concentrate on doing a bang-up job on those duties. Try to become an expert at it. Make such a superior effort that it will be noticed; if you do, your shortcomings in other areas will tend to be overlooked.

Maybe you're a little weak on the paperwork. But customers love you. You recognize their voices on the phone without their having to identify themselves. You go the extra mile to see that their requests, particularly their most unreasonable ones, are dealt with in a prompt, respectful fashion.

Okay, you're a little weak on customer relations, but hey—no one has better paperwork. Every report is on time and letter perfect. What kind of shape would the records be in if it weren't for you?

Play mental games with yourself. Tell yourself how lucky you are to have a job. Remind yourself that in a downsizing environment, a person who hates his job—and lets it show—is not likely to be the person the company goes out of its way to keep.

Mental attitudes turn losing situations into winning ones in the office or at the plant the same way they do on the athletic field. One of my running pals, Dennis Jabs, told me that he motivated himself to jog two miles every day by telling himself that if he didn't feel right at any point in his run, he would quit and walk the rest of the way.

One day, at the half-mile mark, he felt a little uncomfortable, so he stopped running. "Harvey, for about two weeks, every time I got to that half-mile spot, my mind told me to quit, I'd done enough to get by. And some days I did. But on those days I didn't quit, I felt a tremendous sense of accomplishment, like I had done something for myself that I really hadn't expected to be able to do—hadn't even wanted to do—but had achieved because I knew I could do it if I set my mind to it."

If you have hated a job for 10 years, don't expect to talk yourself into loving it overnight. There are going to be times you quit at the half-mile mark, but at least you know you can do it. If you do, and do a good job at it, no matter how much you dislike it, you'll have a feeling of accomplishment.

Mackay's Moral: A job without trials and tribulations
isn't much of a job at all.

Quickie #31
The Principal of It All

Things are not necessarily as we always perceive them to be.

Example: A mother is in the kitchen. She hollers upstairs to her son, who is still in bed. "You are late for school. Get down here right now."

The son hollers back, "I don't want to go to school. The kids don't like me. The teachers don't like me. Everyone talks behind my back. I'm not going to school."

The mother rushes upstairs, opens the bedroom door, points to her son and says, "You get out of bed this very minute. You are going to school for two reasons:

1. You are 41 years old.
2. You're the principal of the school."

Chapter 82

Be Honest

If you have integrity, nothing else matters. If you don't have integrity, nothing else matters.

That pretty much sums up ethics.

As management guru Peter Drucker said: "As to 'ethical problems' in business, I have made myself tremendously unpopular by saying, again and again, that there is no such thing as 'business ethics.' There is only ethics."

Ethics are scrutinized more today than in any previous era. That might be hard for some to believe in light of all the ethical issues we see in the news, such as corporate malfeasance. We are demanding more and higher ethical standards than in the past, and ethical breaches become front-page news. Cheating, under-the-table deals and hoping no one will notice are dangerous practices in the 21st century. The make-money-at-all-costs mentality of the '80s and '90s is now viewed as greedy, excessive and just plain wrong.

Many companies are going beyond the usual degree of ethics. For example, Raytheon has a director of ethics compliance. All wrongdoings, difficult personnel issues and ethical quandaries are reported to the same person. Honeywell also has a corporate director of ethics, whose job is to try to guide employees in what's right and wrong. Companies can't mandate morals, but they can surely ask employees to bring their ethics to work with them.

Time and again, the ethics of a company are judged by its sales force and sales practices.

Many of us may encounter ethical dilemmas in the workplace, whether it's swiping office supplies or witnessing a coworker's questionable actions. To guide you to better ethical decisions, ask yourself these questions:

- **Is it legal?** This is a given, but you'd be surprised how many people don't know local, state and federal laws. Knowing what's right doesn't mean much unless you *do* what's right.
- **How will it make you feel about yourself?** Ask yourself how you will regard yourself if you act or don't act in a given situation. Asked about ethics, Abraham Lincoln once quoted an old man he'd heard speak at a church meeting in Indiana: "When I do good, I feel good. And when I do bad, I feel bad."
- **How do others feel about it?** I have a kitchen cabinet of people whom I can talk to and bounce ideas off. Two heads are better than one, and three heads are better than two. Seek out trusted friends and coworkers. Get their opinions on a situation. You want to see all sides.
- **How would you feel if your actions were made public?** No one ever wants to see his or her name linked to anything bad. Conscience is like a baby. It has to go to sleep before you can. If you don't want coworkers, family or friends to know about something, then it's a sure bet the action is questionable.
- **Does the behavior make sense? Will it hurt others?** If you're worried about getting caught, it doesn't pass the smell test.
- **Is it fair?** Ethical decisions ensure that everyone's best interests are protected. When in doubt, don't.
- **Will people in authority approve?** What would your supervisor say? Get a manager's opinion. We have an open-door policy at MackayMitchell Envelope Company for employees to discuss anything with managers.
- **How would you feel if someone did the same thing to you?** The Golden Rule is always an appropriate standard.
- **Will something negative happen if you don't make a decision?** Sometimes not taking action can result in harm to others.

———

I'm reminded of Hall of Fame golfer Bobby Jones at the 1925 U.S. Open, where he insisted on penalizing himself a stroke when his ball moved slightly in the rough as the blade of his iron touched the turf. No one else could possibly have seen the ball move. The penalty dropped Jones into a tie with Willie MacFarlane, who went on to win the play-off.

Golfer Tom Kite did the same thing 53 years later, in 1978. The self-imposed penalty caused him to lose the Hall of Fame Classic at Pinehurst by one stroke. Reporters asked both men why they'd taken the penalties. And both said essentially the same thing: "There's only one way to play the game."

When ethical questions hit close to home, the same criteria apply.

A mother was invited for dinner at her son Brian's apartment. During the course of the meal, Brian's mother couldn't help but notice how beautiful Brian's roommate, Jennifer, was.

Brian's mom had long suspected a relationship between Brian and Jennifer. Over the course of the evening, while watching the two interact, she started to wonder if there was more between them than met the eye.

Reading his mom's thoughts, Brian volunteered, "I know what you must be thinking, but I assure you Jennifer and I are just roommates."

About a week later, Jennifer came to Brian, saying, "Ever since your mother came to dinner, I've been unable to find the beautiful silver gravy ladle. You don't suppose she took it, do you?"

"Well, I doubt it," Brian said, "but I'll send her an e-mail just to be sure."

So he wrote: "Dear Mom: I'm not saying that you 'did' take the gravy ladle from the house, and I'm not saying that you 'did not' take the gravy ladle. But the fact remains that one has been missing ever since you were here for dinner. Love, Brian."

Several days later, Brian received an e-mail back from his mother: "Dear Son: I'm not saying that you 'do' sleep with Jennifer, and I'm not saying that you 'do not' sleep with Jennifer. But the fact remains that if Jennifer had been sleeping in her own bed, she would have found the ladle by now. Love, Mom."

Mackay's Moral: Honesty is the best policy, but sometimes it has a high premium.

"You're kidding. I thought it was Friday."

Quickie #32
Outfit Your Mind

Shined shoes and a crisp collar still transmit a high-voltage impression when you're applying for a sales job. But it's what's above the collar that counts most of all. The most important thing you need to dress for any sales job interview is your mind. Learn everything you can about the company and its immediate needs. Craft your conversation as carefully as you press your suit.

- **Talk their talk.** What messages has the company CEO emphasized in recent articles, shareholder reports or public speeches? In a natural way, fold some key terminology and concepts into your conversation.
- **Offer a lifeline of hope to an ailing business or market region.** Do you have a workable plan to rejuvenate the soft spot? What can you reliably promise to achieve in your first three months? Companies love salespeople who can make key contributions quickly.
- **Point to your successes in team selling initiatives.** In bigger firms, sales pitches are often shouldered by groups. Show you know how to tap experts in forging a complicated deal. Spotlight your ability to support the success of others in a low-key way. Today's leaner organizations prize team play as never before.
- **Showcase your enthusiasm.** Concentrate on a list of 5–10 "sparkle points" before the interview. Ready your mind to return to these topics if the conversation wanes. They could be key buzzwords in the company's vocabulary or descriptions of a new product line. As a salesperson, you will be judged by your ability to keep a stalled conversation moving along briskly.
- **Close with gusto.** Follow up the interview with an immediate thank-you. Reaffirm your enthusiasm and stress your energetic readiness.

Chapter 83

Make Character
Your Best Characteristic

When somebody says "sales character," what usually pops into mind? Sadly, it's often been the image of a guy with a loud tie in a louder sportcoat with the loudest glad-handing style at a wine and cheese gathering. The image may linger in Hollywood, but gradually the old stereotype is vanishing from our daily experiences.

Sales character is taking on a whole new meaning. The accent is on *character*—doing the right thing in selling. As in: fair practices, stringent quality control and delivering what and when you promise.

Character is a nuclear reactor–sized hot button, and with good reason. Look at every recent national election, and most local ones too. We start out with fundamentally good candidates hitting the campaign trail. Suddenly all these seemingly solid folks become the targets of character assassination 24 hours a day, 7 days a week. The vitriol never ceases. The more vigorously they defend themselves, the more fiercely their opponents attack. Year after year, it feels like we're swimming in a moral meltdown. How do we switch off the friction? By turning the spotlight back on actions, not words.

The business world can be as cutthroat as any political slugfest. When you turn off the lights at the end of the day, you may have made or lost money, you may have won or lost customers, you may have made good or bad decisions. But if you have come through the day with your character intact, you haven't lost anything that can't be regained. Once you compromise your

316

character, however, that's the beginning of the end. And you will always come home a loser.

Coach Lou Holtz describes character this way: "The answers to three questions will determine your success or failure:

1. Can people trust me to do my best?
2. Am I committed to the task at hand?
3. Do I care about other people and show it?

"If the answers to these questions are yes," Lou says, "there is no way you can fail."

Over the years I've learned some very important lessons about character. Let me share a few and give you a jump start:

- **Never compromise character because of your competition.** Occasionally you will discover that your biggest competitor has a better product or a better price or a better salesperson. That should spur you to positive action! Improve your product. Find a responsible way to trim the cost. Hire well. Make your company better.
- **Character follows you wherever you go.** You cannot escape and start over unless you are in the witness protection program, which wouldn't be my first choice. It's getting harder and harder to hide from your past. Don't believe me? Google yourself. Think before you do something silly and have it end up on the Internet. In November 2006, Hollywood celebrity Danny DeVito appeared on ABC's talk show *The View*. He didn't look very sober, and indeed admitted on the air, "I knew it was the last seven limoncellos that was going to get me." In no time, the Web was abuzz with the incident.
- **Building character is difficult, but rebuilding it is even harder.** The inner self usually knows what's right, so you would be wise to listen carefully to the little voices that are telling you to watch yourself. And if you refuse to rely on your own instincts, ask a

trusted friend. Make sure it's someone who will be brutally honest with you.

- **Don't blame your upbringing for your mistakes.** Look around. Do you really believe for one minute that all these people who seem to make good decisions were raised with the Brady Bunch? Of course not. They've accepted that they're adults, take responsibility for their behavior and have learned to bounce back from a few hard knocks.

- **Get used to doing the right thing.** Once it becomes a habit, it's a no-brainer. You'll know you have figured it out when people come to you for advice about the right course to follow.

- **Be honest with yourself.** It is just as easy to be honest as it is to be dishonest. Actually, I think it is easier, since you don't have to have a good memory . . . and you won't have to cover your tracks later. As Teddy Roosevelt said, "I care not what others think of what I do, but I care very much about what I think of what I do. That is character!"

Thomas Jefferson, our third president, put it this way: "Give up money, give up fame, give up science, give up the earth itself and all it contains, rather than do an immoral act. And never suppose, that in any possible situation, or under any circumstances, it is best for you to do a dishonorable thing. Whenever you do a thing, though it can never be known but to yourself, ask yourself how you would act were all the world looking at you, and act accordingly."

That's still good advice, even a couple of hundred years later.

Mackay's Moral: When wealth is lost, nothing is lost; when health is lost, something is lost; when character is lost, all is lost.

Chapter 84

Execution Intelligence

I'm indebted to the ace Internet marketer Alex Mandossian for bringing the idea of "execution intelligence" into my vocabulary. Execution intelligence boils down to this: the ability to convert smarts into action, pronto. Don't focus on comprehensive solutions or even elegant ones. A true business expert knows: The idea is not king. The timely solution is.

Execution intelligence is a management focus skill. It's also a high-yield time-management asset.

Execution intelligence has been at the core of Israel's ability to survive in a hostile Middle East environment. That edge is perceptively described in the book *Start-Up Nation* by Dan Senor and Saul Singer. "If most air forces are designed like a Formula One race car, the Israeli Air Force is a beat-up jeep with a lot of tools in it," says an Israeli air force pilot. "The race car is just not going to" cut it in their geographic environment.

Take the Israeli start-up company Fraud Sciences. This outfit went to PayPal, part of eBay since 2002, with a super plan to stop crooks and frauds on the Internet. The magic was that the solution was already road-tested to spot terrorists in Israel. Adaptive solutions like this score high. They re-channel existing technology into fresh applications.

The inventors didn't dream up a *new* answer. They applied a solid, proven solution to a new type of problem. The accent was on doability, not theory. The Internet has been great in giving everybody new ideas. Today everyone has access to more or less the same knowledge. The edge comes in knowing *how* to put it to work and actually pulling the switch.

A salesperson isn't usually scrapping with tough technology problems. It's amazing, though, how few salespeople really leverage what they already do well—the softer skills of customer relations. The first step to making your proven skill set work harder is knowing exactly where you shine. Take a hard look at your biggest sales successes in the past two years. Are there patterns to your wins and have you put them to work for you?

- What's the ideal amount of time, for example, for you to close a deal? We all tend to remember successes that paid off either instantly or after months of follow through. Far more important, what is the proven optimum deal time? Persistence is admirable, but you may learn that a sale that doesn't close in X months (or X minutes, depending on what you're selling) becomes a long shot. Dedicate the lion's share of your time to your most probable prospects.

- Do your most successful closes have a structure or a pattern? Study the details carefully. Do you succeed by following up your first pitch after a particular interval? Is timing contingent on customer pay or budget cycles? What setting creates the best atmosphere? Hundreds of different variables are at stake. When you pay attention to and make notes about details, patterns emerge. Awareness and application of these patterns can ratchet up your execution intelligence a game-changing notch.

- Collaboration wins ballgames. A no-hitter is a rare experience for any ball club to serve up their fans. The first one in the MLB record book dates back to 1876. The first no-hitter involving more than one pitcher happened in 1917, and there have been a total of nine combined no-hitters since. In June 2012, the Mariners racked up a 1-0 no-hitter against the Dodgers, but it took them six pitchers to do it. Facile teamwork and execution intelligence are often hand-and-glove companions.

Collaborate better within your team and be ready to join forces outside, too. In October 2012 *BusinessWeek* noted: "IBM is pursuing a target of $7 billion in cloud revenue by 2015 after such sales more than tripled last year."

The article reported on a team-up of IBM and ATT "to seek a bigger slice of the $14 billion market for cloud services." Often the execution-smart decision is to link with talent that can immediately supplement your strengths. Translation: Someone else's know-how can jumpstart your own opportunities. As I often point out, where would the Lone Ranger be without Tonto?

People spend their entire lives chasing the wrong rainbow. Execution intelligence forces you to zero in on answers that are easily actionable. Don't stall in the thinking stage. Most brilliant ideas have been thought already. The real genius is in finding a way to put them to work practically.

Mackay's Moral: As philosopher Mortimer Adler succinctly put it: "Nothing short of the doing solves the problem."

Chapter 85

Volunteers Vault Ahead

In the Army, the rule of thumb is: Never, ever volunteer. A volunteer takes a run on his own sword. Volunteers let themselves be victimized. So goes the conventional wisdom at least.

I couldn't disagree more. Smart volunteers get it right. They start with the heart. They love what they do . . . or at least they learn to love it. Never forget: Noah's Ark was built by an amateur who loved what he did. The Titanic was built by professionals.

I love sports, baseball included. In the spring of 1984, I was the point man in a nationally publicized effort to keep the Minnesota Twins in Minnesota. This was a job I volunteered for. Maybe it was the single biggest campaign of my life. Most people considered it a suicide mission.

Our job was to outflank Calvin Griffith. He owned the Twins. Griffith wanted to sell his ball club to a group of Florida businesspeople. They would have then moved the Twins to Tampa.

I helped assemble a group of influential supporters and amassed a $6 million war chest for a blitzkrieg. We held press conferences all over the state. We set up offices to distribute the tickets we were now able to buy.

Then, one day in May, I walked up to the Twins ticket booth in the Hubert H. Humphrey Metrodome. Hot after a tip, a gang of reporters were tailing me. I smiled at the young lady behind the counter and put in my order: "I'd like 15,000 tickets for tonight's game, please!"

That purchase was a game changer. Public sentiment flocked to our side.

Calvin Griffith shook in his boots. Carl Pohlad, banker and PepsiCola-bottling mogul, headed up a local consortium. They bought the team. In fact, they were able to buy it at a bargain-basement price. And we kept the Twins in Minnesota.

It took three years to quietly rebuild the team. When the '87 season began, the Las Vegas bookies' odds were still 150-to-1 against the Twins winning the World Series. Well, that year the Twins nailed the Fall Classic.

The Save-the-Twins experience taught me some of the greatest lessons of my business career:

- How to stare down a big-league cheapskate.
- How to find and tap the wisdom of an owner-mentor like Bill Veeck. My personal meetings with this legendary Chicago White Sox owner were pivotal to our campaign.
- How to martial public opinion. (After all, this was just social networking before there ever was a Twitter.)
- And, the biggest lesson of all: I didn't learn these unbeatable skills sitting in my corner office as CEO. I learned them by volunteering.

Volunteer work ranks among the best real-world sales training platforms available. If you haven't noticed, the volunteer sector is growing like gang-busters. First, why the growth in volunteerism? Government's role as the all-purpose provider of social services is evaporating. Do the math. Which level of government can even afford it? Forget about the national budget debate for a moment. Check out California. Three California cities, including Stockton and San Bernardino, filed for bankruptcy in 2012. Experts have called this "just the tip of the iceberg."

Second, why is the importance of networking soaring? We live in a world of complex relationships. More and more of the human ties that matter are forged helping people who help others. When I was chairman of the American Cancer Society for the state of Minnesota, I volunteered to travel the state for one year. We put on eight cancer informational clinics. Of course, medical professionals were with me all the time.

I can't say that sawbones are great generators of envelope sales. But I can say this: After many years, I can still pick up a phone and call any one of those fellow traveling doctors. They'll give me a "best-in-the-country" medical reference when I need one. I can also get the same medical-care ticket for anyone I need to influence and that has included customers and long-term prospects. That ticket is worth more than all the #10 envelopes in Cucamonga! Often, the gesture—reciprocity without keeping score—may materialize years later in an unexpected business deal coming your way.

Fund-raising is a great way to learn making mega-pitches. CEOs are selling from dawn to dusk. When you volunteer, you often get to rub elbows with business giants in your community and learn their sales techniques. It's the platinum-card leadership companies that drive the style of volunteer work in any community. When I've done volunteer work in the Twin Cities, who's shaped this volunteer culture? The likes of General Mills, 3M, Target, Medtronic, U.S. Bancorp and Carlson.

Why is fund-raising such a central skill in the volunteer sector? Because every volunteer and charitable group needs money. And the last job anyone wants is raising it. Everybody hates the sound of the word "no." The more prestigious the leaders, the more they hate it. They take the rejection personally, and fund-raising is a bottomless pit of rejection.

Especially in fund-raising, you don't have to close every sale to be a success. Making a few unexpected advances in a campaign will usually get appreciative notices. The passion and the fun is not unlike the NCAA Final Four March Madness. A well-orchestrated civic fund-raising campaign has the spark of a Publishers Clearing House campaign. It pays to learn and live that legend: Over 95 percent of Publishers Clearing House mailings got tossed. Those mailings closed only one out of every 25 prospects. And that far outperformed the norm. PCH set standard after standard for the sales industry.

Volunteering can put unexpected polish on a budding sales career. In more than a few cases, I've known salespeople whose volunteer work blossomed into career-changing milestones. It's one of those happy synergies in life—what you owe to your community paying off with more than you might ever expect for yourself.

Mackay's Moral: As Winston Churchill said: "We make a living by what we do, but we make a life by what we give."

Chapter 86

4th-Quarter Game Changers

Are life's record-smashing performances reserved for those sprightly early decades? Not for seasoned vets who know how to strew the seasoning.

- Colonel Harland Sanders began franchising Kentucky Fried Chicken at age 65, using $105 of his first Social Security check.
- TV journalism maven Barbara Walters was 68 in 1997 when she cocreated *The View* and sold ABC on the idea. She and Joy Behar (now 68) are the only cohosts still with the show since its inception, which was lauded as "wildly different" from the get-go for its creative slant.
- Management guru Peter Drucker wrote more than half of the 39 books to his credit when he was past the age of 65. And he was churning out riveting, fresh ideas into his 90s.
- Angela Lansbury, 85 in 2011, wowed Broadway crowds two years earlier as the clairvoyant Madame Arcati in a revival of Noël Coward's *Blithe Spirit*. Therewith Dame Angela carted off her fifth Tony in an illustrious career.
- Roy Neuberger—investor, art collector and philanthropist—made an old-fashioned killing off the 1987 market crash. He was 107 when he died on Christmas Eve 2010. In his autobiography, *So Far, So Good: The First 94 Years*, Neuberger wrote: "I am not as

good a walker as I used to be. When I was 80, I could walk very long distances . . . Three times a week [at age 94] I work out with a personal trainer . . . In 45 minutes I do 42 exercises . . . It costs $45, so it is a dollar a minute—well worth it."

Each embraced the make-it-happen mind-set of the never sidelined former First Lady Eleanor Roosevelt. Formidable "Little Nell," as her pals knew her, served on the National Advisory Committee to the Peace Corps in her 70s and even pitched Good Luck margarine on TV, donating the proceeds to charity. "I could not, at any age," she summed up her life, "be content to take my place in a corner by the fireside and simply look on."

Most of us learn to be our very best only after years of hard-tested effort. Mark Twain nailed it when he said: "The first half of my life I went to school, the second half of my life I got an education."

No one can beat an experienced and determined mind, able and willing to apply new lessons.

Mackay's Moral: It's no accident they're called your golden years.

"That's it? Salesman of the month, August '87?"

Quickie #33
Positive Energy
Is a Chain Reaction

Gordon Dean was a distinguished American lawyer and prosecutor. One of the original members of the Atomic Energy Commission, he became its chairman from 1950 to 1953. It's said that when Dean died in a plane crash in 1958, among his personal effects was an envelope with nine life lessons scribbled on the back. These lessons aren't about the law or about atomic energy. They're wisdom about his philosophy of life:

1. Never lose your capacity for enthusiasm.
2. Never lose your capacity for indignation.
3. Never judge people—don't type them too quickly. But in a pinch never first assume that a man is bad; first assume that he is good and that, at worst, he is in the gray area between bad and good.
4. Never be impressed by wealth alone or thrown by poverty.
5. If you can't be generous when it's hard to be, you won't be when it's easy.
6. The greatest builder of confidence is the ability to do something—almost anything—well.
7. When confidence comes, then strive for humility; you aren't as good as all that.
8. The way to become truly useful is to seek the best that other brains have to offer. Use them to supplement your own, and be prepared to give credit to them when they have helped.
9. The greatest tragedies in the world and personal events stem from misunderstandings. So communicate!

We are all students of life. Want to get to the head of the class? Pay attention and take notes.

Chapter 87

The Average American Thinks He Isn't

Last year, I received a call in late June from a recent college graduate I've been mentoring. She landed a job selling plumbing fixtures to assisted-living facilities. Her first assignment was to make a speech on self-esteem in front of the new sales team she had joined. She looked through my books and columns and didn't find anything specifically related to her topic.

Oh, sure, I've had a few stories on self-esteem here and there. Mostly on not getting too big a head. The line I often use is: "If you think you're indispensable, put your finger in a bowl of water and check out the hole it leaves when you pull it out."

As we talked, this freshly minted BA came up with some mind-bending questions. "How do you stay confident selling, Mr. Mackay?" she asked me. "All it would take is one or two big rejections, and I'd think all that positive attitude would melt away. You call up your sales charts on the laptop, and there's no way to run away from performance that has flatlined for a week or two. How do you hang tough?"

These questions were coming from a rookie, not a hardened vet from the bull pen. I decided it was time for a little research.

One ancient tribe of Australian Aborigines had a unique way of instilling responsibility in its young people. At a predetermined time, each young person would be solemnly entrusted with a secret piece of knowledge vital to the tribe's survival. For example, it might be the location of a hidden spring on their territory, or a secret cave that could serve as a hiding place if the tribe was suddenly attacked.

No one else in the tribe would be entrusted with that particular piece of information, and the young person would be expected to reveal it for the welfare of all when the right occasion presented itself. Imagine what a sense of importance and belonging this custom instilled in the tribe's youth. Each had a unique and important role to play in the tribe's well-being. Wouldn't it be great if we could find modern ways to emulate this ancient tribal custom?

Self-esteem gets a lot of attention in education, but it has come under scrutiny. That's because too many kids are satisfied doing an adequate job rather than their very best. We hear that we shouldn't ruin kids' self-esteem by telling them they aren't doing good enough work. But that's what builds legitimate self-esteem, knowing you are giving your all and accomplishing at your peak. Encouraging your coworkers or employees to give 110 percent isn't a negative; it's proof that you believe they are capable. That's what builds self-esteem.

When I answered my young friend's question, I made one overarching point: You can never allow yourself to retreat from the facts. Don't avoid them. Don't sugarcoat them. But don't let them erode your self-esteem either. If you do, you won't be able to change the facts. It's that simple.

Columnist Erma Bombeck gave us this guidepost for how to live your life and guard your self-esteem: "When I stand before God at the end of my life, I would hope that I would have not a single bit of talent left and could say, 'I used everything You gave me.'" I passed that advice along to my young friend.

Would you sell the product you represent to your mother . . . or to a company in which she was invested? Would you use it yourself, or recommend it to a company if your survival relied on that firm?

> **Self-esteem in the sales world starts with a product in which you are confident.**

Self-esteem is based on a positive attitude and frequent reality checks. Take pride in what you do, whether it's washing dishes or running a major company.

In sales, being able to present your product knowledgeably and with confidence in its quality is tantamount to closing the deal. Would you buy tires from a sales rep who couldn't guarantee their safety in rough conditions? Would you sell for a company that couldn't make that guarantee? I sure wouldn't waste my time or my customers' time with a shoddy product—not if I wanted to hold on to my self-esteem. You see, my customers determine my self-esteem. It's not really about what I do for me—it's what I can do for them.

Mackay's Moral: There are two kinds of people in the world: those who come into a room and say, "Here I am!" and those who come in and say, "Ah, there you are!"

Chapter 88

Use Self-Esteem to Your Advantage

The next time someone calls you an egotistical jerk, you might think that thanking them just confirms their opinion. But that's exactly what you should feel like doing. They have just provided a strong endorsement of your mental health.

Self-esteem has become a lightning rod buzzword these days as a personality flaw. That's *false* self-esteem, the result of heaping praise on people for accomplishing routine or simple tasks. The only thing worse than false self-esteem is false humility. Humility is an important virtue, and certainly one that we all should possess. But please, acting humble just to fish for compliments is a sign of raging insecurity.

Legitimately earned self-esteem comes from performing well, because you have worked so hard to reach the top. It means you have developed your natural talents to their optimal point. The kind that Will Rogers was talking about when he said, "If you done it, it ain't bragging."

> Genuinely deserved self-esteem gives you a crucial competetive edge. The higher your self-esteem is, the better you will get along with yourself and with others.

People with higher self-esteem tend to accomplish more and are more altruistic. Psychotherapist Nathaniel Branden discovered an additional benefit to having high self-esteem: "There is overwhelming evidence that the higher the level of self-esteem, the more likely one will be to treat others with respect, kindness and generosity."

What's the matter with being proud of what we have done or think we can do? When we're young, we're full of the sense that we can and should be able to do almost anything. That enthusiasm shouldn't change as we get older and more experienced. Our accomplishments should reinforce our sense of self-worth.

Anthony Greenwald, a psychologist at the University of Washington, describes what he calls the "egocentricity bias." This is the reinterpretation of events to put ourselves in a favorable light and the belief we have more control over events than we actually do. Greenwald says it is a sign of mental well-being.

Optimism may be self-delusion, a belief that our own abilities are superior to the obstacles that might overcome us. But that's exactly what's needed to perform any heavy-duty assignment. How can you be any good unless you think you can accomplish what you're not supposed to be able to accomplish?

Olympic skating star Scott Hamilton observed, "Adversity, and perseverance, and all these things can shape you. They can give you a value and a self-esteem that is priceless."

There is no better example of the power of positive self-esteem than Muhammad Ali. He called himself "The Greatest"—actually, "The Greatest of All Time." He never doubted his ability to compete at the highest level, and his record proves it.

Top performers in athletics or business are always convinced they can be heroes, even if they don't shout it from the rooftops. And it shows. In fact, baseball scouts call that look "the good face," the sense of self-confidence that radiates from winners. Recruiters often seek the same self-assured look when filling sales slots.

A little boy was talking to himself as he entered his backyard, baseball cap in place and carrying a baseball and bat. "I'm the greatest baseball player in the world," he said proudly. Then he tossed the ball in the air, swung and missed.

Undismayed, he picked up the ball, threw it into the air and said to himself again, "I'm the greatest player ever!" As the ball descended he swung at it again, and again he missed.

He paused a moment to examine the bat and ball carefully. Then once again he threw the ball into the air and said, "I'm the greatest baseball player who ever lived." As the ball came down, he gave another mighty swing and missed the ball again.

"Wow!" he exclaimed. "What a pitcher!"

Mackay's Moral: If you've got what it takes, take it to the top.

Quickie #34
Reciprocity Without Keeping Score

If we're smart, we surround ourselves with talented people . . . the most talented we can find. They are our most powerful asset.

That's why I think of this select group as our own personal brain bank. They include our friends, our mentors, our fellow workers, our industry contacts and—for salespeople—often those customers with whom we have long-term professional ties. You never know when you'll need to draw on the "accounts" you create with those oh-so-valuable resources.

With every contact—every call and every visit—and preferably near the conclusion, sincerely ask the other person what you can do to be helpful to them. Ninety-five times out of a hundred, people will thank you for asking and tell you that there's really nothing they need.

If, however, they do ask you for a favor, then your eyes should flash like the 9,500 LEDs that light up the New Year's ball in Times Square. As you learn what is being asked for, take down every detail with warmth and urgency. Fulfill the request to the best of your ability.

As you do it, and after it's done, expect nothing, *absolutely nothing*, in return. Don't shop for gratitude in your phone calls or e-mails. Do the favor because you like and respect the other person and honestly want to help.

This attitude is what I call Reciprocity Without Keeping Score. There are more than 70,000 words in this book, but none are more important than the 320 on this page.

If you manage your career and live your life in this way, two magical things will happen: Over time, people will find ways to do remarkable and unexpected things for you that make your life easier. And when the sky turns dark and you're hit by a storm in full fury, you are likely to find the most astonishing human network of support you could ever imagine.

Chapter 89

A Club to Aim For

Each year ten Americans are inducted into the prestigious Horatio Alger Association. Past honorees include three presidents—Eisenhower, Ford and Reagan—plus Colin Powell, Bob Hope, Oprah Winfrey, Chuck Yeager and leaders in a host of fields. Several years ago, I was deeply honored to be one of the inductees in a ceremony held in the chambers of our nation's Supreme Court.

This association is phenomenal. Not just for what my fellow members have done, but for what they're still doing. The Horatio Alger Association is all about education and kids. Alger, the namesake, wrote more than 100 novels, mostly rags-to-riches stories in which the heroes overcame adversity through education and the help of role models. The association is the largest private scholarship program in the United States based on need. This year it will award more than $7 million in college scholarships to nearly 1,000 young people across the nation. It is estimated that the association will have awarded more than $87 million in college scholarships between 1984 and 2012.

When I page through the Horatio Alger membership list, I'm overwhelmed by the number of people who have climbed to the top through the stepping-stone of sales, or whose selling and negotiation skills created landmark institutions.

- There's J. B. Fuqua, whose buying and selling expertise built a communications and real estate empire, and who went on to endow the Fuqua School of Business at Duke. His signature quote: "Even with goals, the difference between success and failure often comes down to courage. I had the courage to take risks."

- There's journalism legend Al Neuharth, founder of *USA Today*, who started out peddling papers, as I did. Neuharth maintains, "The sky doesn't fall when you fail. Chicken Little was wrong. The moon and stars are still there. The next time you reach for them, you're more likely to get them in your grasp."

- And there's Carl Pohlad, who started out cleaning houses and milking cows and went on to own a financial empire, a Pepsi bottling giant, and the Minnesota Twins. He lived by this principle: "Work hard and look for opportunity in every life experience."

What can we glean from all these members of such a distinguished organization? When you learn to trust your own self-worth and can sell your credibility and authority to others, you have fashioned the master key that opens the doors to the world's most exclusive clubs. Why will you be admitted? To prove you have the ingenuity to put what you've learned to work for others.

Live your life to broader goals. You'll find something magical in it. Building the biggest client list or the most profitable sales track will be boosted by dedication to a greater goal.

Mackay's Moral: If you're doing well, you should also be doing good.

Chapter 90

Sales Need Flesh and Blood

The salesperson isn't in. Instead, she is in her car or in front of her PC, surrounded by the rest of the work team: a monitor, printer, fax, beeper, phone and scanner. Just master that gleaming collection of electronic tools and let's do *bidness*.

We've been down this road before. Every time there's a new gee-whiz gizmo, we're told that we're about to redesign the Industrial Revolution.

It isn't going to happen.

The Industrial Revolution was not just about making steam do the work of horses, it was also about people moving to cities, where their coworkers and companions were other people, not barnyard animals.

Computers are today's barnyard critters. They can do hard, dumb animal work a lot more quickly than we can, but they make lousy office buddies. Salespeople may not need to go to offices to sell anybody, but they need to go to offices to *be* somebody. That's *be somebody*—not for their own sakes but for the benefit of other people.

Nobody ever went back to their car after closing The Big One and played a CD of the sales manager patting them on the back.

People react to, respond to, brag to, compete with and need other people around them. That's what motivates us. That's what watercoolers and coffee breaks and sales meetings and sales managers are for.

Let's say you've decided to buy a new builder-designed home. There are two types of builders. Builder One wears $1,000 suits and has a beautiful office. There are salespeople rushing in and out. There are plans, models, sketches and awards everywhere. The builder takes you to the site in his Lexus. He builds 50 houses a year. If you were to dig a little, you'd find he makes about $500,000 and, like many builders, has been overextended once or twice, and maybe even gone through Chapter 11.

Builder Two wears jeans. He doesn't drive you to the site, because his office is at the site. It's his construction shack. His bunker looks like it was built with Lincoln Logs, and a Lexus is surely not what this guy drives. His wheels are a clay-crusted pickup. There's only one other person working there, his wife. There are no models or fancy sketches, only blueprints. He builds eight to ten houses a year. If you were to dig a little, you'd find he makes about $500,000 and, like many builders, has been overextended once or twice, and maybe even gone through Chapter 11.

How do the financial statements of these two busy beavers measure up? The houses they build are comparably priced and constructed. They both make the same amount of money and have the same track record as business-people. The first has a higher cost per house, which he overcomes by volume, and the second makes more bucks per house by holding down the overhead.

The only significant difference is you, the customer. I would be willing to bet my last dollar that one of these two builders would be just the sort of person you would be comfortable doing business with, while the other would be a complete turnoff. And no matter which was which, you would get about the same quality house for about the same price. That's the difference selling/marketing/image/human contact makes.

You don't make sales calls to sell somebody. You make them to *be* somebody *for* someone else!

No computer can or ever will be able to duplicate the kind of impression one human being will have on you or on someone else. And, undeniably, there are also people who prefer no human contact at all, but would rather deal with something as impersonal as a computer. And that's where all the buzz is coming from lately. Well, now they've got their salesperson and we have ours.

Mackay's Moral: You can lead the market and succeed.
You can follow the market and succeed. But you can't
buck the market and succeed.

Chapter 91

Sales Success:
The Blue-Ribbon Recipe

I've asked a lot of people over the years what makes a great salesperson. There are many similar answers: passion, persistence, personality and likability, planning, accessibility, trustworthiness, strong work ethic, drive and initiative, quick learner, goal-oriented, follow-up (or, as I say, "The sale begins when the customer says yes"), good communications skills, sense of humor, humility, good timing and strength at building relationships.

Persistence is usually near the top of the list, as it is here. Consider the late Steve Jobs at Apple. Fired as CEO, he returned eleven years later to propel the firm with colossal hits like the iPod, iBook, iTunes, iPhone and iPad. South Africa's *Mail & Guardian Online* dubbed Jobs "The Ultimate Salesman."

When people ask me to name the top three skills of a salesperson, you already know my answers . . .

A good friend who owns a tool distributorship told me enthusiasm is his most important sales trait. He believes that everything you give a client should reflect enthusiasm . . . whether it's a presentation or a piece of paper. He has a mirror in his office so he can look at himself to make sure he is smiling when on the phone with clients. This also forces him to stay focused on what he's doing at all times when talking to a customer.

Showmanship is also important. A first-rate salesperson has to deliver an outstanding performance, even when the customer's mother is the competition and it seems like a lost cause.

Someone else told me that you must be able to ask for the order and close the sale. Her pet peeve is that many salespeople can pop the question, but they can't get customers to the altar.

Other traits aren't so commonplace. Some of these are related to what you do personally—traits that are often invisible to others:

- Having a DVR in your mind so you can review all interactions at the end of the day.
- The ability to think quickly, and think on your feet.
- Paying fanatical attention to detail.
- Handling stress appropriately.
- Mastering cutting-edge computer skills so you manage time to maximum efficiency.
- Flexibility, and being able to multitask.
- Doing your homework to improve your performance.
- Knowing your product line and market, including competitors.
- Being able to recognize and maximize your strengths.
- Being able to deal with rejection. You can't be afraid to fail. In many sales arenas, you get rejected 9 out of 10 times. In baseball, if you're successful 3 out of 10 times, you get a $6 million contract.

Another group of less common characteristics relates to the ability to deal with other people:

- The ability to get the answers if you don't have them on the spot.
- Adding someone to the team who complements your skills.
- The ability to become a friend to your clients.
- Taking care of the customers you have (and they'll take care of you).
- Having empathy for the client.
- Volunteering, which benefits you as well as others.
- Being able to hear what's *not* being said.
- Knowing the decision makers and inner workings of companies so you can position yourself with the person who calls the shots.

- Dealing with each customer differently, but not trying to be all things to all people.

Most of these traits could be applied to almost any business, but the last one really deserves elaboration for salespeople. You have to realize that even if you are doing everything right, your product may not be right for the customer. Think of it this way: Should you sell ice to an Eskimo, just because you can? Ethical behavior is not only highly desirable, it's central to your success.

The ideal salesperson is an ever-evolving creature. We live in an increasingly competitive and transparent world. That means you must have incredible skill and heart to excel. And your heart better be in the right place, too. Sharp-elbowed, out-for-me-and-me-alone types are sure to ring up "No Sale" on the cash register of customer opinion.

Mackay's Moral: Without the right sales skills,
something terrible happens: nothing.

Quickie #35
Why Sellers Morph into Leaders

"'I'm selling every day," General Electric CEO Jeff Immelt said in *The Globalist* in 2006. "I'm getting up and selling turbines, selling jet engines, selling MR scanners—from the time I wake up to the time I go to bed. That's what CEOs do." That's "how you teach your organization to compete."

If you want the short course of Immelt on leadership, Google the following: Immelt things leaders do. Click on the *Fast Company* website result for a ten-item list titled Things Leaders Do. One of them is a theme I especially like: "Stay disciplined and detailed." Both great leaders and superior salespeople keep tabs on the micro "things that are important." Immelt says Dell Computer founder "Michael Dell can tell you how many computers were shipped from Singapore yesterday."

Discipline, detail, and, not to forget, gumption. Stanley Marcus, for years the guiding force of that Dallas-based treasure Neiman Marcus, was one of the great retailing geniuses of all-time. Stanley had lived to the ripe age of 96 when he died in 2002. He was also a buddy of mine whom I esteemed greatly. Stanley had an impeccable eye for the future.

At the end of World War II, Stanley visited five-star General Dwight Eisenhower. This was at the supreme commander's Paris headquarters. Stanley asked Eisenhower to buy his wife Mamie's presidential inaugural gown from Neiman Marcus. This was years before Ike ran for and became president. All Ike said that day was: "If I do, I will."

You guessed it. On Inauguration Day in 1953, Neiman Marcus outfitted new First Lady Mamie Eisenhower. A dozen years later they did the same for President Johnson's wife and two daughters. The Stanley Marcus Lesson: A natural-born closer is always looking for an opening.

Chapter 92

The 7 Cs of Success

On the road to success, you may take a few detours, hit some roadblocks and arrive at a different place than you'd planned. I'm still on my journey, and I'm offering you my map for smooth sailing, traveling the Seven Cs of Success.

Clarity: 80 percent of success comes from being clear about who you are, what you believe in and what you want. But you must remain committed to what you want and make sure those around you understand what you're hoping to accomplish.

A young mathematician was commissioned during wartime as captain of a submarine. Eager to impress his crew and to stress how important it is to strictly observe all safety procedures, the young captain called them all together for a meeting. His instructions went like this:

"I have developed a simple method that you would all do well to learn. Every day, count the number of times the submarine has dived since you boarded. Add to this the number of times it has surfaced. If the sum you arrive at is not an even number—don't open the hatches."

Competence: You can't climb to the next rung on the ladder until you are excellent at what you do now.

Just remember two more things: 1) The person who knows "how" will always have a job, and 2) the person who knows "why" will always be the boss.

Constraints: 80 percent of all obstacles to success come from within. Find out what is constraining you or your company and deal with it.

The Gallup Organization conducted a survey on why quality is difficult to achieve. The greatest percentage listed: financial constraints. Often our lives and careers are shaped by the kind of surroundings we place ourselves in and the challenges we give ourselves.

Consider, for example, the farmer who won a blue ribbon at the county fair. His prize entry? A huge radish the exact shape and size of a quart milk bottle. Asked how he got the radish to look just like a quart milk bottle, the farmer replied, "It was easy. I got the seed growing and then put it into the milk bottle. It had nowhere else to go."

Concentration: The ability to focus on one thing single-mindedly and see it through until it's done is critical to success.

Great athletes are known for their concentration and focus. As golf great Ben Hogan once stood over a crucial putt, a loud train whistle suddenly blared in the distance. After he had sunk the putt, someone asked Hogan if the train whistle had bothered him.

"What whistle?" Hogan replied.

And let's not forget Yankee great and America's favorite philosopher Yogi Berra, who said, "You can't think and hit the ball at the same time."

Creativity: Be open to ideas from many sources. Surround yourself with creative people. Creativity needs to be exercised like a muscle: If you don't use it, you'll lose it.

Studies indicate that, between ages 5 and 17, there is an extreme drop in the creativity level in both male and female students. As you grow older, your creativity level decreases proportionally. The good news is that this trend is reversible, as long as you keep challenging yourself. Consider Grandma Moses, who didn't start painting until age 80 and went on to produce more than 1,500 works of art.

Courage: Most in demand and least in supply, courage is the willingness to do the things you know are right. Courage, contrary to popular belief, is not the absence of fear. Courage is having the heart to act in spite of fear. Don't be afraid to use it.

Continuous learning: Set aside some time every day, every week and every month to improve yourself. To stay miles ahead of the competition, read trade publications or books, or listen to business CDs during your commute to and from work. Go back to school and take additional classes, or join groups or organizations . . . whatever it may be, just never stop learning.

Mackay's Moral: Some people succeed because they are destined to, but most people succeed because they are determined to.

GETTING IT DONE—The Fortune Cookies

If at first you don't succeed . . . you're about average.

———————

Don't let what you can't do interfere with what you *can* do.

———————

Nike said it better than anyone: *Just do it.*

———————

Never let analysis lead to paralysis.

———————

It's the person who has done nothing who is sure that
nothing can be done.

———————

Ideas without action are worthless.

———————

Initiative is important. *Finishative* is vital.

———————

People who say that something is impossible should not interrupt
those who are busy getting it done.

———————

If you're trying to do everything, everything becomes more trying.

———————

To get out of the rut, get off your butt.

———————

Doing beats stewing.

———————

I not only use all the brains I have, but all that I can borrow.
—*Woodrow Wilson*

———————

We are judged by what we finish, not by what we start.

———————

The only thing that matters is if *you* say you can't do it.

———————

AFTERTHOUGHTS

The Mackay Elite 8 (Plus One): A List of Life-Changing Sales Books

As you finish this book, I hope all the advice I've shared will launch your sales career to the moon and back. I've offered the best of my secrets and strategies. Now, as an extra boost, I'm including my reading list of all-time favorite sales books. (You'll notice I haven't included my previous #1 *New York Times* bestseller, *Swim with the Sharks Without Being Eaten Alive*, but you're welcome to add it to your list!)

I've consulted top salespeople, sales trainers and booksellers, and all concur that these volumes belong in every serious salesperson's collection. All are currently in print and readily available; they appear in no particular order below. These authors have inspired me over the years. I know they'll help you too.

Think and Grow Rich by Napoleon Hill, Jeremy P. Tarcher/Penguin, $10 paperback.

This timeless classic is not strictly about sales, but it is without question a book every sales professional must read and study. Although Napoleon Hill wrote this book in 1937, his advice is just as pertinent in today's economy.

He mentions the moneymaking secret that worked for the more than 500 highly successful and wealthy people that he had studied over the years. I won't give away the secret, because he says the reader who is ready and searching for it will pick it up.

His simple 13-step formula provides a guide to identifying goals, mastering the secret of true success, obtaining whatever you want in life, and becoming one of the supersuccessful. The inspiration contained within works for anyone who is willing to commit to an attitude of success. I have turned to Hill's advice many times over my career, and I am a disciple.

Trust me when I say this is one of my two favorite books of all time. (Read about the other one next.)

How to Win Friends and Influence People by Dale Carnegie, Pocket Books, $15 paperback.

Another time-tested jewel, this volume first published in 1937 should be required reading for every high school senior, and then reread annually after that. Carnegie's groundbreaking work arose from the lack of available training materials on the topic at the time. His years of research on human relations provided the basis for the "fine art of getting along with people in everyday business and social contacts."

Carnegie emphasizes positive actions throughout his work. "There is one all-important law of human conduct. If we obey the law, we shall never get into trouble. In fact, that law, if obeyed, will bring us countless friends and constant happiness . . . The law is this: Always make the other person feel important."

Isn't that the slogan every successful salesperson must adopt?

More than 15 million copies of this book have sold in the 70+ years it has been in print. Even though Carnegie died in 1955, his advice is timeless and universally applicable: "Countless numbers of salespeople have sharply increased their sales by use of these principles."

The Greatest Salesman in the World by Og Mandino, Bantam, $7.99 paperback.

First published in 1968, this little treasure says you can change your life "with the priceless wisdom of 10 ancient scrolls handed down for thousands of years." It's a fascinating story divided into short chapters that introduce and explain the 10 concepts that, when turned into good habits, improve every aspect of life.

This book inspired me years ago, and I pick it up every now and then to renew my commitment to being the greatest I can be. The whole book takes less than two hours to read at just over 100 pages, but I guarantee you will have a whole new outlook when you close the cover.

None of these ideas are new, reminding us that selling is the second oldest profession. This may be a low-tech approach, but it's a proven winner in any century.

As Hafid, the greatest salesman in the world, says, "Failure will never overtake me if my determination to succeed is strong enough."

Selling 101 by Zig Ziglar, Thomas Nelson Publishers, $9.99 hardcover.

Zig Ziglar was recognized the world over for his motivational messages on life improvement and balanced living. He published other books on selling, but this is my favorite reference.

He encourages readers to begin each day with the statement, "Today, I will be a successful sales professional, and I will learn something today that will make me even more professional tomorrow." This 100-page how-to book is simple, to-the-point, helpful advice for the beginner or the seasoned salesperson looking to improve.

Zig stresses the "foundation stones of honesty, character, integrity, faith, love, and loyalty," not only for successful sales, but also for life, family and friendship. His four-step formula for a planned-selling process explains how covering the customer's basic needs leads to better results and customer satisfaction. He demonstrates the finer points of closing sales, where most sales presentations fall apart.

Finally, he reminds us that "the sales career is built before, during and after the sale is made." His advice is especially credible, because he has followed his own formula to an extremely successful career.

Jeffrey Gitomer's Little Red Book of Selling, Bar Press, $19.95 hardcover.

The only thing that's "little" about this book is the physical size. The information contained within is huge. Gitomer offers 12.5 principles of sales greatness and a host of other lists to help you organize your priorities and thinking.

Jeffrey says: "The subtle difference in sales between the successful and the unsuccessful is the difference between trying to sell what you have and creating the atmosphere where the prospect will buy what you have. *People don't like to be sold, but they love to buy* has become more than a registered trademark to me—it's my mantra." The short, well-organized chapters offer specific strategies and plenty of encouragement.

Jeffrey's own success is a testament to the quality of his advice. He is a master of the trade. He understands what makes customers tick: "If you make a sale, you can earn a commission. If you make a friend, you can earn a fortune." He is also the author of *Jeffrey Gitomer's Sales Bible*, another fine reference.

SPIN Selling by Neil Rackham, McGraw-Hill Book Company, $29.95 hardcover.

Rackham and his company evaluated 35,000 sales calls in research for this book. The result is specific advice geared toward large sales and why strategies used in smaller sales are ineffective and even detrimental in larger deals.

SPIN stands for Situation, Problem, Implication, and Need-payoff, the four questions a salesperson can use in sales calls to uncover the customer's implied needs and develop them into explicit needs. "In a simple sale, there's usually a straightforward relationship between the product and the problem it solves. It's possible for a solution to match the problem exactly," he says. But in larger sales, "there are likely to be many 'sales calls' where influencers and users sell internally (to their bosses) on your behalf and where there's no opportunity for you to be present."

Rackham presents case studies to illustrate his research conclusions and offers plenty of questions and potential objections to help readers tailor their presentations to larger accounts. The language is straightforward and the examples are clear.

Most of all, he emphasizes the importance of attention to details: "Our research has shown that success is constructed from those important little building blocks called behaviors. More than anything else, it's the hundreds of minute behavioral details in a call that will decide whether it succeeds."

How to Master the Art of Selling by Tom Hopkins, Business Plus, $15.99 paperback.

Perhaps the reason I love to recommend this book is Hopkins' philosophy: "The reason I love selling is its freedom of expression. Sales is one of the few professions left in which you can be yourself and can, in essence, do what you want to do . . . No activity is more vital to the economy's health than selling; no activity is more dependent on individual initiative than selling." No truer words were ever spoken (or written)!

Hopkins is one of the top sales trainers in the country. His practical advice is as clear as can be: If you want to earn more, learn more. He explains the seven basics that will make you as great as you want to be, as well as the 12 sources of sensational selling success in exquisite detail and straightforward language.

One especially helpful chapter that should be read and reread is "Why Don't I Do What I Know I Should Do?"—a great discussion of how to regain your enthusiasm when your motivation lags, every salesperson's challenge.

Hopkins says, "The skills, knowledge, and drive within you are what will make you great . . . These qualities can be expanded and intensified—if you're willing to invest time, effort, and money in yourself . . . You are your greatest asset."

The Psychology of Selling by Brian Tracy, Thomas Nelson, $14.99 paperback.

There is no question in Brian Tracy's mind: "Success is not an accident. Failure is not an accident. In fact, success is predictable. It leaves tracks." Tracy turned his bestselling audio series into a bestselling book that explores the reasons people buy, and how to sell accordingly. "Your job as a sales professional is to win people over to your side by making it clear that you care about them and want the best for them," he says.

He walks readers through the process, explaining the importance of goal-setting, creative selling and understanding why people buy. He explains in detail the six buyer personality profiles and how to deal with each one. Another helpful checklist is his seven-step formula for setting and achieving goals. He wraps it all in a neat little package in the chapter "10 Keys to Success in Selling." The action exercises at the end of each chapter help readers practice the concepts he shares.

Tracy closes his book by reminding his readers, "You have within you, right now, the ability to be more, do more, and have more than you ever have in your life. By becoming absolutely excellent in your chosen profession of selling, you can achieve all your goals and fulfill all your dreams . . . There are no limits."

SUCCESS magazine, Darren Hardy publisher, $24.95/12 issues.

SUCCESS promises to "strive to bring you the thought leaders and success experts, both past and present, and reveal their key ideas and strategies to help you excel in every area of your personal and professional life."

I never leave home without the latest issue, because I get so many terrific ideas from the stories.

The subscription price is an investment in your future. There's a bonus CD in each issue with interviews and more take-home content so you can listen when reading isn't an option. Make it your goal to be one of the feature stories!

Locker Room Fireball

I remember roaming the sidelines with Notre Dame coaching legend Lou Holtz during a pivotal Notre Dame–Florida State game in 1993. I doubt if I will ever live long enough to experience another contest like it.

Here were two supremely talented opposing forces facing off against each other. They were evenly matched in playing-field skills. But one team, Notre Dame, could reach down for something far more rare than mere talent.

When they found that something, it was because Holtz put it there. Holtz thrives on these kinds of contests. A half-hour before the game started, we sat in his office. I asked him how he felt about this electric atmosphere. He said—almost casually—"God, how I love this!"

Dick Rosenthal, the Notre Dame A.D., stopped by to wish Holtz well a moment later. "Big game," said Rosenthal, a point that had not escaped Holtz's notice.

"Big game?" Holtz said, "It's been big since the first moment I got here, and it just keeps getting bigger and bigger. We're adding 12,000 new seats to the stadium. We've got a $27 million TV contract now, and it's just been renewed. At our pep rally on Friday night, we ran out of space and had to lock out 7,000 fans."

I became very close to Holtz since his days as head football coach at the University of Minnesota. In fact, I was instrumental in his hiring. Minnesota was his last stop before Notre Dame. In two years he not only turned around a dead program at the U of M, he got us a bowl invitation for the first time in 25 years.

What makes Lou Holtz special is his combination of three talents: motivation, organization, and focus. He even picked a theme song for the FSU matchup. Holtz had carved the words to Whitney Houston's "One Moment in Time" into the souls of every member of the Notre Dame squad. Every little touch had one target. He wanted to light a fire under his team. He wanted to give them a place to go to find that extra something over and above athletic ability they needed to win. Lou Holtz is a master of sports psychology. In their own way, great sales managers fuel and focus the same energy in the downfield march of a major marketing campaign.

The night before that 1993 FSU game, I eyeballed the master motivator from a corner of an athletic department meeting room. Lou stepped through an oral review of the opposing players with his team, position by position. He matched their individual strengths and weaknesses to each of Notre Dame's own player's individual strengths and weaknesses. No sugar-coating. This was the straight skinny.

Then Coach Holtz wrapped it up by saying: "Now you know about them. Now you know about us. But what it is most important for you to know is this: There is no question in my mind I would rather be your coach. I'd rather be a part of *this* team than *that* team. We are a team, we care about each other.

"We're goal oriented, and we didn't get to be here together in this room because we won our slots in a lottery. We worked for those positions. We are Notre Dame, the greatest tradition in American sports. You are Notre Dame. And this is our one moment in time."

The strains of Whitney Houston—who was then an artist in her prime—echoed through the locker room. Lou passed out copies of the lyrics to each of the players. You could feel the pulse of 63 totally hyped, superbly conditioned American athletes. They were ready to tear the door from its hinges and rush onto the field.

But not quite yet.

Then came Lou's visualization exercises. He asked every team member to replay his assignment. They reaffirmed the priorities of the entire day coming up. What it would feel like before, during and after the game. They locked the whole landscape into their minds: the sights, the sounds, the feeling of victory.

Then came the day of the game.

They were in the locker room. They'd had a night to navigate the road map to victory.

This time the speech was shorter, crisper, more businesslike. The players still carried the emotional high of the previous night's meeting. Now they needed to unload it.

Lou pinpointed the target.

"This is our house," he says, "and *we will not be intimidated.*"

He was ready to let them go.

The locker room door finally opened.

Maybe something similar happened in the visitor's locker room. But it couldn't match what Holtz had produced. And it didn't. Final score: Notre Dame 31, FSU 24.

A manic little 133-pound man pacing the sidelines was the turbine generator behind the victory. This is the steel that forges leadership. Leaders don't leave momentum to chance. They breathe fire into every detail. And it's details that put the ball over the goal line.

Mackay's Moral: With Lou Holtz's twist: "The guy who complains about the bounce of the ball is usually the guy who dropped it."

Second Author's Note

In recent years, I've written two columns about the big picture of selling—and life—that have been particularly popular. Because they summarize so many aspects of selling, they don't fit neatly into any particular section of this book. Every once in a while, there's a benefit to stepping back and gazing at the broad landscape to see how all the parts fit together, because indeed they do. That's why you'll find the following pieces included here.

Harvey Mackay

The ABCs of Selling

Not long ago, I was listening as one of my grandchildren practiced his ABCs. He had a little picture book that helped him remember what the letters stood for, and he studied it intently, determined to be the first in his class to know all the letters and words. With that kind of determination, I knew he would master the alphabet in no time at all.

As he worked, I started thinking about what those letters mean to me after a lifetime in sales and years of helping young hopefuls get started in their careers. I didn't draw pictures, but these are the words my alphabet book would include:

Availability for your customers is essential, so they can reach you with questions, concerns or reorders.

Believe in yourself and your company, or find something else to sell.

Customers aren't always right, but if you want to keep them as your customers, find a way to make them right.

Deliver more than you promise.

Education is for life—never stop learning.

Follow up and follow through. Never leave a customer hanging.

Goals give you a reason to go to work every day. When you reach your goals, set higher ones!

Humanize your selling strategy by learning everything you can about your customers.

I is the least important letter in selling.

Join trade organizations and community groups that will help you both professionally and personally, such as Toastmasters, Chamber of Commerce or Junior Achievement.

Know your competitors and their products as well as you know your own.

Listen to your customers or they'll start talking to someone else.

Maybe is the worst answer a customer can give. No is better than maybe. Find out what you can do to turn it into a yes.

Networking is among the most important skills a salesperson can develop. Someone you know knows someone you need to know.

Opportunities are everywhere. Keep your antennae up.

Price is not the only reason customers buy your product, but it's a good reason.

Quality can never be sacrificed if you want to keep your customers satisfied.

Relationships are precious: They take time to develop and are worth every minute you invest in them.

Service is spelled "serve us" in companies that want to stay in business for a long time.

Trust is central to doing business with anyone. Without it, you have another word that begins with T: Trouble.

Unlimited potential is possible whether you sell computers or candy. You are the only one who can limit your potential.

Volunteer. It's always good to give back. You'll probably find that you get more than you give, and there is no shortage of organizations that need your help.

Winning doesn't necessarily mean beating everyone else. A win-win situation is the best of both worlds.

X-ray and CAT scan your customers so that you know everything about them—so you can serve them better.

You is a word your customers need to hear often, as in "What can I do for you?"

Zeal is a critical element in your presentations, service and life in general. Let your enthusiasm shine through!

Some things never change—including the importance of knowing how to treat your customers and what really matters in your relationships. And as you can see, most of these items cover far more than just sales.

Someday, I think my grandchildren will still be able to use my little alphabet book. Nothing would make me prouder.

Mackay's Moral: Now you know my ABCs—
sales skills from A to Z.

The Second Ten Commandments

We all know about the original Ten Commandments, but have you ever heard of the Second Ten Commandments? These pearls of wisdom, sent to me by a friend, have often been attributed to Elodie Armstrong. I have taken the liberty of putting my spin on them:

I.   **Thou shall not worry, for worry is the most unproductive of all human activities.** You can't saw sawdust. A day of worry is more exhausting than a day of work. People get so busy worrying about yesterday or tomorrow, they forget about today. And today is what you have to work with.

II. **Thou shall not be fearful, for most of the things we fear never come to pass.** Every crisis we face is multiplied when we act out of fear. Fear is a self-fulfilling emotion. When we fear something, we empower it. If we refuse to concede to our fear, there is nothing to fear.

III. **Thou shall not cross bridges before you come to them, for no one yet has succeeded in accomplishing this.** Solve the issues before you right now. Tomorrow's problems may not even be problems when tomorrow comes!

IV. **Thou shall face each problem as it comes. You can handle only one at a time anyway.** In one of my favorite *Peanuts* comic strips, Linus says to Charlie Brown, "There's no problem too big we can't run away from it." I chuckle every time I think about it, because it sounds like such a simple solution to a problem. Problem solving is not easy, so don't make it harder than it is.

V.   **Thou shall not take problems to bed with you, for they make very poor bedfellows.** Just remember that all your problems seem much worse in the middle of the night. If I wake up thinking of a problem, I tell myself that it will seem lighter in the morning. And it always is.

VI. **Thou shall not borrow other people's problems. They can better care for them than you can.** I must confess I have broken this commandment because I wanted to help someone out without being asked, or I thought I was more equipped to handle a situation. But I wouldn't have to deal with the consequences either.

VII. **Thou shall not try to relive yesterday. For good or ill, it is forever gone.** Concentrate on what is happening in your life and be happy now! We convince ourselves that life will be better after we get a better job, make more money, get married, have a baby, buy a bigger house and so on. Yet the accomplishment of any of those events may not make any difference at all. The Declaration of Independence says we are endowed "with certain unalienable rights, that among these are life, liberty and the pursuit of happiness." You are responsible for your own happiness.

VIII. **Thou shall be a good listener, for only when you listen do you hear ideas different from your own.** You can win more friends with your ears than with your mouth. Hearing is one of the body's five senses, but listening is an art. Your success could hinge on whether you have mastered the skill of listening. Most people won't listen to what you're saying unless they already feel that you have listened to them. When we feel we are being listened to, it makes us feel like we are being taken seriously and that what we are saying really matters.

IX. **Thou shall not become bogged down by frustration, for 90 percent of it is rooted in self-pity and will only interfere with positive action.** Seriously, has frustration ever improved a situation? Better to take a break, collect your thoughts and redirect your attention to a positive first step. Then go on from there.

X. **Thou shall count thy blessings, never overlooking the small ones, for a lot of small blessings add up to a big one.** We all have something to be grateful for, even on the worst days. Hey—you're still on the green side of the grass, aren't you?

Mackay's Moral: These may not be chiseled in stone, but try them—they'll make your life less rocky.

INDEX

focus, 7–8, 355
football games, 170
Forbes, 164, 165
Ford, Gerald, 334
Ford, Henry, 25, 80, 101, 108
Fortune, 147, 208
Forum Corporation, 1–2
four-letter words, 150–52
four-minute mile, 12–13, 20
Foxx, Jamie, 121
Frankl, Viktor, 73
Franklin, Ben, 293
Franzén, Johan, 176
Fraud Sciences, 318
Freud, Sigmund, 203–4
Fulton, Robert, 80
fund-raising, 323
Fuqua, J. B., 334–35

Gardner, John, 123
gatekeeper, 251, 257, 277–78
Gates, Bill, 104
Gehrig, Lou, 186
Geisel, Theodore, 302
General Electric, 342
General Mills, 190, 270, 323
Getty, J. Paul, 212
Gielgud, John, 141
Gitomer, Jeffrey, 351–52
Giuliani, Rudy, 146, 147
Gladwell, Malcolm, 103–4
Globalist, The, 342
goals, 2, 13, 85–86, 120, 189, 279, 288, 335
Goldfarb, Harry, 26–27
golf, 22, 71, 74, 111, 154, 158, 185, 191, 193, 269–70, 275, 312, 343
Goodall, Jane, 192
Google, 39, 40, 41, 44, 122, 206–9, 230, 231, 247, 316
Google Analytics, 231
Google Story, The (Vise and Malseed), 206–7
Gove, Bill, 215–16
Graham, Billy, 72

Grant, Ulysses S., 96, 215
Greatest Salesman in the World, The (Mandino), 350–51
Greenwald, Anthony, 331
Gregoire, Jerry, 245
Griffith, Calvin, 321–22
Grossman, Rex, 78
Grove, Andy, 292
gumption, 342
gut feelings, 203–5
gut instinct, 204

Hamilton, Scott, 331
Hamm, Mia, 182
hard work, 7, 8, 182
Harman, Katie, 82
Harry Potter, 164
Hart Trophy, 158
Harvard University, 96, 211
Harvey, Paul, 118
Hatch, Orrin, 53
health and wellness, 291–92
help networks, 243–44
Hemingway, Ernest, 101
Hibbard, Foster, 225
Hill, Napoleon, 112, 225, 349–50
Hill & Knowlton, 241
Hillary, Edmund, 12
Hitler, Adolf, 143
Hogan, Ben, 343
Holiday, Billie, 146
Holtz, Beth, 88
Holtz, Lou, xxi–xxv, 67, 88, 206, 316, 355–57
honesty, 1–2, 10, 310–12, 317
Honeywell, 270
HootSuite, 260
Hope, Bob, 334
Hopkins, Minnesota, 269
Hopkins, Tom, 352–53
Horatio Alger Association, 334–35
Hornung, Paul, 58–59
Houdini, Harry, 233
Houston, Whitney, 356

Money-Back Guarantee

I hope you enjoy my book. I'm so confident of the effectiveness of this advice that if you don't find it beneficial, I will personally refund your purchase price. Just send a letter and your proof of purchase to:

Harvey Mackay
MackayMitchell Envelope Company
2100 Elm St. SE
Minneapolis, MN 55414

Also available from Harvey Mackay:

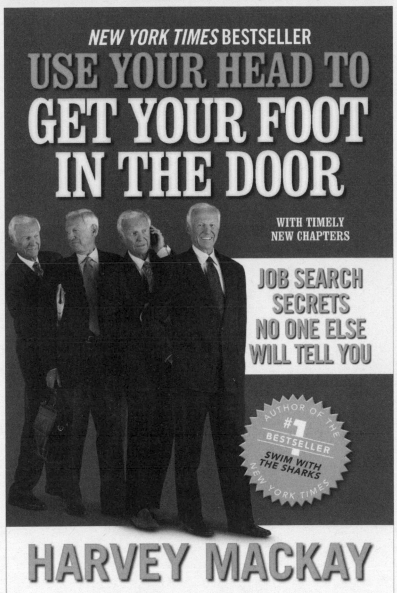

NEW YORK TIMES BESTSELLER

USE YOUR HEAD TO GET YOUR FOOT IN THE DOOR

WITH TIMELY
NEW CHAPTERS

JOB SEARCH SECRETS NO ONE ELSE WILL TELL YOU

AUTHOR OF THE #1 BESTSELLER SWIM WITH THE SHARKS NEW YORK TIMES

HARVEY MACKAY

ISBN: 978-1-59184-343-6

Available wherever books are sold.

Portfolio / Penguin
A member of Penguin Group (USA) Inc.
www.penguin.com

PORTFOLIO
PENGUIN